Study Edition

For Sundays of Year C

LECTIONARY FOR MASS

Annotated by G. B. Harrison

Study Edition

For Sundays of Year C

Pueblo Publishing Company

New York

Nihil Obstat: Daniel V. Flynn, J.C.D.
                  Censor Librorum

Imprimatur: ✣ James P. Mahoney, D.D.
                Vicar General, Archdiocese of New York

Introduction

ADVENT SEASON

CHRISTMAS SEASON

LENTEN SEASON

EASTER TRIDUUM

EASTER SEASON

		1983	1986	1989
Easter Sunday:		*April 3*	*March 30*	*March 26*
Vigil Mass	125			
Mass during the Day	147			
Second Sunday of Easter	152	*April 10*	*April 6*	*April 2*
Third Sunday of Easter	157	*April 17*	*April 13*	*April 9*
Fourth Sunday of Easter	163	*April 24*	*April 20*	*April 16*
Fifth Sunday of Easter	167	*May 1*	*April 27*	*April 23*
Sixth Sunday of Easter	171	*May 8*	*May 4*	*April 30*
Ascension	176	*May 12*	*May 8*	*May 4*
Seventh Sunday of Easter	180	*May 15*	*May 11*	*May 7*
Pentecost Sunday:		*May 22*	*May 18*	*May 14*
Vigil Mass	184			
Mass during the Day	191			

SEASON OF THE YEAR

		1983	1986	1989
Second Sunday	196	*January 16*	*January 19*	*January 15*
Third Sunday	201	*January 23*	*January 26*	*January 22*
Fourth Sunday	206	*January 30*	*February 2*	*January 29*
Fifth Sunday	212	*February 6*	*February 9*	*February 5*
Sixth Sunday	217	*February 13*		
Seventh Sunday	221			
Eighth Sunday	225			
Ninth Sunday	228			*June 4*
Tenth Sunday	232		*June 8*	*June 11*
Eleventh Sunday	236	*June 12*	*June 15*	*June 18*
Twelfth Sunday	242	*June 19*	*June 22*	*June 25*
Thirteenth Sunday	245	*June 26*		*July 2*
Fourteenth Sunday	249	*July 3*	*July 6*	*July 9*
Fifteenth Sunday	254	*July 10*	*July 13*	*July 16*
Sixteenth Sunday	259	*July 17*	*July 20*	*July 23*
Seventeenth Sunday	263	*July 24*	*July 27*	*July 30*
Eighteenth Sunday	268	*July 31*	*August 3*	*August 6*
Nineteenth Sunday	272	*August 7*	*August 10*	*August 13*
Twentieth Sunday	278	*August 14*	*August 17*	*August 20*
Twenty-First Sunday	282	*August 21*	*August 24*	*August 27*
Twenty-Second Sunday	285	*August 28*	*August 31*	*September 3*
Twenty-Third Sunday	289	*September 4*	*September 7*	*September 10*
Twenty-Fourth Sunday	293	*September 11*		*September 17*
Twenty-Fifth Sunday	299	*September 18*	*September 21*	*September 24*

FOREWORD

The Study Edition of the Lectionary for Mass, New American Reader's Lectionary Program, is designed to help the lector prepare for public proclamation of the Word:

A. The text is printed in clear type and in sense lines for easier understanding, and is a line for line reproduction of the Lectionary for Mass.

B. Names likely to cause difficulty are marked for pronunciation.

C. For each reading a guide is provided for such matters as the tone, mood and style to be used, and when needed, a short explanation of the argument or the occasion of writing of the original passage. Key words and phrases are noted as required.

Reading in public is a difficult art and demands much practice and study. No one should ever venture to proclaim the Word without careful preparation at home. If he is not familiar with the book of the Bible from which each reading is taken, then he should read it; at least he should carefully study the whole chapter. This is most necessary because the readings are usually quite short and cannot be understood or read intelligibly unless the lector knows what went before the paragraph he is to read.

In his immediate preparation, the lector needs to grasp the general message of the reading. Then he should examine the text carefully for the exact meaning of every sentence. Next he should decide on the way the reading is to be presented: is it straight story-telling, or exhortation, or lesson, or argument, or prayer, or warning, or encouragement, or condemnation? Every kind demands its own manner of delivery. The lector should also consider each passage for its sound and rhythms, and the words that require special emphasis or special treatment.

Every reader should own and study the Bible in one of the available modern translations, but since THE NEW AMERICAN BIBLE is now used in most Catholic churches in the United States, this version has been chosen for use in the Lectionary for Mass and Study Edition. The lector may also find useful a small book called PROCLAIMING THE WORD, written as a companion to the New American Reader's Lectionary.

Study Edition

For Sundays of Year C

FIRST SUNDAY OF ADVENT

FIRST READING

Jeremiah 33, 14-16   I will cause a good seed to spring forth from David.

During the last days of Jerusalem, just before the city fell to the Babylonians, Jeremiah made this prophecy which was to be fulfilled at the birth of David's descendant—Jesus. Straight declaration of what will be.

A reading from the book of the prophet Je-re-mí-ah

The days are coming, says the Lord,
   when I will fulfill the promise I made
   to the house of Israel and Judah.
In those days, in that time,
   I will raise up for David a just shoot;
   he shall do what is right and just in the land.
In those days Judah shall be safe
   and Je-rú-sa-lem shall dwell secure;
   this is what they shall call her:
   "The Lord our justice."

This is the Word of the Lord.

RESPONSORIAL PSALM

Psalm 25, 4-5. 8-9. 10. 14   After the reading the psalmist sings or says the responsorial verse, and all repeat it. This response is also repeated after each verse of the psalm.

Common Response:

Come, O Lord, and set us free.

Or:

℟. To you, O Lord, I lift my soul.

Your ways, O Lord, make known to me;
   teach me your paths,
Guide me in your truth and teach me,
   for you are God my savior,
   and for you I wait all the day. ℟.

Good and upright is the Lord;
   thus he shows sinners the way.
He guides the humble to justice,
   he teaches the humble his way.   ℟.

All the paths of the Lord are kindness and constancy
   toward those who keep his covenant and his decrees.
The friendship of the Lord is with those who fear him,
   and his covenant, for their instruction.   ℟.

SECOND READING

1Thessalonians 3, 12-4, 2   When Christ comes may he strengthen your hearts in holiness.

Paul exhorts the Thessalonians to be ready, body and soul, for the coming of the Lord. Read this passage as applying to us as we prepare for the feast of the birth of Jesus.

A reading from the first letter of Paul to the Thes-sa-ló-ni-ans

May the Lord increase you
   and make you overflow with love for one another and for all,
   even as our love does for you.
May he strengthen your hearts,
   making them blameless and holy before our God and Father
   at the coming of our Lord Jesus with all his holy ones.

Now, my brothers, we beg and exhort you in the Lord Jesus
   that, even as you learned from us
   how to conduct yourselves in a way pleasing to God—
   which you are indeed doing—
   so you must learn to make still better progress.
You know the instructions we gave you in the Lord Jesus.

   This is the Word of the Lord.

GOSPEL

The cantor sings the alleluia and the people repeat it; the cantor then sings the verse and the people repeat the alleluia. Otherwise the alleluia may be omitted. Reference: Psalm 85, 8.

Al - le - lu - ia.

Lord, let us see your kind - ness, and grant us your sal - va - tion.

Luke 21, 25-28. 34-36   Your redemption is near at hand.

Jesus tells his disciples of the signs that will show the end of the world to be near. The first section is a grave general warning; the second an even more solemn and urgent command to be instantly ready for Christ's second coming.

✠   A reading from the holy gospel according to Luke

Jesus said to his disciples:
  "There will be signs in the sun, the moon and the stars.
On the earth, nations will be in anguish,
    distraught at the roaring of the sea and the waves.
Men will die of fright
    in anticipation of what is coming upon the earth.
The powers in the heavens will be shaken.
After that, men will see the Son of Man
    coming on a cloud with great power and glory.
When these things begin to happen,
    stand up straight and raise your heads,
    for your ransom is near at hand.

  "Be on guard lest your spirits become bloated
    with indulgence and drunkenness and worldly cares.
The great day will suddenly close in on you like a trap.
The day I speak of will come upon all
    who dwell on the face of the earth,
    so be on the watch.
Pray constantly for the strength
    to escape whatever is in prospect,
    and to stand secure before the Son of Man."

    This is the gospel of the Lord.

SECOND SUNDAY OF ADVENT

FIRST READING

Baruch 5, 1-9   Jerusalem—God will show your splendor.

Express the triumph of this prophecy that God will bring his people back from exile to Jerusalem, the holy city.

A reading from the book of the prophet Bá-ruch

Je-rú-sa-lem, take off your robe of mourning and misery;
    put on the splendor of glory from God forever:
Wrapped in the cloak of justice from God,
    bear on your head the mitre
    that displays the glory of the eternal name.
For God will show all the earth your splendor:
    you will be named by God forever
    the peace of justice, the glory of God's worship.

Up, Je-rú-sa-lem! stand upon the heights;
    look to the east and see your children
Gathered from the east and the west
    at the word of the Holy One,
    rejoicing that they are remembered by God.
Led away on foot by their enemies they left you:
    but God will bring them back to you
    borne aloft in glory as on royal thrones.
For God has commanded
    that every lofty mountain be made low,
And that the age-old depths and gorges
    be filled to level ground,
    that Israel may advance secure in the glory of God.
The forests and every fragrant kind of tree
    have overshadowed Israel at God's command;
For God is leading Israel in joy
    by the light of his glory,
    with his mercy and justice for company.

This is the Word of the Lord.

RESPONSORIAL PSALM

Psalm 126, 1-2. 2-3. 4-5. 6   After the reading the psalmist sings or says the responsorial verse, and all repeat it. This response is also repeated after each verse of the psalm.

Common response:

Come, O Lord, and set us free.

Or:

R̸. The Lord has done great things for us;
     we are filled with joy.

When the Lord brought back the captives of Zion,
    we were like men dreaming.
Then our mouth was filled with laughter,
    and our tongue with rejoicing.   R̸.

Then they said among the nations,
    "The Lord has done great things for them."
The Lord has done great things for us;
    we are glad indeed.   R̸.

Restore our fortunes, O Lord,
    like the torrents in the southern desert.
Those that sow in tears
    shall reap rejoicing.   R̸.

Although they go forth weeping,
    carrying the seed to be sown,
They shall come back rejoicing,
    carrying their sheaves.   R̸.

SECOND READING

Philippians 1, 4-6. 8-11   Show yourselves sinless and without blame in the day of Christ.

When Paul wrote this letter, he and most Christians, believed that the return of Christ was near at hand. He exhorts them to increase their love for each other so that they may be ready to greet Christ when he comes. Convey the note of eager expectation.

A reading from the letter of Paul to the Phil-íp-pi-ans

In every prayer I utter,
   I rejoice as I plead on your behalf,
   at the way you have all continually helped
   promote the gospel from the very first day.

I am sure of this much:
   that he who has begun the good work in you
   will carry it through to completion,
   right up to the day of Christ Jesus.
God himself can testify how much I long for each of you
   with the affection of Christ Jesus!
My prayer is that your love may more and more abound,
   both in understanding and wealth of experience,
   so that with a clear conscience and blameless conduct
   you may learn to value the things that really matter,
   up to the very day of Christ.
It is my wish that you may be found rich in the harvest of justice
   which Jesus Christ has ripened in you,
   to the glory and praise of God.

This is the Word of the Lord.

GOSPEL

The cantor sings the alleluia and the people repeat it; the cantor then sings the verse and the people repeat the alleluia. Otherwise the alleluia may be omitted. Reference: Luke 3, 4. 6.

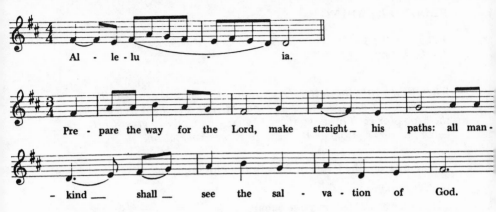

Al - le - lu - ia.

Pre - pare the way for the Lord, make straight _ his paths: all man -

- kind _ shall _ see the sal - va - tion of God.

Luke 3, 1-6   All mankind shall see the salvation of God.

Luke was careful to give historical notes that would enable later readers to fix the date, both of the birth of Jesus and of the beginning of John's preaching. Read as an important historical record.

✚   A reading from the holy gospel according to Luke

In the fifteenth year of the rule of Ti-bé-ri-us Caesar,
    when Pontius Pilate was procurator of Judea,
Herod tét-rarch of Gá-li-lee,
    Philip his brother tét-rarch of the region of I-tur-aé-a and Tra-cho-ní-tis,
    and Ly-sá-ni-as tét-rarch of A-bi-lé-ne,
    during the high-priesthood of An-nas and Cái-a-phas,
    the word of God was spoken to John son of Ze-cha-rí-ah in the
        desert.
He went about the entire region of the Jordan
    proclaiming a baptism of repentance
    which led to the forgiveness of sins,
    as is written in the book of the words of I-saí-ah the prophet:
    "A herald's voice in the desert, crying,
    'Make ready the way of the Lord,
        clear him a straight path.
    Every valley shall be filled
        and every mountain and hill shall be leveled.
The windings shall be made straight
    and the rough ways smooth,
    and all mankind shall see the salvation of God.' "

    This is the gospel of the Lord.

THIRD SUNDAY OF ADVENT

FIRST READING

Zephaniah 3, 14-18 The Lord will exult with you, over you, he will renew you by his love.

The concluding verses of the prophecy of Zephaniah. The prophet laments the idolatry and faithlessness of the people which must inevitably lead to destruction. Yet the Lord will save a remnant of those who are faithful, and then joy will return to Jerusalem. A song of joyful hope.

A reading from the book of the prophet Ze-phan-í-ah

Shout for joy, O daughter Zion!
  sing joyfully, O Israel!
Be glad and exult with all your heart,
  O daughter Je-rú-sa-lem!
The Lord has removed the judgment against you,
  he has turned away your enemies;
The King of Israel, the Lord, is in your midst,
  you have no further misfortune to fear.
On that day, it shall be said to Je-rú-sa-lem:
  Fear not, O Zion, be not discouraged!
The Lord, your God, is in your midst,
  a mighty savior;
He will rejoice over you with gladness,
  and renew you in his love.
He will sing joyfully because of you,
  as one sings at festivals.

  This is the Word of the Lord.

RESPONSORIAL PSALM

*Isaiah 12, 2-3. 4. 5-6 After the reading the psalmist sings or says the
responsorial verse, and all repeat it. This response is also repeated
after each verse of the psalm.*

Common response:

Come, O   Lord,   and set   us   free.

Or:

℟. Cry out with joy and gladness:
   for among you is the great and Holy One of Israel.

God indeed is my savior;
   I am confident and unafraid.
My strength and my courage is the Lord,
   and he has been my savior.
With joy you will draw water
   at the fountain of salvation. ℟.

Give thanks to the Lord, acclaim his name;
   among the nations make known his deeds,
   proclaim how exalted is his name. ℟.

Sing praise to the Lord for his glorious achievement;
   let this be known throughout all the earth.
Shout with exultation, O city of Zion,
   for great in your midst is the Holy One of Israel. ℟.

SECOND READING

Philippians 4, 4-7   The Lord is near.

A note of joyful excitement.   Christ is coming; be ready.   Stress
especially the last sentence: God's peace.

A reading from the letter of Paul to the Phil-íp-pi-ans

Rejoice in the Lord always!
I say it again. Rejoice!
Everyone should see how unselfish you are.
The Lord himself is near.
Dismiss all anxiety from your minds.
Present your needs to God in every form of prayer
    and in petitions full of gratitude.
Then God's own peace, which is beyond all understanding,
    will stand guard over your hearts and minds, in Christ Jesus.

This is the Word of the Lord.

GOSPEL

The cantor sings the alleluia and the people repeat it; the cantor then
sings the verse and the people repeat the alleluia. Otherwise the alleluia
may be omitted. Reference: Isaiah 61, 1.

Al - le - lu - ia.

The — Spir - it of the Lord is up - on me: he
sent me to bring Good News to the poor.

Luke 3, 10-18   What, then, must we do?

John the Baptist's straight answers to those who ask what they ought to do. In the second part make clear John's humility as the messenger of Christ, and the vigor of his words and personality.

✠   A reading from the holy gospel according to Luke

The crowds asked John, "What ought we to do? "
In reply he said,
   "Let the man with two coats give to him who has none.
The man who has food should do the same."

Tax collectors also came to be baptized, and they said to him,
   "Teacher, what are we to do? "
He answered them,
   "Exact nothing over and above your fixed amount."

Soldiers likewise asked him,
   "What about us? "
He told them, "Do not bully anyone.
Denounce no one falsely.
Be content with your pay."

The people were full of anticipation,
   wondering in their hearts whether John might be the Mes-sí-ah.
John answered them all by saying:
   "I am baptizing you in water,
   but there is one to come who is mightier than I.˙
I am not fit to loosen his sandal strap.
He will baptize you in the Holy Spirit and in fire.
His winnowing-fan is in his hand to clear his threshing floor
   and gather the wheat into his granary,
   but the chaff he will burn in unquenchable fire."
Using exhortations of this sort,
   he preached the good news to the people.

   This is the gospel of the Lord.

FOURTH SUNDAY OF ADVENT

FIRST READING

Micah 5, 1-4   Out of you will be born the one who is to rule over Israel.

Micah lived at the time of the fall of the kingdom of Israel. He denounced the corrupt ways of the leaders of the people both in Samaria and in Jerusalem, but yet, he prophesied, a savior would come from Bethlehem—the birthplace of David. As preparation for the reading, see I Samuel 16: 1-13 and 17: 12-15, and Matthew chapter 2. Convey the importance of this passage as a prophecy that "the Messiah will be descended from (or, be of the family of) David, the Hero King."

A reading from the book of the prophet Mí-cah

Thus says the Lord:
You, Béth-le-hem-Éph-ra-thah
   too small to be among the clans of Judah,
   From you shall come forth for me
   one who is to be ruler in Israel;
Whose origin is from of old,
   from ancient times.
(Therefore the Lord will give them up, until the time
   when she who is to give birth has borne,
And the rest of his brethren shall return
   to the children of Israel.)
He shall stand firm and shepherd his flock
   by the strength of the Lord,
   in the majestic name of the Lord, his God;
And they shall remain, for now his greatness
   shall reach to the ends of the earth;
   he shall be peace.

This is the Word of the Lord.

RESPONSORIAL PSALM

Psalm 80, 2-3. 15-16. 18-19   After the reading the psalmist sings or says the responsorial verse, and all repeat it. This response is also repeated after each verse of the psalm.

Common response:

Come, O   Lord,   and set   us   free.

Or:

℟.   Lord, make us turn to you,
    let us see your face and we shall be saved.

O shepherd of Israel, hearken,
    from your throne upon the cherubim, shine forth.
Rouse your power,
    and come to save us.   ℟.

Once again, O Lord of hosts,
    look down from heaven, and see;
Take care of this vine,
    and protect what your right hand has planted
        [the son of man whom you yourself made strong.]   ℟.

May your help be with the man of your right hand,
    with the son of man whom you yourself made strong.
Then we will no more withdraw from you;
    give us new life, and we will call upon your name.   ℟.

SECOND READING

Hebrews 10, 5-10   I am coming to do your will.

One of the themes of the letter to the Hebrews is that Jesus was the one acceptable sacrifice for the sins of the world that superseded all others. Give a quiet reading to this difficult passage which is part symbol, part theology, to be comprehended rather than analyzed

A reading from the letter of Paul to the Hebrews

On coming into the world Jesus said:
   "Sacrifice and offering you did not desire,
   but a body you have prepared for me;
Holocausts and sin offerings you took no delight in.
Then I said, ' As is written of me in the book,
   I have come to do your will, O God.' "
First he says,
   "Sacrifices and offerings, holocausts and sin offerings
   you neither desired nor delighted in."
(These are offered according to the prescriptions of the law.)
Then he says,
   "I have come to do your will."
In other words,
   he takes away the first covenant to establish the second.
By this "will," we have been sanctified
   through the offering of the body of Jesus Christ once for all.

   This is the Word of the Lord.

GOSPEL

The cantor sings the alleluia and the people repeat it; the cantor then sings the verse and the people repeat the alleluia. Otherwise the alleluia may be omitted. Reference: Luke 1, 38.

Al - le - lu - ia.

I am the _ ser - vant of the Lord: may his will for me be done.

Luke 1, 39-45   Why should it happen that I am honored with a visit from the mother of my Lord?

Prepare by reading the whole chapter. Mary was already with child when she went to visit Elizabeth in her pregnancy. Bring out the human relations of these two women.

✠   A reading from the holy gospel according to Luke

Mary set out, proceeding in haste into the hill country
    to a town of Judah,
        where she entered Ze-cha-rí-ah's house and greeted Elizabeth.
When Elizabeth heard Mary's greeting,
    the baby stirred in her womb.
Elizabeth was filled with the Holy Spirit,
    and cried out in a loud voice:

    "Blessed are you among women
    and blessed is the fruit of your womb.
But who am I that the mother of my Lord should come to me?
The moment your greeting sounded in my ears,
    the baby stirred in my womb for joy.
Blessed is she who trusted
    that the Lord's words to her would be fulfilled."

    This is the gospel of the Lord.

CHRISTMAS VIGIL

FIRST READING

Isaiah 62, 1-5 The Lord takes delight in you.

The original passage refers to Zion, the Citadel of Jerusalem, in ruins after the destruction of Jerusalem, but soon to be rebuilt and become glorious again. Read as poetry in a tone of hopeful joy.

A reading from the book of the prophet I-saí-ah

For Zí-on's sake I will not be silent,
  for Jer-ú-sa-lem's sake I will not be quiet,
Until her vindication shines forth like the dawn
  and her victory like a burning torch.
Nations shall behold your vindication,
  and all kings your glory;
You shall be called by a new name
  pronounced by the mouth of the Lord.
You shall be a glorious crown in the hand of the Lord,
  a royal diadem held by your God.
No more shall men call you "Forsaken,"
  or your land "Desolate,"
But you shall be called "My Delight,"
  and your land "Espoused."
For the Lord delights in you,
  and makes your land his spouse.
As a young man marries a virgin,
  your Builder shall marry you;
And as a bridegroom rejoices in his bride
  so shall your God rejoice in you.

  This is the Word of the Lord.

RESPONSORIAL PSALM

Psalm 89, 4-5. 16-17. 27. 29 After the reading the psalmist sings or says the responsorial verse, and all repeat it. This response is also repeated after each verse of the psalm.

Common response:

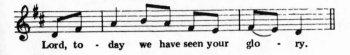

Lord, to - day we have seen your glo - ry.

Or:

℟. For ever I will sing the goodness of the Lord.

I have made a covenant with my chosen one,
    I have sworn to David my servant:
Forever will I confirm your posterity
    and establish your throne for all generations. ℟.

Happy the people who know the joyful shout;
    in the light of your countenance, O Lord, they walk.
At your name they rejoice all the day,
    and through your justice they are exalted. ℟.

He shall say of me, "You are my father,
    my God, the Rock, my savior."
Forever I will maintain my kindness toward him,
    and my covenant with him stands firm. ℟.

SECOND READING

Acts 13, 16-17. 22-25 Paul spoke of Christ, the son of David.

In the synagogue at Pisidia, Paul preached Christ to his fellow Jews. The reading is a short extract from his talk, which began with an account of the history of the Jews and culminated in the preaching of John the Baptist and his recognition of Jesus, the crucifixion, and the resurrection. For an audience of devout Jews, it was natural to point out that Jesus was descended from David. Read as a brief extract from a lecture-sermon.

A reading from the Acts of the Apostles

[When Paul came to An-ti-och Pi-sí-di-a, he entered the synagogue there]
    and motioning to them for silence, he began:

"Fellow Israelites and you others who reverence our God,
  listen to what I have to say!
The God of the people Israel once chose our fathers.
He made this people great during their sojourn in the land of Egypt,
  and 'with an outstretched arm' he led them out of it.
God raised up David as their king;
  on his behalf God testified,
  'I have found David son of Jés-se
  to be a man after my own heart who will fulfill my every wish.'
"According to his promise,
  God has brought forth from this man's descendants
  Jesus, a savior for Israel.
John heralded the coming of Jesus
  by proclaiming a baptism of repentance
  to all the people of Israel.
As John's career was coming to an end, he would say,
  'What you suppose me to be I am not.
Rather, look for the one who comes after me.
I am not worthy to unfasten the sandals on his feet.' "

This is the Word of the Lord.

GOSPEL

The cantor sings the alleluia and the people repeat it; the cantor then sings the verse and the people repeat the alleluia. Otherwise the alleluia may be omitted.

Al - le - lu - ia, al - le - lu - ia, al - le - lu - ia.

To - mor - row the wick - ed - ness of the earth will be de - stroyed: the Sav - ior of the world _ will _ be our King.

Long Form: Matthew 1, 1-25   A genealogy of Jesus Christ, son of David.

It is hardly possible for a reader to make this passage, a pedigree of forty-two generations, interesting to the average layman, but if he is familiar with the pronunciation of the names, he can at least avoid unnecessary stumbling. The second part of the reading is a short, straight account of events before the birth of Jesus. Read simply and with conviction, with slight emphasis on the words of the angel. The sentence beginning, "All this . . . God is with us," is Matthew's comment, underlining the fact—so important to Jewish converts—that Jesus showed that he was indeed the Messiah because he fulfilled the ancient prophecies. Pause before and after the comment.

✠   The beginning of the holy gospel according to Matthew

A family record of Jesus Christ, son of David, son of A-bra-ham.
A-bra-ham was the father of I-saac, I-saac the father of Jacob,
   Jacob the father of Jú-dah and his brothers.
Jú-dah was the father of Pé-rez and Zé-rah, whose mother was Tá-mar.
Pé-rez was the father of Héz-ron,
   Héz-ron the father of Rám.
Rám was the father of Am-mín-a-dab,
   Am-mín-a-dab the father of Náh-shon,
Náh-shon the father of Sál-mon. Sál-mon was the father of Bó-az,
    whose mother was Rá-hab,
   Bó-az was the father of Ó-bed, whose mother was Ruth.
Ó-bed was the father of Jés-se, Jés-se the father of King David.
David was the father of Sól-o-mon,
   whose mother had been the wife of U-rí-ah.
Sól-o-mon was the father of Rehó-bo-am, Rehó-bo-am the father of
    Abí-jah, Abí-jah the father of A-sa.
    A-sa was the father of Je-hó-sha-phat,
   Je-hó-sha-phat the father of Jó-ram, Jó-ram the father of Uz-zí-ah.
Uz-zí-ah was the father of Jó-tham, Jó-tham the father of Á-haz,
   Á-haz the father of Hez-ekí-ah.
Hez-ekí-ah was the father of Ma-nás-seh,
   Ma-nás-seh the father of A-mos,
   A-mos the father of Jo-sí-ah.
Jo-sí-ah became the father of Je-cho-ní-ah and his brothers
    at the time of the Babylonian exile. After the Babylonian exile
     Je-cho-ní-ah was the father of She-ál-tiel,
     She-ál-tiel the father of Ze-rúb-ba-bel.

Ze-rúb-ba-bel was the father of Abí-ud,
Abí-ud the father of E-lí-a-kim, E-li-a-kim the father of À-zor.
À-zor was the father of Zá-dok, Zá-dok the father of Á-chim,
A-chim the father of E-lí-ud. E-lí-ud was the father of E-lé-azar,
E-lé-azar the father of Mát-than, Mát-than the father of Jacob.
Jacob was the father of Joseph the husband of Mary.
It was of her that Jesus who is called the Mes-sí-ah was born.

Thus the total number of generations is:
   from A-bra-ham to David, fourteen generations;
   from David to the Babylonian captivity, fourteen generations;
   from the Babylonian captivity to the Mes-sí-ah, fourteen generations.

Now this is how the birth of Jesus Christ came about.
When his mother Mary was engaged to Joseph,
   but before they lived together, she was found with child
   through the power of the Holy Spirit.
Joseph her husband, an upright man unwilling to expose her to the law,
   decided to divorce her quietly.
Such was his intention
   when suddenly the angel of the Lord appeared in a dream
      and said to him:
"Joseph, son of David, have no fear about taking Mary as your wife.
It is by the Holy Spirit that she has conceived this child.
She is to have a son and you are to name him Jesus
   because he will save his people from their sins."
All this happened
   to fulfill what the Lord had said through the prophet:
   "The virgin shall be with child
   and give birth to a son,
   and they shall call him Em-má-nu-el,"
   a name which means "God is with us."
When Joseph awoke he did as the angel of the Lord had directed him
   and received her into his home as his wife.
He had no relations with her at any time
   before she bore a son, whom he named Jesus.

   This is the gospel of the Lord.

Short Form: Matthew 1, 18-25   This is how Jesus came to be born.

✠ A reading from the holy gospel according to Matthew

Now this is how the birth of Jesus Christ came about.
When his mother Mary was engaged to Joseph,
   but before they lived together,
     she was found with child through the power of the Holy Spirit.
Joseph her husband, an upright man
   unwilling to expose her to the law, decided to divorce her quietly.
Such was his intention when suddenly the angel of the Lord
     appeared to him in a dream and said to him:
   "Joseph, son of David, have no fear about taking Mary as your wife.
   It is by the Holy Spirit that she has conceived this child.
She is to have a son and you are to name him Jesus
   because he will save his people from their sins."
All this happened to fulfill what the Lord had said through the prophet:
   "The virgin shall be with child
   and give birth to a son,
   and they shall call him Emmanuel,"
   a name which means "God is with us."
When Joseph awoke he did as the angel of the Lord had directed him
   and received her into his home as his wife.
He had no relations with her at any time
   before she bore a son, whom he named Jesus.

   This is the gospel of the Lord.

CHRISTMAS:MASS AT MIDNIGHT

FIRST READING

Isaiah 9, 1-3. 5-6   A son is given to us.

*After the spoliation of the kingdom, the people will enjoy a new
freedom when the Messiah is born, for he will bring peace and justice. Read as a poem of great rejoicing. In the first stanza, bring
out the feeling of relief because the tyranny of the oppressor has
been overthrown; in the second, triumphant welcome to the newborn King.*

A reading from the book of the prophet I-sai-ah

The people who walked in darkness
   have seen a great light;
Upon those who dwelt in the land of gloom
   a light has shone.
You have brought them abundant joy
   and great rejoicing,
As they rejoice before you as at the harvest,
   as men make merry when dividing spoils.
For the yoke that burdened them,
      the pole on their shoulder,
And the rod of their taskmaster
   you have smashed, as on the day of Midian.

For a child is born to us, a son is given us;
   upon his shoulder dominion rests.
They name him Wonder-Counselor, God-Hero,
   Father-Forever, Prince of Peace.
His dominion is vast
   and forever peaceful,
From David's throne, and over his kingdom,
   which he confirms and sustains
By judgment and justice,
   both now and forever.
The zeal of the Lord of hosts will do this!

   This is the Word of the Lord.

RESPONSORIAL PSALM

Psalm 96, 1-2. 2-3. 11-12. 13 After the reading the psalmist sings or says the responsorial verse, and all repeat it. This response is also repeated after each verse of the psalm.

Common response:

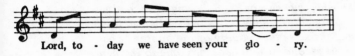

Lord, to - day we have seen your glo - ry.

Or:

℟. Today is born our Savior, Christ the Lord.

Sing to the Lord a new song;
  sing to the Lord, all you lands.
Sing to the Lord; bless his name.   ℟.

Announce his salvation, day after day.
Tell his glory among the nations;
  Among all peoples, his wondrous deeds.   ℟.

Let the heavens be glad and the earth rejoice;
  let the sea and what fills it resound;
  let the plains be joyful and all that is in them!
Then shall all the trees of the forest exult.   ℟.

They shall exult before the Lord, for he comes;
  for he comes to rule the earth.
He shall rule the world with justice
  and the peoples with his constancy.   ℟.

SECOND READING

Titus 2, 11-14 God's grace has been revealed to all men.

Christ was born to redeem us by sacrificing himself. Read as a simple passage of explanation—a short note on what Christ's coming really signifies.

A reading from the letter of Paul to Tí-tus

The grace of God has appeared, offering salvation to all men.
It trains us to reject godless ways and worldly desires,
   and live temperately, justly, and devoutly in this age
   as we await our blessed hope,
    the appearing of the glory of the great God
      and of our Savior Christ Jesus.
It was he who sacrificed himself for us,
   to redeem us from all unrighteousness
   and to cleanse for himself a people of his own,
   eager to do what is right.

This is the Word of the Lord.

GOSPEL

The cantor sings the alleluia and the people repeat it; the cantor then sings the verse and the people repeat the alleluia. Otherwise the alleluia may be omitted. Reference: Luke 2, 10-11.

Al - le - lu - ia, al - le - lu - ia, al - le - lu - ia.

Good News and great joy to all the world: to-day is born our Sav-ior, Christ the Lord.

Luke 2, 1-14   Today a savior has been born for you.

This is the clearer of the two accounts of Christ's birth (the other being Matthew 1: 18-25). Luke explains how Jesus came to be born in Bethlehem and not in Nazareth. The first two paragraphs are straight narrative of events. The third paragraph is full of feeling, which culminates in the angels' triumphant message, announcing the birth of the Messiah.

✠   A reading from the holy gospel according to Luke

In those days Caé-sar Au-gús-tus published a decree
   ordering a census of the whole world.
This first census took place while Qui-rín-i-us was governor of Syria.
Everyone went to register, each to his own town.
And so Joseph went from the town of Ná-za-reth in Gál-i-lee to Judea,
   to David's town of Béth-le-hem—
     because he was of the house and lineage of David—
   to register with Mary, his espoused wife, who was with child.

While they were there the days of her confinement were completed.
She gave birth to her first-born son
   and wrapped him in swaddling clothes and laid him in a manger,
   because there was no room for them
     in the place where travelers lodged.

There were shepherds in the locality,
   living in the fields and keeping night watch
     by turns over their flocks.
The angel of the Lord appeared to them,
   as the glory of the Lord shone around them,
   and they were very much afraid.
The angel said to them: "You have nothing to fear!
I come to proclaim good news to you—
   tidings of great joy to be shared by the whole people.
This day in David's city a savior has been born to you,
   the Messiah and Lord.
Let this be a sign to you:
   in a manger you will find an infant wrapped in swaddling clothes."
Suddenly, there was with the angel a multitude of the heavenly host,
   praising God and saying,
     "Glory to God in high heaven,
   peace on earth to those on whom his favor rests."

This is the gospel of the Lord.

CHRISTMAS:MASS AT DAWN

FIRST READING

Isaiah 62, 11-12   Your savior is born.

The conclusion of a poem on Jerusalem, restored after its destruction, as the Lord's bride.   The Messiah, her savior, is coming.   "Frequented" in the ninth line means "full of people."

A reading from the book of the prophet I-sai-ah

See, the Lord proclaims
   to the ends of the earth:
Say to daughter Zí-on,
   your savior comes!
Here is his reward with him,
   his recompense before him.
They shall be called the holy people,
   the redeemed of the Lord,
and you shall be called "Frequented,"
   a city that is not forsaken.

   This is the Word of the Lord.

RESPONSORIAL PSALM

Psalm 97, 1. 6. 11-12 After the reading the psalmist sings or says the responsorial verse, and all repeat it. This response is also repeated after each verse of the psalm.

Common response:

Lord, to - day we have seen your glo - ry.

Or:

℟. A light will shine on us this day: the Lord is born for us.

The Lord is king; let the earth rejoice;
    let the many isles be glad.
The heavens proclaim his justice,
    and all peoples see his glory. ℟.

Light dawns for the just;
    and gladness, for the upright of heart.
Be glad in the Lord, you just,
    and give thanks to his holy name. ℟.

SECOND READING

Titus 3, 4-7 His own compassion saved us.

God saved us because he is loving and merciful. He saved us by baptism and the Holy Spirit which Christ gave us. Read as an extract from a personal letter of advice to a newly appointed Bishop, on matters of pastoral duty and essential Christian doctrine.

A reading from the letter of Paul to Tí-tus

When the kindness and love of God our Savior appeared,
    he saved us, not because of any righteous deeds we had done,
    but because of his mercy.
He saved us through the baptism of new birth
    and renewal by the Holy Spirit.
This Spirit he lavished on us through Jesus Christ our Savior,
    that we might be justified by his grace
    and become heirs, in hope, of eternal life.

This is the Word of the Lord.

GOSPEL

*The cantor sings the alleluia and the people repeat it; the cantor then
sings the verse and the people repeat the alleluia. Otherwise the alleluia
may be omitted. Reference: Luke 2, 14.*

Al - le - lu - ia, al - le - lu - ia, al - le - lu - ia.

Glo - ry to God in heav - en, peace and grace to His peo - ple on earth.

*Luke 2, 15-20 The shepherds found Mary and Joseph, and the baby
lying in the manger.*

*The end of the story of the shepherds of Bethlehem. Straight
story telling. Slight stress on "Mary treasured. . . . heart."*

✠ A reading from the holy gospel according to Luke

When the angels had returned to heaven,
 the shepherds said to one another:
  "Let us go over to Béth-le-hem and see this event
  which the Lord has made known to us."
They went in haste and found Mary and Joseph,
 and the baby lying in the manger;
 once they saw, they understood
 what had been told them concerning this child.
All who heard of it were astonished
 at the report given them by the shepherds.
Mary treasured all these things and reflected on them in her heart.
The shepherds returned, glorifying and praising God
 for all they had heard and seen,
 in accord with what had been told them.

This is the gospel of the Lord.

CHRISTMAS: MASS DURING THE DAY

FIRST READING

Isaiah 52, 7-10 All the ends of the earth shall see the salvation of our God.

A song of excited rejoicing that the exiles in Babylon are coming back to Jerusalem. The watchmen cry out in joy, for now the Lord will restore the Holy City.

A reading from the book of the prophet I-sai-ah

How beautiful upon the mountains
   are the feet of him who brings glad tidings,
Announcing peace, bearing good news,
   announcing salvation, and saying to Zi-on,
   "Your God is King! "

Hark!   Your watchmen raise a cry,
   together they shout for joy,
For they see directly, before their eyes,
   the Lord restoring Zi-on.
Break out together in song,
   O ruins of Jer-ú-sa-lem!
For the Lord comforts his people,
   he redeems Jer-ú-sa-lem.
The Lord has bared his holy arm
   in the sight of all the nations;
All the ends of the earth will behold
   the salvation of our God.

   This is the word of the Lord.

RESPONSORIAL PSALM

Psalm 98, 1. 2-3. 3-4. 5-6 After the reading the psalmist sings or says the responsorial verse and all repeat it. This response is also repeated after each verse of the psalm.

Common response:

Lord, to - day we have seen your glo - ry.

Or:

℟. All the ends of the earth have seen the saving power of God.

Sing to the Lord a new song,
 for he has done wondrous deeds;
His right hand has won victory for him,
 his holy arm. ℟.

The Lord has made his salvation known:
 in the sight of the nations he has revealed his justice.
He has remembered his kindness and his faithfulness
 toward the house of Israel. ℟.

All the ends of the earth have seen
 the salvation by our God.
Sing joyfully to the Lord, all you lands;
 break into song; sing praise. ℟.

Sing praise to the Lord with the harp,
 with the harp and melodious song.
With trumpets and the sound of the horn
 sing joyfully before the King, the Lord. ℟.

SECOND READING

Hebrews 1, 1-6   In our own time, God speaks to us through his Son.

Straight triumphant proclamation that Jesus is the Son to whom God the Father has entrusted all things.

A reading from the letter of Paul to the Hebrews

In times past, God spoke in fragmentary and varied ways
    to our fathers through the prophets;
    in this, the final age, he has spoken to us
    through his Son, whom he has made heir of all things
    and through whom he first created the universe.
This Son is the reflection of the Father's glory,
    the exact representation of the Father's being,
    and he sustains all things by his powerful word.
When he had cleansed us from our sins,
    he took his seat at the right hand of the Majesty in heaven,
    as far superior to the angels
    as the name he has inherited is superior to theirs.

To which of the angels did God ever say,
    "You are my son; today I have begotten you"?
Or again,
    "I will be his father, and he shall be my son"?
And again when he leads his first-born into the world, he says,
    "Let all the angels of God worship him."

    This is the Word of the Lord.

GOSPEL

The cantor sings the alleluia and the people repeat it; the cantor then sings the verse and the people repeat the alleluia. Otherwise the alleluia may be omitted.

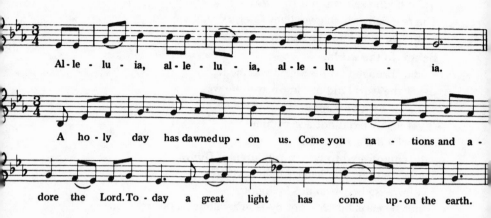

Al - le - lu - ia, al - le - lu - ia, al - le - lu - ia.

A ho - ly day has dawned up - on us. Come you na - tions and a -

dore the Lord. To - day a great light has come up - on the earth.

Long Form: John 1, 1-18 The Word was made flesh, he lived among us, and we saw his glory.

The opening of the fourth Gospel. John's general theme is that Jesus, born in the stable at Bethlehem, is not only a man but also Christ, the Messiah, the Son of God. John's Gospel opens: "In the beginning was the Word . . . " By the "Word," is meant "God's creative wisdom," personified in the Son, the second person of the Trinity.

This passage, and indeed every reading from the fourth Gospel, calls for very special skill in conveying both the simplicity of the language and the depth of the thought. Read sentence by sentence slowly, and so clearly that everyone present can comprehend the words and their meaning.

✠ The beginning of the holy gospel according to John

In the beginning was the Word;
   the Word was in God's presence,
    and the Word was God.
He was present to God in the beginning.
Through him all things came into being,
   and apart from him nothing came to be.
Whatever came to be in him, found life,
   life for the light of men.
The light shines on in darkness,
   a darkness that did not overcome it.

There was a man named John sent by God,
   who came as a witness to testify to the light,
   so that through him all men might believe—
   but only to testify to the light,
   for he himself was not the light.
The real light which gives light to every man
   was coming into the world.

He was in the world,
   and through him the world was made,
   yet the world did not know who he was.
   To his own he came,
   yet his own did not accept him.
Any who did accept him
   he empowered to become children of God.
These are they who believe in his name—
   who were begotten not by blood,
   nor by carnal desire, nor by man's willing it, but by God.
The Word became flesh
   and made his dwelling among us,
   and we have seen his glory:
   the glory of an only Son coming from the Father, filled with enduring love.
John testified to him by proclaiming,
   "This is he of whom I said,
'The one who comes after me ranks ahead of me,
for he was before me.' "
Of his fullness we have all had a share—
   love following upon love.
For while the law was given through Moses,
   this enduring love came through Jesus Christ.
No one has ever seen God.
It is God the only Son, ever at the Father's side,
   who has revealed him.

   This is the gospel of the Lord.

Short Form: *John 1, 1-5. 9-14* *The Word was made flesh, he lived among us, and we saw his glory.*

✠ The beginning of the holy gospel according to John

In the beginning was the Word;
   the Word was in God's presence,
   and the Word was God.
He was present to God in the beginning.
Through him all things came into being,
   and apart from him nothing came to be.
Whatever came to be in him, found life,
   life for the light of men.
The light shines on in darkness,
   a darkness that did not overcome it.
The real light which gives light to every man
   was coming into the world.
He was in the world
   and through him the world was made,
   yet the world did not know who he was.
To his own he came,
   yet his own did not accept him.
Any who did accept him
   he empowered to become children of God.
These are they who believe in his name—
   who were begotten not by blood,
   nor by carnal desire, nor by man's willing it, but by God.
The Word became flesh
   and made his dwelling among us,
   and we have seen his glory:
   the glory of an only Son coming from the Father,
   filled with enduring love.

This is the gospel of the Lord.

SUNDAY IN THE OCTAVE OF CHRISTMAS: HOLY FAMILY

FIRST READING

Sirach 3, 2-6. 12-14   He who fears the Lord honors his parents.

The Book of Sirach (also called Ecclesiaticus) is a collection of wise sayings, mainly on human behavior. This passage comes from a section on a son's duty to his parents. Bring out the style one line paralleled by the next, and each couplet making a proverb. Pause slightly after each.

A reading from the book of Sí-rach

The Lord sets a father in honor over his children;
   a mother's authority he confirms over her sons.
He who honors his father atones for sins;
   he stores up riches who reveres his mother.
He who honors his father is gladdened by children,
   and when he prays he is heard.
He who reveres his father will live a long life;
   he obeys the Lord who brings comfort to his mother.
My son, take care of your father when he is old;
   grieve him not as long as he lives.
Even if his mind fail, be considerate with him;
   revile him not in the fullness of your strength.
For kindness to a father will not be forgotten,
   it will serve as a sin offering—it will take lasting root.

This is the Word of the Lord.

RESPONSORIAL PSALM

Psalm 128, 1-2. 3. 4-5 After the reading the psalmist sings or says the responsorial verse, and all repeat it. This response is also repeated after each verse of the psalm.

Common response:

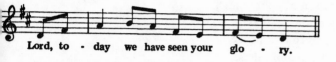

Lord, to - day we have seen your glo - ry.

Or:

℟. Happy are those who fear the Lord
   and walk in his ways.

Happy are you who fear the Lord,
   who walk in his ways!
For you shall eat the fruit of your handiwork;
   happy shall you be, and favored.   ℟.

Your wife shall be like a fruitful vine
   in the recesses of your home;
Your children like olive plants
   around your table.   ℟.

Behold, thus is the man blessed
   who fears the Lord.
The Lord bless you from Zí-on:
   may you see the prosperity of Jerusalem
   all the days of your life.   ℟.

SECOND READING

Colossians 3, 12-21 Concerning the Christian life in the world.

Paul's advice on how Christians should behave towards each other and particularly in the family. The message is full of warm affection, made more effective if you pause slightly and often to stress every shade of meaning.——e.g. "clothe yourselves with heart-felt mercy,/ with kindness,/ humility,/ meekness,/ and patience."

A reading from the letter of Paul to the Co-lós-si-ans

Because you are God's chosen ones, holy and beloved,
   clothe yourselves with heartfelt mercy,
      with kindness, humility, meekness, and patience.

Bear with one another;
  forgive whatever grievances you have against one another.

Forgive as the Lord has forgiven you.
Over all these virtues put on love,
  which binds the rest together and makes them perfect.
Christ's peace must reign in your hearts,
  since as members of the one body
  you have been called to that peace.
Dedicate yourselves to thankfulness.
Let the word of Christ, rich as it is, dwell in you,
In wisdom made perfect, instruct and admonish one another.
Sing gratefully to God from your hearts.
  in psalms, hymns, and inspired songs.
Whatever you do, whether in speech or in action,
  do it in the name of the Lord Jesus.
Give thanks to God the Father through him.

You who are wives, be submissive to your husbands.
This is your duty in the Lord.
Husbands, love your wives.
Avoid any bitterness toward them.
You children, obey your parents in everything
  as the acceptable way in the Lord.
And fathers, do not nag your children lest they lose heart.

  This is the Word of the Lord.

GOSPEL

The cantor sings the alleluia and the people repeat it; the cantor then
sings the verse and the people repeat the alleluia. Otherwise the alleluia
may be omitted. Reference: Colossians 3, 15. 16.

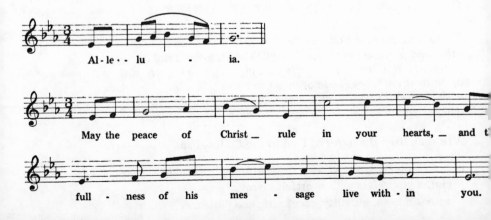

Al - le - - lu - ia.

May the peace of Christ _ rule in your hearts, _ and the

full - ness of his mes - sage live with - in you.

Luke 2, 41-52 His parents found him in the temple, sitting among the doctors, listening to them.

This very human story is the only recorded incident in the boyhood of Jesus. Contrast the growing anxiety of Mary and her protest with the boy's calmness and surprise that his Mother should not have understood how natural it was for him to be found in the Temple. Stress the contrast between "your father" and "my Father's house."

✠ A reading from the holy gospel according to Luke

The parents of Jesus used to go every year to Je-rú-sa-lem
   for the feast of the Pás-so-ver,
   and when he was twelve
   they went up for the celebration as was their custom.
As they were returning at the end of the feast,
   the child Jesus remained behind unknown to his parents.
Thinking he was in the party,
   they continued their journey for a day,
   looking for him among their relatives and acquaintances.

Not finding him, they returned to Je-rú-sa-lem in search of him.
On the third day they came upon him in the temple
   sitting in the midst of the teachers,
   listening to them and asking them questions.
All who heard him were amazed
   at his intelligence and his answers.

When his parents saw him they were astonished,
   and his mother said to him:
   "Son, why have you done this to us?
You see that your father and I
   have been searching for you in sorrow."
He said to them:
   "Why did you search for me?
Did you not know I had to be in my Father's house? "
But they did not grasp what he said to them.

He went down with them then, and came to Ná-za-reth,
   and was obedient to them.
His mother meanwhile kept all these things in memory.
Jesus, for his part, progressed steadily
   in wisdom and age and grace before God and men.

   This is the gospel of the Lord.

OCTAVE OF CHRISTMAS:
SOLEMNITY OF MARY, MOTHER OF GOD

FIRST READING

*Numbers 6, 22-27   They will call down my name on the sons of Israel
and I will bless them.*

*The form of the words to be used all call down God's blessing on
his people. The name of God is Yahweh (I am), but "the Lord"
was substituted by those who regarded "Yahweh" as too sacred
to be mentioned. Yahweh is used by many modern scholars, as
in the Jerusalem Bible. It is not allowed in the liturgy of the
Church.*

Read the blessings slowly and distinctly, with a pause after each.

A reading from the book of Numbers

The Lord said to Moses:
   "Speak to Aaron and his sons and tell them:
   This is how you shall bless the Israelites. Say to them:
   The Lord bless you and keep you!
The Lord let his face shine upon you, and be gracious to you!
The Lord look upon you kindly and give you peace!
So shall they invoke my name upon the Israelites,
   and I will bless them."

   This is the Word of the Lord.

RESPONSORIAL PSALM

*Psalm 67, 2-3. 5. 6. 8   After the reading the psalmist sings or says
the responsorial verse, and all repeat it. This response is also
repeated after each verse of the psalm.*

Common response:

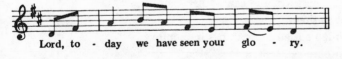

Lord, to - day we have seen your glo - ry.

Or:

℞. May God bless us in his mercy.

May God have pity on us and bless us;
   may he let his face shine upon us.
So may your way be known upon earth;
   among all nations, your salvation. ℟.

May the nations be glad and exult
   because you rule the peoples in equity;
   the nations on the earth you guide. ℟.

May the peoples praise you, O God;
   may all the peoples praise you!
May God bless us,
   and may all the ends of the earth fear him! ℟.

SECOND READING

*Galatians 4, 4-7 When the appointed time came, God sent his son,
born of a woman.*

*Jewish converts to Christianity often insisted that Gentile con-
verts be bound by the Mosaic Law, and follow all its ritual observances, otherwise they could not receive the promised blessings. Paul contradicts them, saying that God sent his Son to
deliver believers from the Old Law. All who accept Christ are
God's adopted sons. Read with vigor as a straight declaration
to the Galation converts from paganism that they are as much
God's sons as the Jewish Christians.*

A reading from the letter of Paul to the Gal-á-tians

When the designated time had come,
   God sent forth his Son born of a woman,
   born under the law, to deliver from the law
   those who were subjected to it,
   so that we might receive our status as adopted sons.
The proof that you are sons
   is the fact that God has sent forth into our hearts
   the spirit of his Son which cries out "Ab-ba! " ("Father! ").
You are no longer a slave but a son!
And the fact that you are a son
   makes you an heir, by God's design.

   This is the Word of the Lord.

GOSPEL

*The cantor sings the alleluia and the people repeat it; the cantor then
sings the verse and the people repeat the alleluia. Otherwise the alleluia
may be omitted. Reference: Hebrews 1, 1-2.*

Al - le - lu - ia.

In   the   past   God spoke   to   our   fa - thers through the proph-ets;

now   he speaks to   us   through   his   Son.

*Luke 2, 16-21   The shepherds found Mary and Joseph, and the infant
lying in the crib. . .When the eighth day came they gave him the name
of Jesus.*

The end of the story of the shepherds of Bethlehem.

✤ A reading from the holy gospel according to Luke

The shepherds went in haste to Béth-le-hem and found Mary and Joseph,
   and the baby lying in the manger;
   once they saw, they understood
   what had been told them concerning this child.
All who heard of it were astonished
   at the report given them by the shepherds.

Mary treasured all these things
   and reflected on them in her heart.
The shepherds returned, glorifying and praising God
   for all they had heard and seen,
   in accord with what had been told them.

When the eighth day arrived for his circumcision,
   the name Jesus was given the child,
   the name the angel had given him before he was conceived.

This is the gospel of the Lord.

SECOND SUNDAY AFTER CHRISTMAS

FIRST READING

Sirach 24, 1-2. 8-12　The wisdom of God lives in his people.

This reading needs careful study to bring out its full meaning. Wisdom is singing her own praise. She came forth from God's mouth as a separate spiritual being. God sent her to live with his people of Israel. She served him in the holy tent (i.e. the tabernacle which was constructed in the desert, and then in Solomon's Temple in Zion. Jerusalem, God's own holy city, is her natural home. Read as a song of praise.

A reading from the book of Sí-rach

Wisdom sings her own praises,
    before her own people she proclaims her glory;
In the assembly of the Most High she opens her mouth,
    in the presence of his hosts she declares her worth:
Then the Creator of all gave me his command,
    and he who formed me chose the spot for my tent,
Saying, "In Jacob make your dwelling,
    in Israel your inheritance."
Before all ages, in the beginning, he created me,
    and through all ages I shall not cease to be.
In the holy tent I ministered before him,
    and in Zion I fixed my abode.
Thus in the chosen city he has given me rest,
    in Jer-ú-sa-lem is my domain.
I have struck root among the glorious people,
    in the portion of the Lord, his heritage.

    This is the Word of the Lord.

RESPONSORIAL PSALM

*Psalm 147, 12-13. 14-15. 19-20   After the reading the psalmist sings or
says the responsorial verse, and all repeat it. This response is also
repeated after each verse of the psalm.*

Common response:

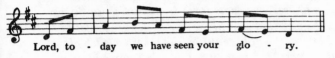

Lord, to - day   we   have seen your   glo - ry.

Or:

℟. The Word of God became man,
        and lived among us.

Glorify the Lord, O Jerusalem;
    praise your God, O Zion.
For he has strengthened the bars of your gates;
    he has blessed your children within you.   ℟.

He has granted peace in your borders;
    with the best of wheat he fills you.
He sends forth his command to the earth;
    swiftly runs his word!   ℟.

He has proclaimed his word to Jacob,
    his statutes and his ordinances to Israel.
He has not done thus for any other nation;
    his ordinances he has not made known to them. Alleluia.   ℟.

SECOND READING

Ephesians 1, 3-6. 15-18   He has blessed us with all the spiritual blessings of heaven in Jesus.

Read the first section as an expression of triumph, almost a hymn, praising God the Father for choosing us as his adopted sons. In the second section, Paul becomes more personal as he thanks God for the Christian spirit of the Ephesians. He prays that God will grant them the wisdom to know him clearly. Be ready for the long sentences.

A reading from the letter of Paul to the E-phé-si-ans

Praised be the God and Father of our Lord Jesus Christ,
    who has bestowed on us in Christ
    every spiritual blessing in the heavens!
God chose us in him before the world began
    to be holy and blameless in his sight,
    to be full of love;
    he likewise predestined us through Christ Jesus to be his adopted sons—
    such was his will and pleasure—
    that all might praise the glorious favor
    he has bestowed on us in his beloved.

For my part, from the time I first heard of your faith in the Lord Jesus
    and your love for all the members of the church,
    I have never stopped thanking God for you
    and recommending you in my prayers.
May the God of our Lord Jesus Christ, the Father of glory,
    grant you a spirit of wisdom and insight to know him clearly.
May he enlighten your innermost vision
    that you may know the great hope to which he has called you,
    the wealth of his glorious heritage
    to be distributed among the members of the church.

    This is the Word of the Lord.

GOSPEL

*The cantor sings the alleluia and the people repeat it; the cantor then
sings the verse and the people repeat the alleluia. Otherwise the alleluia
may be omitted. Reference: 1 Timothy 3, 16.*

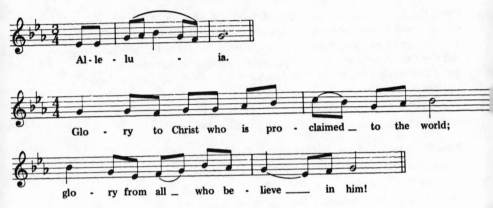

Al - le - lu - ia.

Glo - ry to Christ who is pro - claimed _ to the world;
glo - ry from all _ who be - lieve ____ in him!

*Long Form: John 1, 1-18   The Word was made flesh,
he lived among us, and we saw his glory.*

*The opening of the fourth Gospel. John's general theme is that
Jesus, born in the stable at Bethlehem, is not only a man but also
Christ, the Messiah, the Son of God. John's Gospel opens: "In
the beginning was the Word . . . " By the "Word" is meant "God's
creative Wisdom," personified in the Son, the second person of the
Trinity.*

*This passage, and indeed every reading from the fourth Gospel,
calls for very special skill in conveying both the simplicity of the
language and the depth of the thought. Read sentence by sentence
slowly, and so clearly that everyone present can comprehend the
words and their meaning.*

✠ The beginning of the holy gospel according to John

In the beginning was the Word;
  the Word was in God's presence,
  and the Word was God.
He was present to God in the beginning.
Through him all things came into being,
  and apart from him nothing came to be.
Whatever came to be in him, found life,
  life for the light of men.
The light shines on in darkness,
  a darkness that did not overcome it.

There was a man named John sent by God,
   who came as a witness to testify to the light,
   so that through him all men might believe—
   but only to testify to the light,
   for he himself was not the light.
The real light which gives light to every man
   was coming into the world.
He was in the world,
   and through him the world was made,
   yet the world did not know who he was.
To his own he came,
   yet his own did not accept him.
Any who did accept him
   he empowered to become children of God.
These are they who believe in his name—
   who were begotten not by blood,
   nor by carnal desire, nor by man's willing it, but by God.
The Word became flesh
   and made his dwelling among us,
   and we have seen his glory:
   the glory of an only Son coming from the Father,
   filled with enduring love.
John testified to him by proclaiming:
   "This is he of whom I said,
   'The one who comes after me ranks ahead of me,
   for he was before me.' "
Of his fullness
   we have all had a share—
   love following upon love.
For while the law was a gift through Moses,
   this enduring love came through Jesus Christ.
No one has ever seen God.
It is God the only Son,
   ever at the Father's side,
   who has revealed him.

   This is the gospel of the Lord.

Short Form: John 1, 1-5. 9-14 The Word was made flesh,
he lived among us, and we saw his glory.

✠ The beginning of the holy gospel according to John

In the beginning was the Word;
    the Word was in God's presence,
    and the Word was God.
He was present to God in the beginning.
Through him all things came into being,
    and apart from him nothing came to be.
Whatever came to be in him, found life,
    life for the light of men.
The light shines on in darkness,
    a darkness that did not overcome it.
The real light which gives light to every man
    was coming into the world.
He was in the world,
    and through him the world was made,
    yet the world did not know who he was.
To his own he came,
    yet his own did not accept him.
Any who did accept him
    he empowered to become children of God.
These are they who believe in his name—
    who were begotten not by blood,
    nor by carnal desire, nor by man's willing it, but by God.
The Word became flesh
    and made his dwelling among us,
    and we have seen his glory:
    the glory of an only Son coming from the Father,
    filled with enduring love.

    This is the gospel of the Lord.

EPIPHANY

FIRST READING

Isaiah 60, 1-6   The glory of the Lord shines upon you.

A song about the New Jerusalem. Read with enthusiasm, observ-ing the poetic pattern of this song of praise for Jerusalem made glorious by the coming of the Lord to his own city. Slight empha-sis on the words denoting light, radiance and magnificence.

A reading from the book of the prophet I-saí-ah

Rise up in splendor, Jer-ú-sa-lem! Your light has come,
   the glory of the Lord shines upon you.
See, darkness covers the earth,
   and thick clouds cover the peoples;
But upon you the Lord shines,
   and over you appears his glory.
Nations shall walk by your light,
   and kings by your shining radiance.
Raise your eyes and look about;
   they all gather and come to you:
Your sons come from afar,
   and your daughters in the arms of their nurses.

Then you shall be radiant at what you see,
   your heart shall throb and overflow,
For the riches of the sea shall be emptied out before you,
   the wealth of nations shall be brought to you.
Caravans of camels shall fill you,
   dromedaries from Míd-ian and Éph-ah;
All from Shé-ba shall come
   bearing gold and frankincense,
   and proclaiming the praises of the Lord.

   This is the Word of the Lord.

RESPONSORIAL PSALM

Psalm 72, 1-2. 7-8. 10-11. 12-13   After the reading the psalmist sings or says the responsorial verse, and all repeat it.   This response is also repeated after each verse of the psalm.

Common response:

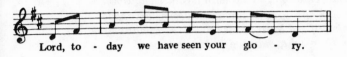

Lord, to - day we have seen your glo - ry.

Or:

℞. Lord, every nation on earth will adore you.

O God, with your judgment endow the king,
    and with your justice, the king's son;
He shall govern your people with justice
    and your afflicted ones with judgment.   ℞.

Justice shall flower in his days,
    and profound peace, till the moon be no more.
May he rule from sea to sea,
    and from the River to the ends of the earth.   ℞.

The kings of Tár-shish and the Isles shall offer gifts;
    the kings of A-rá-bi-a and Sé-ba shall bring tribute.
All kings shall pay him homage,
    all nations shall serve him.   ℞.

For he shall rescue the poor man when he cries out,
    and the afflicted when he has no one to help him.
He shall have pity for the lowly and the poor;
    the lives of the poor he shall save.   ℞.

SECOND READING

Ephesians 3, 2-3. 5-6   The revelation means that pagans now share the same inheritance, that they are parts of the same body.

Paul's special mission was to bring the good news to the pagans (the Gentiles), for by Christ's coming, they were to be made co-heirs of the promises made to the Jews. To Jewish converts, brought up in the old law, this was not always an acceptable teaching.

Read as a straight statement.

A reading from the letter of Paul to the E-phé-si-ans

I am sure you have heard of the ministry
   which God in his goodness gave me in your regard.
God's secret plan, as I have briefly described it,
   was revealed to me, unknown to men in former ages
   but now revealed by the Spirit to the holy apostles and prophets.
It is no less than this:
   in Christ Jesus the Gén-tiles are now co-heirs with the Jews,
   members of the same body and sharers of the promise
   through the preaching of the gospel.

   This is the Word of the Lord.

GOSPEL

*The cantor sings the alleluia and the people repeat it; the cantor then
sings the verse and the people repeat the alleluia. Otherwise the alleluia
may be omitted. Reference: Matthew 2, 2.*

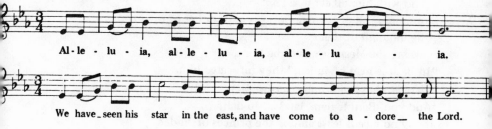

Matthew 2, 1-12 We have come from the East to worship the king.

*Wise Men from the East come searching for the Christ Child.
Bring out the drama of this story. Herod was a ruthless, suspi-
cious usurper and is naturally disturbed when strangers from the
East come looking for the newborn King of the Jews. He wants
to know more and consults the men learned in the Scriptures.
They reply with a passage from Micah 5: 1, 3*

*But you, Bethlehem—Ephrath
   too small to be among the clans of Judah,
From you shall come forth for me
   one who is to be ruler in Israel;
Whose origin is from old,
   from ancient times.
He shall stand firm and shepherd his flock
   by the strength of the Lord,
in the majestic name of the Lord, his God;
   And they shall remain, for now his greatness*

shall reach to the ends of the earth;
  he shall be peace.

Herod sends the Wise Men to Bethlehem hoping for further news
so that he may identify and kill the Child.
Straight, lively story-telling culminating in the symbolic gifts of
gold (for a king), frankincense (used in worshipping a God) and
myrrh (for suffering.)

✠   A reading from the holy gospel according to Mát-thew

After Jesus' birth in Béth-le-hem of Judea
  during the reign of King Herod,
    astrologers from the east arrived one day in Jer-ú-sa-lem inquiring,
    "Where is the newborn king of the Jews?
We observed his star at its rising
  and have come to pay him homage."
At this news King Herod became greatly disturbed,
  and with him all Jer-ú-sa-lem.
Summoning all of the chief priests and scribes of the people,
  he inquired of them
    where the Messiah was to be born.
"In Béth-le-hem of Judea," they informed him.
"Here is what the prophet has written:
'And you, Béth-le-hem, land of Jú-dah,
are by no means least among the princes of Jú-dah
  since from you shall come a ruler
    who is to shepherd my people Israel.' "
Herod called the astrologers aside
  and found out from them
    the exact time of the star's appearance.
Then he sent them to Béth-le-hem,
  after having instructed them:
    "Go and get detailed information about the child.
When you have found him,
  report it to me
    so that I may go and offer him homage too."

After their audience with the king, they set out.
The star which they had observed at its rising
  went ahead of them until it came to a standstill over the place where
    the child was.

They were overjoyed at seeing the star,
  and on entering the house,
  found the child with Mary his mother.
They prostrated themselves and did him homage.
Then they opened their coffers
  and presented him with gifts of gold, frankincense, and myrrh.

They received a message in a dream not to return to Herod,
  so they went back to their own country by another route.

  This is the gospel of the Lord.

BAPTISM OF THE LORD

FIRST READING

*Isaiah 42, 1-4. 6-7   Here is my servant, my chosen one in whom my
soul delights.*

*A brief extract from the first of the Songs of the Suffering Ser-
vant. Read as poetry in a solemn, almost somber tone. The
first stanza is spoken about the Servant; stress that he will be
quiet, meek and inconspicuous. In the second, the Lord
speaks to the Servant; his mission is to bring light and comfort.*

A reading from the book of the prophet I-saí-ah

Here is my servant whom I uphold,
  my chosen one with whom I am pleased,
Upon whom I have put my spirit;
  he shall bring forth justice to the nations,
Not crying out, not shouting,
  not making his voice heard in the street.
A bruised reed he shall not break,
  and a smoldering wick he shall not quench,
Until he establishes justice on the earth;
  the coastlands will wait for his teaching.

I, the Lord, have called you for the victory of justice,
  I have grasped you by the hand;
  I formed you, and set you
  as a covenant of the people,
  a light for the nations,
To open the eyes of the blind,
  to bring out prisoners from confinement,
  and from the dungeon, those who live in darkness.

  This is the Word of the Lord.

RESPONSORIAL PSALM

Psalm 29, 1-2. 3-4. 3. 9-10 After the reading the psalmist sings or says the responsorial verse, and all repeat it. This response is also repeated after each verse of the psalm.

Common response:

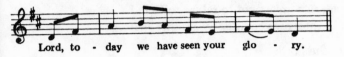

Lord, to - day we have seen your glo - ry.

Or:

℟. The Lord will bless his people with peace.

Give to the Lord, you sons of God,
  give to the Lord glory and praise,
Give to the Lord the glory due his name;
  adore the Lord in holy attire. ℟.

The voice of the Lord is over the waters,
  the Lord, over vast waters.
The voice of the Lord is mighty;
  the voice of the Lord is majestic. ℟.

The God of glory thunders,
  and in his temple all say, "Glory! "
The Lord is enthroned above the flood;
  the Lord is enthroned as king forever. ℟.

SECOND READING

Acts 10, 34-38   God anointed him with the Holy Spirit and with power.

Cornelius, a Roman centurion, is sent to ask if Peter would preach the Gospel to the household. As a strict Jew, Peter had not hitherto realized that the good news was intended for any but the Jews. Nevertheless, after a remarkable dream, he went, preached, and baptized the whole household. This is the first recorded sermon to pagans; the previous addresses in Acts had been to convince the Jews.

In reading, realize what Peter is feeling. He is still surprised that God should have called a pagan. In speaking to Cornelius and his people, he remembers that they have a very different background from the Jews whom he has hitherto addressed.

A reading from the Acts of the Apostles

Peter addressed Cor-né-li-us and the people assembled at his house
    in these words:
  "I begin to see how true it is
  that God shows no partiality.
Rather, the man of any nation
  who fears God and acts uprightly is acceptable to him.
This is the message he has sent to the sons of Israel,
  'the good news of peace' proclaimed through Jesus Christ
    who is Lord of all.
I take it you know what has been reported
  all over Judea about Jesus of Ná-za-reth,
  beginning in Gá-li-lee with the baptism John preached;
  of the way God anointed him with the Holy Spirit and power.
He went about doing good works
  and healing all who were in the grip of the devil,
  and God was with him."

This is the Word of the Lord.

GOSPEL

The cantor sings the alleluia and the people repeat it; the cantor then sings the verse and the people repeat the alleluia. Otherwise the alleluia may be omitted. Reference: Mark 9, 6.

Al - le - lu - ia.

The heavens were o - pened and the Fa - ther's voice ⸻ was heard: this is my be - lov - ed Son hear ⸻ him.

Luke 3, 15-16. 21-22   Someone is coming who is more powerful than I am, he will baptize you with the Holy Spirit and with fire.

This brief account of the baptism of Jesus is a reminder of an event well-known to Christians. Stress the final sentence.

✠   A reading from the holy gospel according to Luke

The people were full of anticipation,
    wondering in their hearts
    whether John might be the Mes-sí-ah.
John answered them all by saying:
    "I am baptizing you in water,
    but there is one to come who is mightier than I.
I am not fit to loosen his sandal strap.
He will baptize you in the Holy Spirit and in fire.

When all the people were baptized,
    and Jesus was at prayer
    after likewise being baptized,
    the skies opened and the Holy Spirit
    descended on him in visible form like a dove.
A voice from heaven was heard to say,
    "You are my beloved Son.
On you my favor rests."

    This is the gospel of the Lord.

FIRST SUNDAY OF LENT

FIRST READING

Deuteronomy 26, 4-10   The confession of faith of the elect.

Regulations for a rite of thanksgiving after harvest. The people must remember all that the Lord has done for them, from the call of Abraham to this day. The reminder applies also at the beginning of our season of penance.

A reading from the book of Deu-ter-ón-o-my

Moses told the people:
  "The priest shall receive the basket from you
  and shall set it in front of the altar of the Lord, your God.
Then you shall declare before the Lord, your God,
  'My father was a wandering A-ra-mé-an
  who went down to Egypt with a small household
  and lived there as an alien.
But there he became a nation great, strong, and numerous.
When É-gyp-ti-ans maltreated and oppressed us,
  imposing hard labor upon us,
  we cried to the Lord, the God of our fathers,
  and he heard our cry and saw our affliction,
  our toil and our oppression.
He brought us out of Egypt with his strong hand and outstretched arm,
  with terrifying power, with signs and wonders;
  and bringing us into this country,
  he gave us this land flowing with milk and honey.
Therefore, I have now brought you the first fruits
  of the products of the soil which you, O Lord, have given me.'
And having set them before the Lord, your God,
  you shall bow down in his presence.
Then you and your family,
  together with the Levite and the aliens who live among you,
  shall make merry over all these good things
  which the Lord, your God, has given you.

  This is the Word of the Lord.

RESPONSORIAL PSALM

*Psalm 91, 1-2. 10-11. 12-13. 14-15   After the reading the psalmist sings or
says the responsorial verse, and all repeat it. This response is also
repeated after each verse of the psalm.*

Common response:

Re - mem - ber your love   and   your   faith - ful - ness,   Lord.

Or:

℟. Be with me, Lord, when I am in trouble.

You who dwell in the shelter of the Most High,
   who abide in the shadow of the Almighty,
Say to the Lord, "My refuge and my fortress,
   my God, in whom I trust."   ℟.

No evil shall befall you,
   nor shall affliction come near your tent,
For to his angels he has given command about you,
   that they guard you in all your ways.   ℟.

Upon their hands they shall bear you up,
   lest you dash your foot against a stone.
You shall tread upon the asp and the viper;
   you shall trample down the lion and the dragon.   ℟.

Because he clings to me, I will deliver him;
   I will set him on high because he acknowledges my name.
He shall call upon me, and I will answer him;
   I will be with him in distress;
I will deliver him and glorify him.   ℟.

SECOND READING

Romans 10, 8-13   The confession of faith of the believers in Christ.

*Christians, whatever their origin, must openly and freely profess
their faith, of which the two most important facts are that Jesus
is Lord, and that God raised him from the dead. State all this
clearly and emphatically, sentence by sentence.*

A reading from the letter of Paul to the Romans

What does Scripture say?
"The word is near you,
> on your lips and in your heart
> (that is, the word of faith which we preach)."
For if you confess with your lips that Jesus is Lord,
> and believe in your heart that God raised him from the dead,
> you will be saved.
Faith in the heart leads to justification,
> confession on the lips to salvation.
Scripture says, "No one who believes in him
> will be put to shame."
Here there is no difference between Jew and Greek;
> all have the same Lord,
> rich in mercy toward all who call upon him.
"Everyone who calls on the name of the Lord
> will be saved."

> This is the Word of the Lord.

GOSPEL

*The cantor sings the response and the people repeat it; the cantor
then sings the verse before the gospel and the people repeat the
response. Otherwise the verse before the gospel may be omitted.
Reference: Matthew 4, 4.*

Praise and hon - or to you, Lord___ Je - sus Christ.

For other responses to the verse see page 436.

Man does not live on bread a - lone, but on ev - 'ry word that

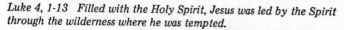

comes from the mouth _ of ___ God.

*Luke 4, 1-13 Filled with the Holy Spirit, Jesus was led by the Spirit
through the wilderness where he was tempted.*

*Before beginning his ministry, Jesus withdrew into the desert
and fasted for forty days. Here the Devil tempted him to show
his divine power in three ways; by satisfying his hunger; to
satisfy human ambition by seeking power over men; by showing*

a spectacular sign that he is more than human. Unlike Adam,
Christ rebuffed the enemy. Read without emotion, for this is
not a story of a clash of human wills, but a cosmic contest between
Good and Evil.

✠   A reading from the holy gospel according to Luke

Jesus, full of the Holy Spirit, returned from the Jordan
    and was led by the Spirit into the desert for forty days,
    where he was tempted by the devil.
During that time he ate nothing,
    and at the end of it he was hungry.
The devil said to him,
    "If you are the Son of God,
    command this stone to turn into bread."
Jesus answered him, "Scripture has it,
    'Not on bread alone shall man live.' "

Then the devil took him up higher
    and showed him all the kingdoms of the world in a single instant.
He said to him,
    "I will give you all this power
    and the glory of these kingdoms;
    the power has been given to me
    and I give it to whomever I wish.
Prostrate yourself in homage before me,
    and it shall all be yours."
In reply, Jesus said to him, "Scripture has it,
    'You shall do homage to the Lord your God;
    him alone shall you adore.' "

Then the devil led him to Je-rú-sa-lem,
    set him on the parapet of the temple,
    and said to him,
    "If you are the Son of God,
    throw yourself down from here, for Scripture has it,
    'He will bid his angels watch over you'; and again,
    'With their hands they will support you,
    that you may never stumble on a stone.' "

Jesus said to him in reply,
    "It also says,
    'You shall not put the Lord your God to the test.' "
When the devil had finished all this tempting
    he left him, to await another opportunity.

    This is the gospel of the Lord.

SECOND SUNDAY OF LENT

FIRST READING

Genesis 15, 5-12. 17-18 Abraham put his faith in the Lord.

*From the account of a vision granted to Abraham, in which the
Lord promised that he would be given the long desired son and
that his descendants would become a great people. Suggest the
atmosphere of the vision, and especially the dreamlike appearance
of the brazier and the torch. At the same time indicate that the
call and the promises given to Abraham mark the beginning of the
events that lead up to the birth of the Messiah.*

A reading from the book of Gé-ne-sis

God took Abram outside and said:
"Look up at the sky and count the stars, if you can.
Just so," he added, "shall your descendants be."
Abram put his faith in the Lord,
  who credited it to him as an act of righteousness.

He then said to him,
  "I am the Lord who brought you from Ur of the Chal-dé-ans
  to give you this land as a possession."
"O Lord God," he asked,
  "how am I to know that I shall possess it? "
He answered him,
  "Bring me a three-year-old heifer,
  a three-year-old she-goat, a three-year-old ram,
  a turtledove, and a young pigeon."
He brought him all these,
  split them in two,
  and placed each half opposite the other;
  but the birds he did not cut up.
Birds of prey swooped down on the carcasses,
  but Abram stayed with them.
As the sun was about to set,
  a trance fell upon Abram,
  and a deep, terrifying darkness enveloped him.

When the sun had set and it was dark,
  there appeared a smoking brazier and a flaming torch,
  which passed between those pieces.
It was on that occasion
  that the Lord made a covenant with Abram, saying:
  "To your descendants I give this land
  from the Wá-di of Egypt to the Great River [the Eu-phrá-tes.]
This is the Word of the Lord.

RESPONSORIAL PSALM

*Psalm 27, 1. 7-8. 8-9. 13-14 After the reading the psalmist sings or
says the responsorial verse, and all repeat it. This response is also
repeated after each verse of the psalm.*

Common response:

Re - mem - ber your love and your faith - ful - ness, Lord

Or:

R̸. The Lord is my light and my salvation.

The Lord is my light and my salvation;
   whom should I fear?
The Lord is my life's refuge;
   of whom should I be afraid? R̸.

Hear, O Lord, the sound of my call;
   have pity on me, and answer me.
Of you my heart speaks; you my glance seeks. R̸.

Your presence, O Lord, I seek.
Hide not your face from me;
   Do not in anger repel your servant.
You are my helper: cast me not off. R̸.

I believe that I shall see the bounty of the Lord
   in the land of the living.
Wait for the Lord with courage;
   be stouthearted, and wait for the Lord. R̸.

SECOND READING

*Long Form: Philippians 3, 17-4. 1   Christ will transfigure these
wretched bodies of ours into copies of his glorious body.*

*Paul exhorts his converts in Philippi to remember that Christians
must live after the model he has shown them; they must not
follow those who indulge in every kind of easy living in the world,
for Christians are citizens of heaven. An earnest plea for self
discipline.*

A reading from the letter of Paul to the Phil-íp-pi-ans

Be imitators of me, my brothers.
Take as your guide
   those who follow the example that we set.
Unfortunately, many go about
   in a way which shows them to be enemies of the cross of Christ.
I have often said this to you before;
   this time I say it with tears.
Such as these will end in disaster!
Their god is their belly
   and their glory is in their shame.
I am talking about those
   who are set upon the things of this world.
As you well know,
   we have our citizenship in heaven;
   it is from there that we eagerly await
   the coming of our savior, the Lord Jesus Christ.
He will give a new form to this lowly body of ours
   and remake it according to the pattern of his glorified body,
   by his power to subject everything to himself.
For these reasons, my brothers,
   you whom I so love and long for,
   you who are my joy and my crown,
   continue, my dear ones, to stand firm in the Lord.

   This is the Word of the Lord.

Or Short Form: Philippians 3, 20-4, 1   Christ will transfigure these wretched bodies of ours into copies of his glorious body.

A reading from the letter of Paul to the Phil-íp-pi-ans

As you well know,
> we have our citizenship in heaven;
> it is from there that we eagerly await
> the coming of our savior, the Lord Jesus Christ.

He will give a new form to this lowly body of ours
> and remake it according to the pattern of his glorified body,
> by his power to subject everything to himself.

For the rest, my brothers,
> rejoice in the Lord.
> I find writing you these things no burden,
> and for you it is a safeguard.

This is the Word of the Lord.

GOSPEL

*The cantor sings the response and the people repeat it; the cantor
then sings the verse before the gospel and the people repeat the response.
Otherwise the verse before the gospel may be omitted.*

Praise and hon - or to you, Lord___ Je - sus Christ.

For other responses to the verse see page 436.

From the shin - ing cloud the Fa - ther's voice is heard:

this is my be - lov - ed Son; hear him.

Luke 9, 28-36 As Jesus prayed, the aspect of his face was changed and his clothing became brilliant as lightning.

The vision of Jesus glorified should be read as if you had heard it from one of the eyewitnesses, as the true account of a mystical experience that is beyond analysis or explanation. Slightly emphasize the brightness, and have in mind that this divine manifestation is a parallel to the visions of God himself recorded in various places in the Old Testament.

☩   A reading from the holy gospel according to Luke

Jesus took Peter, John and James,
   and went up onto a mountain to pray.
While he was praying, his face changed in appearance
   and his clothes became dazzlingly white.
Suddenly two men were talking with him—Moses and E-lí-jah.
They appeared in glory and spoke of his passage
   which he was about to fulfill in Jerusalem.
Peter and those with him had fallen into a deep sleep;
   but awakening, they saw his glory
   and likewise saw the two men who were standing with him.
When these were leaving, Peter said to Jesus,
   "Master, how good it is for us to be here.
Let us set up three booths,
   one for you, one for Moses, and one for E-lí-jah."
(He did not really know what he was saying.)
While he was speaking, a cloud came and overshadowed them,
   and the disciples grew fearful as the others entered it.
Then from the cloud came a voice which said,
   "This is my Son, my Chosen One. Listen to him."
When the voice fell silent, Jesus was there alone.
The disciples kept quiet,
   telling nothing of what they had seen at that time to anyone.

   This is the gospel of the Lord.

THIRD SUNDAY OF LENT

FIRST READING

Exodus 3, 1-8. 13-15   This is what you must say to the sons of Israel:
"I am has sent me to you."

Moses had been brought up as the adopted son of the Princess of
Egypt; but he killed an Egyptian and was forced to flee into the
deserts of Sinai. Here from a burning bush God called him to
rescue his people from the Egyptians. Read Chapters 2 and 3 as
preparation. This reading demands great skill, for you must convey
the presence of God. Begin with straight narrative, which changes
into awe as Moses hears himself called. Then follows a profound
religious experience as God reveals his own name. The intensity
deepens to the end: "This is my name for ever; this is my title for
all generations. A longer pause than usual before you add "This is
the Word of the Lord."

A reading from the book of Éx-o-dus

Moses was tending the flock of his father-in-law Jéth-ro, the priest
     of Mí-di-an.
Leading the flock across the desert,
     he came to Hó-reb, the mountain of God.
There an angel of the Lord appeared to him in fire flaming out of a bush.
As he looked on, he was surprised
     to see that the bush, though on fire, was not consumed.
So Moses decided,
     "I must go over to look at this remarkable sight,
     and see why the bush is not burned."
When the Lord saw him coming over to look at it more closely,
     God called out to him from the bush, "Moses! Moses! "
He answered, "Here I am."
God said, "Come no nearer!
Remove the sandals from your feet,
     for the place where you stand is holy ground.
I am the God of your father," he continued,
     "the God of Abraham, the God of Í-saac, the God of Jacob."
Moses hid his face, for he was afraid to look at God.

But the Lord said,
"I have witnessed the affliction of my people in Egypt
and have heard their cry of complaint against their slave drivers,
so I know well what they are suffering.
Therefore I have come down to rescue them
from the hands of the E-gýp-tians and lead them out of that land
into a good and spacious land,

a land flowing with milk and honey."

"But," said Moses to God,
"when I go to the Ís-ra-el-ites and say to them,

'The God of your fathers has sent me to you,'

if they ask me, 'What is his name? "
what am I to tell them? "
God replied, "I am who am."
Then he added,
"This is what you shall tell the Ís-ra-el-ites:
I AM sent me to you."

God spoke further to Moses,
"Thus shall you say to the Ís-ra-el-ites:
The Lord, the God of your fathers,
the God of Abraham, the God of Í-saac,
the God of Jacob, has sent me to you.
"This is my name forever;
this is my title for all generations."

This is the Word of the Lord.

RESPONSORIAL PSALM

*Psalm 103, 1-2. 3-4. 6-7. 8-11 After the reading the psalmist sings
or says the responsorial verse, and all repeat it. This response is also
repeated after each verse of the psalm.*

Common response:

Re - mem - ber your love and your faith - ful - ness, Lord.

Or:

℟. The Lord is kind and merciful.

Bless the Lord, O my soul;
    and all my being, bless his holy name.
Bless the Lord, O my soul,
    and forget not all his benefits. ℟.

He pardons all your iniquities,
    he heals all your ills.
He redeems your life from destruction,
    he crowns you with kindness and compassion. ℟.

The Lord secures justice
    and the rights of all the oppressed.
He has made known his ways to Moses,
    and his deeds to the children of Israel. ℟.

Merciful and gracious is the Lord,
    slow to anger and abounding in kindness.
For as the heavens are high above the earth,
    so surpassing is his kindness toward those who fear him. ℟.

SECOND READING

1 Corinthians 10, 1-6. 10-12   All this that happened to the people of Moses in the desert was written for our benefit.

Paul often wrote of events in the past history of the Jews as types or symbols of what happened in the life of Christ or of a Christian. Here he has in mind the years spent in the desert after the escape from Egypt. By day the people were led by a cloud; they passed through the Red Sea—a symbol of baptism; when there was no water Moses struck a rock, and water gushed out; many of the people were destroyed in the desert because they rebelled. In reading be conscious of what is in Paul's mind and of his final message: do not be too sure of yourself, these things may happen to you.

A reading from the first letter of Paul to the Co-rín-thi-ans

I want you to remember this:
    our fathers were all under the cloud
    and all passed through the sea;
    by the cloud and the sea
    all of them were baptized into Moses.

All ate the same spiritual food.

All drank the same spiritual drink

(they drank from the spiritual rock that was following them,
and the rock was Christ),

yet we know that God was not pleased with most of them,
for "they were struck down in the desert."

These things happened as an example

to keep us from wicked desires such as theirs.

Nor are you to grumble as some of them did,

to be killed by the destroying angel.

The things that happened to them serve as an example.

They have been written as a warning to us,

upon whom the end of the ages has come.

For all these reasons,

let anyone who thinks he is standing upright
watch out lest he fall!

This is the Word of the Lord.

GOSPEL

*The cantor sings the response and the people repeat it; the cantor
then sings the verse before the gospel and the people repeat the response.
Otherwise the verse before the gospel may be omitted.*

Praise and hon - or to you, Lord___ Je - sus Christ.

For other responses to the verse see page 436.

Cre-ate a clean heart in me, O God; give back to me the joy of your sal - va - tion.

Luke 13, 1-9 Unless you repent you will all perish as they did.

*Two discourses of Jesus; the first that we are not to suppose that
the misfortunes of others are a sign that they were worse sinners
than we are; and secondly the parable of the barren fig tree,
symbolising that God in his mercy was very patient with the failings,
of Israel, his chosen people. Bring out the humanity of Jesus in
both passages.*

✠ A reading from the holy gospel according to Luke

At that time some were present
   who told Jesus about the Gal-i-lé-ans
   whose blood Pilate had mixed with their sacrifices.
He said in reply:
   "Do you think that these Gal-i-lé-ans
   were the greatest sinners in Gá-li-lee
   just because they suffered this?
By no means!
But I tell you, you will all come to the same end
   unless you reform.
Or take those eighteen
   who were killed by a falling tower in Sí-lo-am.
Do you think they were more guilty
   than anyone else who lived in Jerusalem?
Certainly not!
But I tell you, you will all come to the same end
   unless you begin to reform."

Jesus spoke this parable:
   "A man had a fig tree growing in his vineyard,
   and he came out looking for fruit on it
   but did not find any.
He said to the vinedresser,
   'Look here! For three years now
   I have come in search of fruit on this fig tree and found none.
Cut it down.
Why should it clutter up the ground? '
In answer, the man said,
   'Sir, leave it another year
   while I hoe around it and manure it;
   then perhaps it will bear fruit.
If not, it shall be cut down.' "

   This is the gospel of the Lord.

Or the readings given for Year A, page 415, may be used in place of the above.

FOURTH SUNDAY OF LENT

FIRST READING

Joshua 5, 9a. 10-12   The people of God went to the promised land and there kept the passover.

After the death of Moses, Joshua became the leader of the people of Israel. They crossed over the river Jordan and began the siege of the city of Jericho. Joshua now ordered a solemn rededication to the Lord. During the years in the desert the rite of circumcision, which especially marked the descendants of Abraham, had been neglected. Now all males are circumcised, and thereby the "reproach of Egypt" is removed. Then they celebrate the feast of the Passover. Read as a historical note.

A reading from the book of Jósh-u-a

The Lord said to Jósh-u-a,
    "Today I have removed the reproach of Egypt from you."

While the Ís-ra-el-ites were encamped at Gíl-gal
    on the plains of Jé-ri-cho,
    they celebrated the Páss-o-ver on the evening of the fourteenth
        of the month.
On the day after the Páss-o-ver
    they ate of the produce of the land
    in the form of unleavened cakes and parched grain.
On that same day after the Páss-o-ver
    on which they ate of the produce of the land,
    the manna ceased.
No longer was there manna for the Ís-ra-el-ites,
    who that year ate of the yield of the land of Cá-na-an.

    This is the Word of the Lord.

RESPONSORIAL PSALM

*Psalm 34, 2-3. 4-5. 6-7   After the reading the psalmist sings or says
the responsorial verse, and all repeat it. This response is also
repeated after each verse of the psalm.*

Common response:

Re - mem - ber your love   and   your   faith - ful - ness,   Lord.

Or:

℟. Taste and see the goodness of the Lord.

I will bless the Lord at all times;
  his praise shall be ever in my mouth.
Let my soul glory in the Lord;
  the lowly will hear me and be glad.   ℟.

Glorify the Lord with me,
  let us together extol his name.
I sought the Lord, and he answered me
  and delivered me from all my fears.   ℟.

Look to him that you may be radiant with joy,
  and your faces may not blush with shame.
When the afflicted man called out, the Lord heard,
  and from all his distress he saved him.   ℟.

SECOND READING

2 Corinthians 5, 17-21   God reconciled us to himself through Christ.

*To understand what Paul is saying, study the whole chapter with
the aid of a commentary. Paul means that one who accepts Christ,
becomes a new creature. In his mercy, God has appointed us, his
apostles, to bring about the reconciliation between men and God.
We beg you to be reconciled, remembering that God caused his own
sinless Son to become Sin that we might be saved. Clarify the argument
by slow, clear, forceful reading.*

A reading from the second letter of Paul to the Cor-ín-thi-ans

If anyone is in Christ, he is a new creation.
The old order has passed away; now all is new!
All this has been done by God,
    who has reconciled us to himself through Christ
    and has given us the ministry of reconciliation.
I mean that God, in Christ,
    was reconciling the world to himself,
    not counting men's transgressions against them,
    and that he has entrusted the message of reconciliation to us.
This makes us ambassadors for Christ,
    God as it were appealing through us.
We implore you, in Christ's name:
    be reconciled to God!
For our sakes God made him who did not know sin to be sin,
    so that in him we might become the very holiness of God.

    This is the Word of the Lord.

GOSPEL

*The cantor sings the response and the people repeat it; the cantor then
sings the verse before the gospel and the people repeat the response.
Otherwise the verse before the gospel may be omitted.*

Praise and hon - or to you, Lord— Je - sus Christ.

For other responses to the verse see page 436.

I will rise and go to my— Fa - ther and tell— him: Fa - ther
I have — sinned a - gainst heav - en and a - gainst you.

Luke 15, 1-3. 11-32 Your brother here was dead and has come to life.

*The Pharisees and scribes condemned Jesus because he was always
so friendly towards sinners of all kinds. He replies by telling the
story of how a father forgave his spendthrift son and rejoiced when
he came home. Read with zest, as if the story was quite unfamiliar
to your hearers; bring out the very different characters of the two
brothers, and stress the conclusion with its message: God rejoices
when a sinner is reconciled.*

✠   A reading from the holy gospel according to Luke

The tax collectors and the sinners
   were all gathering around Jesus to hear him,
   at which the Pharisees and the scribes murmured,
   "This man welcomes sinners and eats with them."
Then he addressed this parable to them:
   "A man had two sons.
The younger of them said to his father,
   'Father, give me the share of the estate that is coming to me.'
So the father divided up the property.
Some days later this younger son collected all his belongings
   and went off to a distant land,
   where he squandered his money on dissolute living.
After he had spent everything,
   a great famine broke out in that country
   and he was in dire need.
So he attached himself to one of the propertied class of the place,
   who sent him to his farm to take care of the pigs.
He longed to fill his belly with the husks
   that were fodder for the pigs,
   but no one made a move to give him anything.
Coming to his senses at last,
   he said: 'How many hired hands at my father's place
   have more than enough to eat,
   while here I am starving!
I will break away and return to my father, and say to him,
   'Father I have sinned against God and against you;
   I no longer deserve to be called your son.
Treat me like one of your hired hands.'
With that he set off for his father's house.
While he was still a long way off,
   his father caught sight of him and was deeply moved.
He ran out to meet him,
   threw his arms around his neck, and kissed him.

The son said to him,
'Father, I have sinned against God and against you;
I no longer deserve to be called your son.'
The father said to his servants:
'Quick! bring out the finest robe and put it on him;
put a ring on his finger and shoes on his feet.
Take the fatted calf and kill it.
Let us eat and celebrate
because this son of mine was dead and has come back to life.
He was lost and is found.'
Then the celebration began.

"Meanwhile the elder son was out on the land.
As he neared the house on his way home,
he heard the sound of music and dancing.
He called one of the servants
and asked him the reason for the dancing and the music.
The servant answered, 'Your brother is home,
and your father has killed the fatted calf
because he has him back in good health.'
The son grew angry at this and would not go in;
but his father came out and began to plead with him.

"He said in reply to his father:
'For years now I have slaved for you.
I never disobeyed one of your orders,
yet you never gave me so much as a kid goat
to celebrate with my friends.
Then, when this son of yours returns
after having gone through your property with loose women,
you kill the fatted calf for him.'

" 'My son', replied the father,
'you are with me always, and everything I have is yours.
But we had to celebrate and rejoice!
This brother of yours was dead,
and has come back to life.
He was lost, and is found.' "

This is the gospel of the Lord.

Or the readings given for Year A, page 424, may be used in place of the above.

FIFTH SUNDAY OF LENT

FIRST READING

Isaiah 43, 16-21   I am doing a new thing and I will give drink to my people.

A prophecy made to the exiles in Babylon that they will return to Jerusalem. In lines 1-7 the thought is 'forget the story of how the Lord led you out of Egypt' for now (lines 8-20) the Lord will give you a new exodus through the other desert back to your homeland.' Read as poetry that conveys its meaning by emotion rather than clear statement.

A reading from the book of the prophet I-saí-ah

Thus says the Lord,
   who opens a way in the sea
   and a path in the mighty waters,
Who leads out chariots and horsemen,
   a powerful army,
Till they lie prostrate together, never to rise,
   snuffed out and quenched like a wick.
Remember not the events of the past,
   the things of long ago consider not;
See, I am doing something new!
   Now it springs forth, do you not perceive it?
In the desert I make a way,
   in the wasteland, rivers.
Wild beasts honor me,
   jackals and ostriches,
For I put water in the desert
   and rivers in the wasteland
   for my chosen people to drink,
The people whom I formed for myself,
   that they might announce my praise.

This is the Word of the Lord.

RESPONSORIAL PSALM

*Psalm 126, 1-2. 2-3. 4-5. 6 After the reading the psalmist sings or says
the responsorial verse, and all repeat it. This response is also repeated
after each verse of the psalm.*

Common response:

Re - mem - ber your love and your faith - ful - ness, Lord.

Or:

℟. The Lord has done great things for us;
   we are filled with joy.

When the Lord brought back the captives of Zion,
   we were like men dreaming.
Then our mouth was filled with laughter,
   and our tongue with rejoicing. ℟.

Then they said among the nations,
   "The Lord has done great things for them."
The Lord has done great things for us;
   we are glad indeed. ℟.

Restore our fortunes, O Lord,
   like the torrents in the southern desert.
Those that sow in tears
   shall reap rejoicing. ℟.

Although they go forth weeping,
   carrying the seed to be sown,
They shall come back rejoicing,
   carrying their sheaves. ℟.

SECOND READING

Philippians 3, 8-14   Because of Christ I look upon everything else as useless in order to gain him.

Paul's meaning is that nothing has any value except to know Christ. Before he was a Christian, Paul relied on 'justice', based on the law, that is, that he would be saved by knowing and strictly following the Law of Moses. Now justice (salvation) comes from his faith in Jesus; now he hopes for the life to come through knowledge of Christ.

He has not yet fully achieved Christ but, like the runner in a race, he pushes on to the finish to gain the prize, that is, resurrection from the dead and eternal union with the risen Christ. A difficult reading which needs full understanding of Paul's argument: salvation comes from Christ and not from the Old Law.

A reading from the letter of Paul to the Phil-íp-pi-ans

I have come to rate all as loss
   in the light of the surpassing knowledge
   of my Lord Jesus Christ.
For his sake I have forfeited everything;
   I have accounted all else rubbish
   so that Christ may be my wealth and I may be in him,
   not having any justice of my own
   based on observance of the law.
The justice I possess is that which comes through faith in Christ.

It has its origin in God and is based on faith.
I wish to know Christ
   and the power flowing from his resurrection;
   likewise to know how to share in his sufferings
   by being formed into the pattern of his death.
Thus do I hope that I may arrive at resurrection from the dead.

It is not that I have reached it yet,
   or have already finished my course;
   but I am racing to grasp the prize if possible,
   since I have been grasped by Christ [Jesus].
Brothers, I do not think of myself
   as having reached the finish line.
I give no thought to what lies behind
   but push on to what is ahead.

My entire attention is on the finish line
   as I run toward the prize to which God calls me
   life on high in Christ Jesus.

   This is the Word of the Lord.

GOSPEL

*The cantor sings the response and the people repeat it; the cantor then
sings the verse before the gospel and the people repeat the response.
Otherwise the verse before the gospel may be omitted.*

Praise and hon - or to you, Lord___ Je - sus Christ.

For other responses to the verse see page 436.

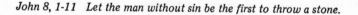

Re - pent, ___ says the Lord, the ___ king - dom of heav-en is at hand. ___

John 8, 1-11 Let the man without sin be the first to throw a stone.

*Bring out the vivid details of this well told story. Jesus has so
often preached forgiveness of sin that the Pharisees believe that
they can confound him with an actual case. If he forgives this
woman who has been caught in the act of adultery, then he goes
contrary to the strict law laid down by Moses: "if a man is
discovered having relations with a woman married to another,,
both the man and the woman shall die. Thus shall you purge
the evil from your midst." (Deuteronomy 22: 22)." Stress the
crafty question "what do you have to say about this case?" As
often, Jesus makes no direct reply, but his words confuse his
questioners for no one can claim never to have broken any of
the laws. Give full meaning to Jesus' final words: he forgives
the sinner but not the sin.*

✠   A reading from the holy gospel according to John

Jesus went out to the Mount of Olives.
At daybreak he reappeared in the temple area;
   and when the people started coming to him,
   he sat down and began to teach them.

The scribes and the Phár-isees led a woman forward
    who had been caught in adultery.
They made her stand there in front of everyone.
"Teacher," they said to him,
    "this woman has been caught in the act of adultery.
In the law, Moses ordered such women to be stoned.
What do you have to say about the case? "
(They were posing this question to trap him,
    so that they could have something to accuse him of.)
Jesus simply bent down
    and started tracing on the ground with his finger.
When they persisted in their questioning,
    he straightened up and said to them,
    "Let the man among you who has no sin
    be the first to cast a stone   at her."
A second time he bent down and wrote on the ground.
Then the audience drifted away one by one,
    beginning with the elders.
This left him alone with the woman,
    who continued to stand there before him.
Jesus finally straightened up again and said to her,
    "Woman, where did they all disappear to?
Has no one condemned you? "
"No one, sir," she answered.
Jesus said, "Nor do I condemn you.
You may go. But from now on, avoid this sin."

    This is the gospel of the Lord.

Or the readings given for Year A, page 432, may be used in place of the above.

PASSION SUNDAY
(PALM SUNDAY)
THE PROCESSION WITH PALMS

GOSPEL

Luke 19, 28-40 Blessed is he who comes in the name of the Lord.

*Jesus' triumphant entry into Jerusalem. Begin with straight
story telling which becomes full of noise and enthusiasm until
—as the last words show—Jesus himself is moved by the excitement.*

✠   A reading from the holy gospel according to Luke

Jesus went ahead with his ascent to Je-rú-sa-lem.
As he approached Béth-pha-ge and Béth-a-ny on the mount called
   Ol-i-vet,
    he sent two of the disciples with these instructions:
    "Go into the village straight ahead of you.
Upon entering it you will find an ass tied there
    which no one has yet ridden.
Untie it and lead it back.
If anyone should ask you,
    'Why are you untying the beast? '
    say, 'The Master has need of it.' "

They departed on their errand
    and found things just as he had said.
As they untied the ass, its owners said to them,
    "Why are you doing that? "
They explained that the Master needed it.
Then they led the animal to Jesus,
    and laying their cloaks on it,
    helped him mount.
They spread their cloaks on the roadway as he moved along;
    and on his approach to the descent from Mount Ol-i-vet,
    the entire crowd of disciples
    began to rejoice and praise God loudly
    for the display of power they had seen, saying:
    "Blessed be he who comes as king in the name of the Lord!
Peace in heaven and glory in the highest! "

Some of the Phár-isees in the crowd said to him,
    "Teacher, rebuke your disciples."
He replied, "If they were to keep silence,
    I tell you the very stones would cry out!"

    This is the gospel of the Lord

PASSION SUNDAY
(PALM SUNDAY)

MASS

FIRST READING

Isaiah 50, 4-7   I did not cover my face against insult and I know I will not be ashamed (Third song of the Servant of Yahweh).

From the third Song of the Suffering Servant. The tone of the first stanza is quiet, unresisting sadness. Slight pause. In the second stanza the tone changes to subdued, confident hope.

A reading from the book of the prophet I-saí-ah

The Lord God has given me
   a well-trained tongue,
That I might know how to speak to the weary
   a word that will rouse them.
Morning after morning
   he opens my ear that I may hear;
And I have not rebelled,
   have not turned back.
I gave my back to those who beat me,
   my cheeks to those who plucked my beard;
My face I did not shield
   from buffets and spitting.

The Lord God is my help,
   therefore I am not disgraced;
I have set my face like flint,
   knowing that I shall not be put to shame.

   This is the Word of the Lord.

RESPONSORIAL PSALM

Psalm 22, 8-9. 17-18. 19-20. 23-24 After the reading the psalmist sings or says the responsorial verse, and all repeat it. This response is also repeated after each verse of the psalm.

Common response:

Re - mem - ber your love and your faith - ful - ness, Lord.

Or:

℞. My God, my God, why have you abandoned me?

All who see me scoff at me;
    they mock me with parted lips, they wag their heads:
    "He relied on the Lord; let him deliver him,
    let him rescue him, if he loves him." ℞.

Indeed, many dogs surround me,
    a pack of evildoers closes in upon me;
They have pierced my hands and my feet;
    I can count all my bones. ℞.

They divide my garments among them,
    and for my vesture they cast lots.
But you, O Lord, be not far from me;
    O my help, hasten to aid me. ℞.

I will proclaim your name to my brethren;
    in the midst of the assembly I will praise you:
"You who fear the Lord, praise him;
all you descendants of Jacob, give glory to him." ℞.

SECOND READING

*Philippians 2, 6-11   He humbled himself to become like us and God
raised him on high.*

*Except for the first line, "Your attitude must be Christ's," this
is a very early Christian hymn and should be read as such. Show
that each stanza expresses a different clause in the creed; Jesus
is the only Son of God, he became man, he was crucified, died and
was buried, he rose again, he ascended into heaven, and is seated
at the right hand of the Father; all leading to the triumphant
conclusion that we therefore worship Jesus Lord.*

A reading from the letter of Paul to the Phil-íp-pians

Your attitude must be Christ's:
   though he was in the form of God
   he did not deem equality with God
   something to be grasped at.
Rather, he emptied himself
   and took the form of a slave,
   being born in the likeness of men.
He was known to be of human estate,
   and it was thus that he humbled himself,
   obediently accepting even death,
   death on a cross!
Because of this,
   God highly exalted him
   and bestowed on him the name
   above every other name,
So that at Jesus' name
   every knee must bend
   in the heavens, on the earth,
   and under the earth,
   and every tongue proclaim
   to the glory of God the Father:
   JESUS CHRIST IS LORD!

   This is the Word of the Lord.

GOSPEL

*The cantor sings the response and the people repeat it; the cantor then
sings the verse before the gospel and the people repeat the response.
Otherwise the verse before the gospel may be omitted.
Reference: Philippians 2, 8-9*

Praise and hon - or to you, Lord___ Je - sus Christ.

For other responses to the verse see page 436.

Christ be - came o - be - di - ent for us e - ven to death ___

dy - ing on the cross. There - fore ___ God raised ___ him on high and

gave him a name a - bove all oth - er names.

Long Form: Luke 22, 14-23, 56 The passion of our Lord Jesus Christ.

Luke's account of the Passion is a careful compilation and includes some incidents and sayings not given in the versions of Matthew or Mark. If this Gospel is read by three readers, the words of Jesus himself should be spoken with a special sensitive distinction. The Narrator is responsible for stimulating each hearer to use his imagination, and to feel, hear and see the events as they are unfolded in the narrative. Both Narrator and Speaker need to be conscious of the characters of the chief persons in the story—Peter, Pilate and Herod.

The narrative falls into sixteen episodes which should be separated by a slight pause after each.

Jesus and his disciples begin the last supper. Before the meal Jesus blesses and distributes the wine. Then he establishes the eucharist by blessing and distributing the bread, and likewise the cup when the meal is ended.

℣. The passion of our Lord Jesus Christ according to Luke

When the hour arrived, Jesus took his place at table,
    and the apostles with him.
He said to them:

✠   "I have greatly desired to eat this Passover with you before
         I suffer.
     I tell you, I will not eat again
         until it is fulfilled in the kingdom of God."

C.   Then taking a cup he offered a blessing in thanks and said:

✠   "Take this and divide it among you;
         I tell you, from now on I will not drink
         of the fruit of the vine until the coming of the reign of God."

C.   Then taking bread and giving thanks,
         he broke it and gave it to them, saying:

✠   "This is my body to be given for you.
     Do this as a remembrance of me."

C.   He did the same with the cup after eating, saying as he did so:

✠   "This cup is the new covenant in my blood,
     which will be shed for you.

He tells them that one of them will betray him.

✠   "And yet the hand of my betrayer is with me at this table.
     The Son of Man is following out his appointed course,
         but woe to that man by whom he is betrayed."

C.   Then they began to dispute among themselves
         as to which of them would do such a deed.

*The disciples dispute who will be the greatest. Jesus rebukes
them and warns Simon Peter that he must strengthen his brothers.
Peter declares that he is ready to die for Jesus, and is told that
before cockcrow he will deny his Lord three times. Convey Peter's
impetuous self-confidence.*

C.   A dispute arose among them
         about who would be regarded as the greatest.
     He said:

✠   "Earthly kings lord it over their people.
     Those who exercise authority over them are called their benefactors.
     Yet it cannot be that way with you.
     Let the greater among you be as the junior,
         the leader as the servant.

Who, in fact, is the greater—

he who reclines at table or he who serves the meal?
Is it not the one who reclines at table?

Yet I am in your midst as the one who serves you.

You are the ones who have stood loyally by me in my temptations.

I for my part assign to you the dominion
my Father has assigned to me.

In my kingdom, you will eat and drink at my table,

and you will sit on thrones judging the twelve tribes of Israel.

"Simon, Simon!   Remember that Satan has asked for you
to sift you all like wheat.

But I have prayed for you that your faith may never fail.

You in turn must strengthen your brothers."

C.   He said to him,

S.   "Lord, at your side I am prepared to face imprisonment
and death itself."

C.   Jesus replied,

✠   "I tell you, Peter,

the rooster will not crow today
until you have three times denied that you know me."

Jesus warns them that the scriptures must be fulfilled. Convey the impression that so far the disciples have no sense of what is about to happen.

C.   He asked them,

✠   "When I sent you on mission

without purse or traveling bag or sandals,
were you in need of anything? "

C.   They replied.

SS.   "Not a thing,"

C.   He said to them:

✠   "Now, however, the man who has a purse must carry it;
the same with the traveling bag.

And the man without a sword must sell his coat and buy one.

It is written in Scripture,

'He was counted among the wicked,'

and this, I tell you, must come to be fulfilled in me.

All that has to do with me approaches its climax."

C.   They said,

SS.   "Lord, here are two swords! "

C.   He answered,

✠   "Enough."

The agony in the Mount of Olives. Quiet but distinct reading.

C.   Then he went out and made his way,
        as was his custom, to the Mount of Olives;
        his disciples accompanied him.
      On reaching the place he said to them,

✠   "Pray that you may not be put to the test."

C.   He withdrew from them about a stone's throw,
        then went down on his knees and prayed in these words:

✠   "Father, if it is your will,
        take this cup from me;
        yet not my will but yours be done."

C.   An angel then appeared to him from heaven to strengthen him.
      In his anguish he prayed with all the greater intensity,
        and his sweat became like drops of blood falling to the ground.
      Then he rose from prayer and came to his disciples,
        only to find them asleep, exhausted with grief.
      He said to them,

✠   "Why are you sleeping?
      Wake up, and pray that you may not be subjected to the trial."

*By contrast suggest the noise and confusion of the betrayal
and the arrest of Jesus.*

C.   While he was still speaking a crowd came,
        led by the man named Judas, one of the Twelve
      He approached Jesus to embrace him.
      Jesus said to him,

✠   "Judas, would you betray the Son of Man with a kiss? "

C.   When the companions of Jesus saw what was going to happen,
        they said,

SS.   "Lord, shall we use the sword? "

C.   One of them went so far as to strike the high priest's servant
      and cut off his right ear.
   Jesus said in answer to their question,

✠   "Enough! "

C.   Then he touched the ear and healed the man.
   But to those who had come out against him—
      the chief priests, the chiefs of the temple guard, and the
        ancients—
      Jesus said,

✠   "Am I a criminal that you come out after me
      armed with swords and clubs?
   When I was with you day after day in the temple
      you never raised a hand against me.
   But this is your hour—the triumph of darkness! "

*Peter denies his Master. Read with vigor and bluster but change
to quiet emphasis at "the Lord turned and looked at Peter.";
and Peter's breakdown.*

C.   They led him away under arrest
      and brought him to the house of the high priest,
      while Peter followed at a distance.
   Later they lighted a fire in the middle of the courtyard
      and were sitting beside it, and Peter sat among them.
   A servant girl saw him sitting in the light of the fire.
   She gazed at him intently, then said,

S.   "This man was with him."

C.   He denied the fact, saying,

S.   "Woman, I do not know him."

C.   A little while later someone else saw him and said,

S.   "You are one of them too."

C.   But Peter said,

S.   "No, sir, not I! "

C.   About an hour after that another spoke more insistently:

S.   "This man was certainly with him, for he is a Gal-i-lé-an."

C.   Peter responded,

S.   "My friend, I do not know what you are talking about."

C.   At the very moment he was saying this,
      a rooster crowed.
    The Lord turned around and looked at Peter,
      and Peter remembered the word
      that the Lord had spoken to him,
      "Before the rooster crows today you will deny me three times."
    He went out and wept bitterly.

The guards illtreat Jesus.

C.   Meanwhile the men guarding Jesus
      amused themselves at his expense.
    They blindfolded him first, slapped him, and then taunted him:

SS.   "Play the prophet; which one struck you? "

C.   And they directed many other insulting words at him.

*Jesus is brought before the Council. Stress their eagerness
to condemn him. They take him to Pilate and accuse him of
subverting the nation. Pilate is not impressed by the charge.
He sends Jesus to Herod.*

C.   At day break, the elders of the people, the chief priests,
      and the scribes assembled again.
    Once they had brought him before their council,
    they said,

SS.   "Tell us, are you the Mes-sí-ah? "

C.   He replied,

✠   "If I tell you, you will not believe me,
      and if I question you, you will not answer.
    This much only will I say:
      'From now on, the Son of Man will have his seat
      at the right hand of the Power of God. "

C.   They asked in chorus.

SS.   "So you are the Son of God? "

C.   He answered,

✠   "It is you who say I am."

C.   They said,

SS.   "What need have we of witnesses?
       We have heard it from his own mouth."

C.   Then the entire assembly rose up and led him before Pilate.
       They started his prosecution by saying,

SS.   "We found this man subverting our nation,
       opposing the payment of taxes to Caesar,
           and calling himself the Mes-si-ah, a king."

C.   Pilate asked him,

S.   "Are you the king of the Jews? "

C.   He answered,

✠   "That is your term."

C.   Pilate reported to the chief priests and the crowds,

S.   "I do not find a case against this man."

C.   But they insisted,

S.   "He stirs up the people by his teaching
           throughout the whole of Judea, from Gá-li-lee,
           where he began, to this very place."

C.   On hearing this Pilate asked if the man was a Gal-i-lé-an;
           and when he learned that he was under Herod's jurisdiction,
           he sent him to Herod,
           who also happened to be in Jerusalem at the time.

*Jesus is dragged before Herod. Stress Herod's vulgar and
vindictive nature.*

C.   Herod was extremely pleased to see Jesus.
       From the reports about him he had wanted for a long time to see him,
           and he was hoping to see him work some miracle.
       He questioned Jesus at considerable length,
           but Jesus made no answer.
       The chief priests and scribes were at hand to accuse him vehemently.
       Herod and his guards then treated him with contempt and insult,
           after which they put a magnificent robe on him
           and sent him back to Pilate.
       Herod and Pilate, who had previously been set against each other,
           became friends from that day.

*The second appearance before Pilate. Convey the increasing
malice of Jesus' accusers, and Pilate's weak, callous irresponsibilities
as he consents to the crucifixion of a man he knows to be innocent.*

C.   Pilate then called together the chief priests,
       the ruling class, and the people, and said to them:

S.   "You have brought this man before me
       as one who subverts the people.
     I have examined him in your presence
       and have no charge against him arising from your allegations.
     Neither has Herod, who therefore has sent him back to us;
       obviously this man has done nothing to deserve death.
     Therefore I mean to release him,
       once I have taught him a lesson."

C.   The whole crowd cried out,

SS. "Away with this man; release Ba-ráb-bas for us! "

C.   This Ba-ráb-bas had been thrown in prison
       for causing an uprising in the city, and for murder.
     Pilate addressed them again,
       for he wanted Jesus to be the one he released.
     But they shouted back,

SS. "Crucify him, crucify him! "

C.   He said to them for the third time,

S.   "What wrong is this man guilty of?
     I have not discovered anything about him deserving the death
          penalty.
     I will therefore chastise him and release him."

C.   But they demanded with loud cries that he be crucified,
       and their shouts increased in violence.
     Pilate then decreed that what they demanded should be done.
     He released the one they asked for,
       who had been thrown in prison for insurrection and murder,
       and delivered Jesus up to their wishes.

The way of the cross. Jesus speaks to the women of Jerusalem.

C.   As they led him away,
       they laid hold of one Simon the Cy-re-né-an who was coming

in from the fields.
They put a crossbeam on Simon's shoulder
 for him to carry along behind Jesus.
A great crowd of people followed him,
 including women who beat their breasts and lamented over him.
Jesus turned to them and said:

"Daughters of Jerusalem, do not weep for me.
Weep for yourselves and for your children.
The days are coming when they will say,
 'Happy are the sterile, the wombs that never bore
 and the breasts that never nursed.'
Then they will begin saying to the mountains,
 'Fall on us, and to the hills, 'Cover us.'
If they do these things in the green wood, what will happen in the dry? "

Two others who were criminals
 were led along with him to be crucified.
When they came to Skull Place, as it was called,
 they crucified him there and the criminals as well,
 one on his right and the other on his left.
Jesus said,

"Father, forgive them;
 they do not know what they are doing."]

*Jesus is crucified and mocked by all except the penitent and
sympathetic fellow victim.*

They divided his garments, rolling dice for them.
The people stood there watching,
 and the leaders kept jeering at him, saying,

"He saved others; let him save himself
 if he is the Mes-si-ah of God, the chosen one."

The soldiers also made fun of him,
 coming forward to offer him their sour wine and saying,

"If you are the king of the Jews, save yourself."

There was an inscription over his head:

"THIS IS THE KING OF THE JEWS."
One of the criminals hanging in crucifixion blasphemed him,

"Aren't you the Messiah? Then save yourself and us."

C.   But the other one rebuked him:

S.   "Have you no fear of God,
          seeing you are under the same sentence?
      We deserve it, after all.
      We are only paying the price for what we've done,
          but this man has done nothing wrong."

C.   He then said,

S.   "Jesus, remember me when you enter upon your reign."

C.   And Jesus replied,

✠   "I assure you:
          this day you will be with me in paradise."

The narrative now becomes even more somber as Jesus dies.
At this point, without being too dramatic, the Narrator must
make the whole scene vivid to his hearers; it calls for deep empathy
and understanding.

C.   It was now around midday,
          and darkness came over the whole land
          until midafternoon with an eclipse of the sun.
      The curtain in the sanctuary was torn in two.
      Jesus uttered a loud cry and said,

✠   "Father, into your hands I commend my spirit."

C.   After he said this, he expired.
      The centurion, upon seeing what had happened,
          gave glory to God by saying,

S.   "Surely this was an innocent man."

C.   After the crowd assembled for this spectacle
          witnessed what had happened,
          they returned beating their breasts.
      All his friends and the women who had accompanied him
          from Gá-li-lee
      were standing at a distance watching everything.

Joseph of Arimathea begs the body of Jesus which is laid in
the new tomb.

C There was a man named Joseph,
　　an upright and holy member of the Sán-hed-rin,
　　who had not been associated with their plan or their action.
He was from A-ri-ma-thé-a, a Jewish town,
　　and he looked expectantly for the reign of God.
This man approached Pilate with a request for Jesus' body.
He took it down, wrapped it in fine linen,
　　and laid it in a tomb hewn out of the rock,
　　in which no one had yet been buried.

All is finished. The women go back to wait for the end of
the Sabbath rest. Conclude on a quiet note of sadness but leave
the hearer in a state of anticipation that after tomorrow the sadness
will give place to the joy of Easter when Jesus returns to his own.

C. That was the day of Preparation,
　　and the sabbath was about to begin.
The women who had come with him from Gá-li-lee followed
　　along behind.
They saw the tomb and how his body was buried.
Then they went back home to prepare spices and perfumes.
They observed the sabbath as a day of rest,
　　in accordance with the law.

　　This is the gospel of the Lord.

Short Form: Luke 23, 1-49 The passion of our Lord Jesus Christ.

✠ A reading from the holy gospel according to Luke

The elders of the people and chief priests and scribes
　　rose up and led Jesus before Pilate.
They started his prosecution by saying,
　　"We found this man subverting our nation,
　　opposing the payment of taxes to Caesar,
　　and calling himself the Mes-sí-ah, a king."
Pilate asked him, "Are you the king of the Jews? "
He answered, "That is your term."
Pilate reported to the chief priests and the crowds,
　　"I do not find a case against this man."

But they insisted, "He stirs up the people by his teaching
  throughout the whole of Judea, from Gá-li-lee,
  where he began, to this very place."
On hearing this Pilate asked if the man was a Gal-i-lé-an;
  and when he learned that he was under Herod's jurisdiction,
  he sent him to Herod,
  who also happened to be in Jerusalem at the time.

Herod was extremely pleased to see Jesus.
From the reports about him he had wanted for a long time
  to see him,
  and he was hoping to see him work some miracle.
He questioned Jesus at considerable length,
  but Jesus made no answer.
The chief priests and scribes were at hand to accuse him vehemently.
Herod and his guards then treated him with contempt and insult,
  after which they put a magnificent robe on him
  and sent him back to Pilate.
Herod and Pilate, who had previously been set against each other,
  became friends from that day.

Pilate then called together the chief priests,
  the ruling class, and the people, and said to them:
  "You have brought this man before me as one who subverts
    the people.
I have examined him in your presence
  and have no charge against him arising from your allegations.
Neither has Herod, who therefore has sent him back tó us;
  obviously this man has done nothing to deserve death.
Therefore I mean to release him,
  once I have taught him a lesson."
The whole crowd cried out,
  "Away with this man; release Ba-ráb-bas for us! "
This Ba-ráb-bas had been thrown in prison
  for causing an uprising in the city, and for murder.
Pilate addressed them again,
  for he wanted Jesus to be the one he released.

But they shouted back, "Crucify him, crucify him! "
He said to them for the third time,
  "What wrong is this man guilty of?
I have not discovered anything about him deserving the death penalty.
I will therefore chastise him and release him." '
But they demanded with loud cries that he be crucified,
  and their shouts increased in violence.

Pilate then decreed that what they demanded should be done.
He released the one they asked for,
>who had been thrown in prison for insurrection and murder,
>and delivered Jesus up to their wishes.

As they led him away,
>they laid hold of one Simon the Cy-re-né-an who was coming
>>in from the fields.

They put a crossbeam on Simon's shoulder
>for him to carry along behind Jesus.
A great crowd of people followed him,
>including women who beat their breasts and lamented over him.
Jesus turned to them and said:
>"Daughters of Jerusalem, do not weep for me.
Weep for yourselves and for your children.
The days are coming when they will say,
>'Happy are the sterile, the wombs that never bore
>and the breasts that never nursed.'
Then they will begin saying to the mountains,
>'Fall on us,' and to the hills, 'Cover us.'
If they do these things in the green wood, what will happen
>in the dry? "

Two others who were criminals
>were led along with him to be crucified.
When they came to Skull Place, as it was called,
>they crucified him there and the criminals as well,
>one on his right and the other on his left.
>[Jesus said, "Father, forgive them;
>they do not know what they are doing."]
They divided his garments, rolling dice for them.

The people stood there watching,
>and the leaders kept jeering at him, saying,
>"He saved others; let him save himself
>if he is the Mes-si-ah of God, the chosen one."
The soldiers also made fun of him,
>coming forward to offer him their sour wine and saying,
>"If you are the king of the Jews, save yourself."
There was an inscription over his head:
>"THIS IS THE KING OF THE JEWS."
One of the criminals hanging in crucifixion blasphemed him,
>"Aren't you the Mes-si-ah? Then save yourself and us."

But the other one rebuked him:
"Have you no fear of God,
    seeing you are under the same sentence?
We deserve it, after all.
We are only paying the price for what we've done,
    but this man has done nothing wrong."
He then said,"Jesus, remember me
    when you enter upon your reign."
And Jesus replied, "I assure you:
    this day you will be with me in paradise."

It was now around midday,
    and darkness came over the whole land
    until midafternoon with an eclipse of the sun.
The curtain in the sanctuary was torn in two.
Jesus uttered a loud cry and said,
    "Father, into your hands I commend my spirit."
After he said this, he expired.
The centurion, upon seeing what had happened,
    gave glory to God by saying,
    "Surely this was an innocent man."
After the crowd assembled for this spectacle
    witnessed what had happened,
    they returned beating their breasts.
All his friends and the women who had accompanied him from
        Gá-li-lee
    were standing at a distance watching everything.

    This is the gospel of the Lord.

HOLY THURSDAY
CHRISM MASS
FIRST READING

Isaiah 61, 1-3. 6. 8-9 The Lord has anointed me, he has sent me to bring Good News to the poor, to give them the oil of gladness.

Verses extracted from a poem declaring the mission of the prophet to those in trouble and sorrow.

A reading from the book of the prophet I-saí-ah

The spirit of the Lord God is upon me,
  because the Lord has anointed me;
He has sent me to bring glad tidings to the lowly,
  to heal the brokenhearted,
To proclaim liberty to the captives
  and release to the prisoners,
To announce a year of favor from the Lord
  and a day of vindication by our God,
  to comfort all who mourn;
To place on those who mourn in Zí-on
  a diadem instead of ashes,
To give them oil of gladness in place of mourning,
  a glorious mantle instead of a listless spirit.

You yourselves shall be named priests of the Lord,
  ministers of our God you shall be called.
I will give them their recompense faithfully,
  a lasting covenant I will make with them.
Their descendants shall be renowned among the nations,
  and their offspring among the peoples;
All who see them shall acknowledge them
  as a race the Lord has blessed.

This is the Word of the Lord.

RESPONSORIAL PSALM

Psalm 89, 21-22. 25. 27   After the reading the psalmist sings or says the
responsorial verse, and all repeat it.   This response is repeated after each
verse of the psalm.

Common response:

Re - mem-ber your love   and   your   faith-ful-ness,   Lord.

Or:

℟. For ever I will sing the goodness of the Lord.

I have found David, my servant;
   with my holy oil I have anointed him,
That my hand may be always with him,
   and that my arm may make him strong.   ℟.

My faithfulness and my kindness shall be with him,
   and through my name shall his horn be exalted.
"He shall say of me, 'You are my father,
   my God, the rock, my savior.'   ℟.

SECOND READING

Revelation 1, 5-8   Christ has made us a line of kings, priests to serve his
God and Father.

From the opening words of the vision of John. Jesus Christ has
made us all priests in the service of the Father. An ecstatic vision
of the second coming. God is the beginning and the ending—
Alpha is the first letter of the Greek alphabet, and Omega the last.
Passages from the Book of Revelation should be read in a special
tone of triumph or warning.

A reading from the book of Revelation

[Grace and peace to you] from Jesus Christ the faithful witness,
   the first-born from the dead and ruler of the kings of earth.
To him who loves us and freed us from our sins by his own blood,
   who has made us a royal nation of priests
   in the service of his God and Father—
   to him be glory and power forever and ever! Amen.
See, he comes amid the clouds!
Every eye shall see him,
   even of those who pierced him.
All the peoples of the earth
   shall lament him bitterly.
So it is to be! Amen!
The Lord God says, "I am the Alpha and the Omega,
   the One who is and who was and who is to come, the Almighty! "

   This is the Word of the Lord.

GOSPEL

*The cantor sings the response and the people repeat it; the cantor then
sings the verse before the gospel and the people repeat the response.
Otherwise the verse before the gospel may be omitted. Reference:
Isaiah 61, 1: cited in Luke 4, 18.*

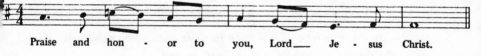

Praise and hon - or to you, Lord___ Je - sus Christ.

For other responses to the verse see page 436.

The spir - it of the Lord is up - on me; he
sent me to bring Good___ News to the poor.

104 Holy Thursday: Chrism Mass

*Luke 4, 16-21   The spirit of the Lord has been given to me, for he has
anointed me.*

*Jesus' first appearance as teacher before the people of his own
home town. He identifies himself as the prophet of Reading I.
Begin as straight narrative, and rise to a climax on the last sentence.
In the quotation from Isaiah, the key words are the same as
in Reading I. Stress the final words: "Today this Scripture passage
is fulfilled in your hearing."*

✢   A reading from the holy gospel according to Luke

Jesus came to Ná-za-reth where he had been reared,
   and entering the synagogue on the sabbath
   as he was in the habit of doing,
   he stood up to do the reading.
When the book of the prophet I-sai-ah was handed him,
   he unrolled the scroll and found the passage where it was written:
   "The spirit of the Lord is upon me;
   therefore he has anointed me.
   He has sent me to bring glad tidings to the poor,
   to proclaim liberty to captives,
   Recovery of sight to the blind
   and release to prisoners,
   To announce a year of favor from the Lord."

Rolling up the scroll, he gave it back to the assistant and sat down.
All in the synagogue had their eyes fixed on him.
Then he began by saying to them,
"Today this Scripture passage is fulfilled in your hearing."

   This is the gospel of the Lord.

EASTER TRIDUUM
MASS OF THE LORD'S SUPPER

FIRST READING

Exodus 12, 1-8. 11-14   The law for the passover meal.

Each year, in remembrance of the deliverance from Egypt, Jews everywhere celebrate the feast of the Passover. In preparation for this reading, and also for a fuller understanding of much of the language in the Easter Vigil, reread Exodus, chapters 11 and 12. This reading has a special importance for Christians because Jesus established a new Paschal Feast is the Eucharist with himself as the Lamb. Read in the formal and meaningful tone used for the organization of a ritual.

A reading from the book of Exodus

The Lord said to Moses and Aaron in the land of Egypt,
  "This month shall stand at the head of your calendar;
  you shall reckon it the first month of the year.
Tell the whole community of Israel:
  On the tenth of this month every one of your families
  must procure for itself a lamb, one apiece for each household.
If a family is too small for a whole lamb,
  it shall join the nearest household in procuring one
  and shall share in the lamb
  in proportion to the number of persons who partake of it.
The lamb must be a year-old male and without blemish.
You may take it from either the sheep or the goats.
You shall keep it until the fourteenth day of this month,
  and then, with the whole assembly of Israel present,
  it shall be slaughtered during the evening twilight.
They shall take some of its blood
  and apply it to the two doorposts
  and the lintel of every house in which they partake of the lamb.
That same night they shall eat its roasted flesh with unleavened bread
    and bitter herbs.

"This is how you are to eat it:
  with your loins girt, sandals on your feet and your staff in hand,
  you shall eat like those who are in flight.
It is the Pass-over of the Lord.

For on this same night I will go through Egypt,
  striking down every first-born of the land, both man and beast,
  and executing judgment on all the gods of Egypt—I, the Lord!
But the blood will mark the houses where you are.
Seeing the blood, I will pass over you;
  thus, when I strike the land of Egypt, no destructive blow will come
    upon you.
"This day shall be a memorial feast for you,
  which all your generations shall celebrate
  with pilgrimage to the Lord, as a perpetual institution."

  This is the Word of the Lord.

RESPONSORIAL PSALM

*Psalm 116, 12-13. 15-16. 17-18   After the reading the psalmist sings
or says the responsorial verse, and all repeat it. This response is
also repeated after each verse of the psalm.*

Common response:

Re - mem - ber your love   and   your   faith - ful - ness,   Lord.

Or:

℟. Our blessing-cup is a communion with the blood of Christ.

How shall I make a return to the Lord
  for all the good he has done for me?
The cup of salvation I will take up,
  and I will call upon the name of the Lord.   ℟.

Precious in the eyes of the Lord
  is the death of his faithful ones.
I am your servant, the son of your handmaid;
  you have loosed my bonds.   ℟.

To you will I offer sacrifice of thanksgiving,
  and I will call upon the name of the Lord.
My vows to the Lord I will pay
  in the presence of all his people.   ℟.

SECOND READING

*1 Corinthians 11, 23-26   Until the Lord comes, every time you eat
this bread and drink this cup, you proclaim his death.*

*Paul's account of the eucharist, as he had received it. It occurs
in a passage where he is rebuking the Corinthian converts for
lack of reverence for the sacrament. This is the earliest known
account of the first eucharist; the first gospel accounts were
written down some years later. Read reverently in an even tone.*

A reading from the first letter of Paul to the Cor-ín-thi-ans

I received from the Lord what I handed on to you,
   namely, that the Lord Jesus on the night in which he was betrayed
   took bread, and after he had given thanks, broke it and said,
   "This is my body, which is for you.
Do this in remembrance of me."
In the same way, after the supper, he took the cup, saying,
   "This cup is the new covenant in my blood.
Do this, whenever you drink it, in remembrance of me."
Every time, then, you eat this bread and drink this cup,
   you proclaim the death of the Lord until he comes!

   This is the Word of the Lord.

GOSPEL

*The cantor sings the response and the people repeat it; the cantor then
sings the verse before the gospel and the people repeat the response.
Otherwise the verse before the gospel may be omitted. Reference:
John 13, 34.*

Praise and hon - or to you, Lord— Je - sus Christ.

For other responses to the verse see page 436.

I — give you a new com - mand - ment: love — one an -

oth - er as I have loved you.

John 13, 1-15   Now he showed how perfect was his love.

*"Before the feast of Passover began, Jesus washed the disciples'
feet." This is the beginning of the narrative of the Passion in
John's Gospel. Read in a slow, even tone, with a feeling for
what is to come. Peter is embarrassed because he does not
perceive the significance of Jesus' action, for usually only slaves
or servants washed the feet of the guests at a banquet. Jesus'
reply is full of depth which the disciples did not realize till
afterwards.*

✠ A reading from the holy gospel according to John

Before the feast of Páss-over, Jesus realized
   that the hour had come for him to pass from this world to the Father.
He had loved his own in this world,
   and would show his love for them to the end.
The devil had already induced Judas,
   son of Simon Is-cár-i-ot, to hand Jesus over;
   and so, during the supper, Jesus—fully aware
   that he had come from God
   and was going to God, the Father
   who had handed everything over to him—
   rose from the meal and took off his cloak.
He picked up a towel and tied it around himself.
Then he poured water into a basin and began to wash his disciples' feet
   and dry them with the towel he had around him.
Thus he came to Simon Peter, who said to him,
   "Lord, are you going to wash my feet? "
Jesus answered, "You may not realize now what I am doing,
   but later you will understand."
Peter replied, "You shall never wash my feet! "
"If I do not wash you," Jesus answered,
   "you will have no share in my heritage."
"Lord," Simon Peter said to him,
   "then not only my feet, but my hands and head as well."
Jesus told him, "The man who has bathed
   has no need to wash [except for his feet];
   he is entirely cleansed, just as you are; though not all."
(The reason he said, "Not all are washed clean,"
   was that he knew his betrayer.)

After he had washed their feet, he put his cloak back on
  and reclined at table once more.
He said to them:
  "Do you understand what I just did for you?
You address me as 'Teacher' and 'Lord',
  and fittingly enough,
  for that is what I am.
But if I washed your feet—
  I who am Teacher and Lord—
  then you must wash each other's feet.
What I just did was to give you an example:
  as I have done, so you must do.

  This is the gospel of the Lord.

GOOD FRIDAY
THE PASSION OF THE LORD

FIRST READING

Isaiah 52, 13-53. 12   He surrendered himself to death, while bearing the faults of many (Fourth song of the Servant of Yahweh).

The fourth of the Songs of the Suffering Servant.   To give a good reading of this beautiful but difficult poem, careful study of the meaning is essential, a marked copy is desirable.

The passage begins with the final glory of the Servant, and then goes back to his degradation and suffering; who could believe that one who suffered so much would ever be exalted?

A reading from the book of the prophet I-sai-ah

See, my servant shall prosper,
   he shall be raised high and greatly exalted.
Even as many were amazed at him—
   so marred was his look beyond that of man,
   and his appearance beyond that of mortals—
So shall he startle many nations,
   because of him kings shall stand speechless;
For those who have not been told shall see,
   those who have not heard shall ponder it.

He was modest and insignificant.   Men despised him for his suffering (which they took as proof that he must have been a sinner.)

Who would believe what we have heard?
To whom has the arm of the Lord been revealed?
He grew up like a sapling before him,
   like a shoot from the parched earth;
There was in him no stately bearing to make us look at him,
   nor appearance that would attract us to him.
He was spurned and avoided by men,
   a man of suffering, accustomed to infirmity,
One of those from whom men hide their faces,
   spurned, and we held him in no esteem.

Yet he suffered as a victim for us; our sins were laid on him. We thought of him as stricken, as one smitten by God (i.e. we thought he was a sinner whom God had punished).

Yet it was our infirmities that he bore,
  our sufferings that he endured,
While we thought of him as stricken,
  as one smitten by God and afflicted.
But he was pierced for our offenses,
  crushed for our sins;
Upon him was the chastisement that makes us whole,
  by his stripes we were healed.
We had all gone astray like sheep,
  each following his own way;
But the Lord laid upon him
  the guilt of us all.

Though he was guiltless, he submitted without protest. He was buried, like a criminal, in a shameful grave.

Though he was harshly treated, he submitted
  and opened not his mouth;
Like a lamb led to the slaughter
  or a sheep before the shearers,
  he was silent and opened not his mouth.
Oppressed and condemned, he was taken away,
  and who would have thought any more of his destiny?
When he was cut off from the land of the living,
  and smitten for the sin of his people,
A grave was assigned him among the wicked
    and a burial place with evildoers,
Though he had done no wrong
  nor spoken any falsehood.
[But the Lord was pleased to crush him in infirmity.]

The meaning is now reversed. Since he gave his life for us, he will see his descendants for many generations (the greatest reward for a good man).

If he gives his life as an offering for sin,
  he shall see his descendants in a long life,
    and the will of the Lord shall be accomplished through him.

He will be greatly honored because he suffered for the sins of so many.

Because of his affliction
   he shall see the light in fullness of days;
Through his suffering, my servant shall justify many,
   and their guilt he shall bear.
Therefore I will give him his portion among the great,
   and he shall divide the spoils with the mighty,
Because he surrendered himself to death
   and was counted among the wicked;
And he shall take away the sins of many,
   and win pardon for their offenses.

   This is the Word of the Lord.

RESPONSORIAL PSALM

Psalm 31, 2. 6. 12-13. 15-16. 17. 25   After the reading the psalmist sings or says the responsorial verse, and all repeat it. This response is also repeated after each verse of the psalm.

Common response:

Re - mem - ber your love and your faith - ful - ness, Lord

Or:

℟. Father, I put my life in your hands.

In you, O Lord, I take refuge;
   let me never be put to shame.
In your justice rescue me.
Into your hands I commend my spirit;
   you will redeem me, O Lord, O faithful God.   ℟.

For all my foes I am an object of reproach,
   a laughingstock to my neighbors, and a dread to my friends;
   they who see me abroad flee from me.
I am forgotten like the unremembered dead;
   I am like a dish that is broken.   ℟.

But my trust is in you, O Lord;
   I say, "You are my God."
In your hands is my destiny; rescue me
   from the clutches of my enemies and my persecutors.   ℟.

Let your face shine upon your servant;
   save me in your kindness.
Take courage and be stouthearted,
   all you who hope in the Lord.   ℟.

SECOND READING

Hebrews 4, 14-16; 5, 7-9 He submitted humbly and became for all the source of eternal salvation.

Jesus, our high priest, can sympathize with us for he was a man. Though he was the Son of God, he suffered because he obeyed God's will. Use a tone of persuasive instruction.

A reading from the letter of Paul to the Hebrews

We have a great high priest who has passed through the heavens,
   Jesus, the Son of God;
   let us hold fast to our profession of faith.
For we do not have a high priest
   who is unable to sympathize with our weakness,
   but one who was tempted in every way that we are,
   yet never sinned.
So let us confidently approach the throne of grace
   to receive mercy and favor and to find help in time of need.

In the days when he was in the flesh,
   Christ offered prayers and supplications with loud cries and tears
     to God,
   who was able to save him from death,
   and he was heard because of his reverence.
Son though he was, he learned obedience from what he suffered;
   and when perfected he became the source of eternal salvation for
     all who obey him.

   This is the Word of the Lord.

GOSPEL

The cantor sings the response and the people repeat it; the cantor then sings the verse before the gospel and the people repeat the response. Otherwise the verse before the gospel may be omitted. Reference: Philippians 2, 8-9.

Praise and hon - or to you, Lord___ Je - sus Christ.

For other responses to the verse see page 436.

Christ be - came o - be - di - ent for us e - ven to death ___ dy - ing on the cross. There - fore ___ God raised ___ him on high and gave him a name a - bove all oth - er names.

John 18, 1-19. 42   The Passion of our Lord Jesus Christ according to John.

John was particularly concerned with showing that Jesus is the Son of God. He gives five chapters to Jesus' words to his disciples at the Last Supper. Then all go out to the garden. Here the reading for the Good Friday gospel begins. It falls into 14 sections, each of which can best be read as a separate episode, with a slight pause after each. The lector should be counscious of the vivid details in the story.

Through the darkness Judas' party approaches carrying lanterns and and torches. Jesus comes forward and asks, "Who is it you want?" "Jesus the Nazorean." "I am he." At the reply those with Judas draw back and fall to the ground. Show here, and throughout, Jesus' calm, overpowering dignity. Peter wounds the high priest's servant. "Am I not to drink the cup the Father has given me?"

2. The Passion of our Lord Jesus Christ according to John

Jesus went out with his disciples across the Kí-dron valley.
There was a garden there, and he and his disciples entered it.
The place was familiar to Judas as well (the one who was to hand him
     over)
  because Jesus had often met there with his disciples.

Judas took the cohort as well as guards
  supplied by the chief priests and the Phá-ri-sees,
  and came there with lanterns, torches and weapons.
Jesus, aware of all that would happen to him,
  stepped forward and said to them,

"Who is it you want? "

"Jesus the Na-zo-ré-an,"

They replied.

"I am he,"

He Answered.

(Now Judas, the one who was to hand him over, was right there with
     them.)
As Jesus said to them, "I am he,"
  they retreated slightly and fell to the ground.
Jesus put the question to them again,

"Who is it you want? "

"Jesus the Na-zo-ré-an,"

They repeated.

"I have told you, I am he,"

Jesus said.

"If I am the one you want, let these men go."

(This was to fulfill what he had said, "I have not lost one of those you
     gave me.")
Then Simon Peter, who had a sword,
  drew it and struck the slave of the high priest, severing his right ear.
(The slave's name was Mál-chus.)

At that Jesus said to Peter,

"Put your sword back in its sheath.
Am I not to drink the cup the Father has given me? "

Jesus is led to the house of Annas, father-in-law of Caiaphas, the high priest. Peter follows and is admitted into the yard, where he lightly denies that he is one of Jesus' followers. Now the night is cold. Peter stands with the others around the charcoal fire.

C.   Then the soldiers of the cohort, their tribune, and the Jewish guards
        arrested Jesus and bound him.
    They led him first to An-nas, the father-in-law of Caí-a-phas
        who was high priest that year.
    (It was Caí-a-phas who had proposed to the Jews
        the advantage of having one man die for the people.)
    Simon Peter, in company with another disciple, kept following
        Jesus closely.
    This disciple, who was known to the high priest,
        stayed with Jesus as far as the high priest's courtyard,
        while Peter   was left standing at the gate.
    The disciple known to the high priest
        came out and spoke to the woman at the gate, and then brought
            Peter in.
    This servant girl who kept the gate said to Peter,

S.   "Aren't you one of this man's followers? "

C.   He replied.

S.   "Not I,"

C.   Now the night was cold,
        and the servants and the guards who were standing around
        had made a charcoal fire to warm themselves by.
    Peter joined them and stood there warming himself.

*The high priest questions Jesus, who replies, "I have always spoken
publicly to any who would listen. I always taught in a synagogue
or in the temple area . . . . Question those who heard me." One of
the guards strikes Jesus. Annas sends him, bound, to Caiaphas.*

C.   The high priest questioned Jesus, first about his disciples, then about
        his teaching.
    Jesus answered by saying:

✠   "I have spoken publicly to any who would listen.
    I always taught in a synagogue or in the temple area
        where all the Jews come together.
    There was nothing secret about anything I said.

✠   Why do you question me? Question those who heard me when I spoke.
It should be obvious they will know what I said."

C.   At this reply, one of the guards who was standing nearby
        gave Jesus a sharp blow on the face.
He said.

S.   "Is that any way to answer the high priest"

C.   Jesus replied,

✠   "If I said anything wrong produce the evidence,
but if I spoke the truth why hit me? "

C.   An-nas next sent him, bound, to the high priest Caí-a-phas.

*Meanwhile Peter has been warming himself. Twice again he
denies that he is one of Jesus' disciples. At that moment a cock
begins to crow.*

C.   All through this, Simon Peter had been standing there warming himself.
They said to him,

SS.   "Are you not a disciple of his? "

C.   He denied:

S.   "I am not! "

S.   "But did I not see you with him in the garden? "

C.   insisted one of the high priest's slaves—
as it happened, a relative of the man whose ear Peter had severed.
Peter denied it again.
At that moment a cock began to crow.

*Next morning Jesus is brought before Pilate, the Roman governor,
who loathes the Jews as much as they loathe him. Each party tries
to get the upper hand. Pilate comes out to them and asks coldly,
"What accusation do you bring against this man? " The reply is
indirect and cautious: "If he were not a criminal, we would certainly
not have handed him over to you." Pilate is curious. He goes inside
with Jesus.*

C.   At daybreak they brought Jesus from Caiaphas to the praetorium.
They did not enter the praetorium themselves,
    for they had to avoid ritual impurity
        if they were to eat the Páss-over supper.
Pilate came out to them.

S.   "What accusation do you bring against this man? " he demanded.

C.   They retorted,

SS.   "If he were not a criminal,"
"we would certainly not have handed him over to you."

C.   At this Pilate said,

S.   "Why do you not take him
and pass judgment on him according to your law? "

C.   The Jews answered.

SS.   "We may not put anyone to death,"

(This was to fulfill what Jesus had said, indicating the sort of death
he would die.)

Pilate begins to question Jesus by himself. "Are you the King of the
Jews? " Jesus replies, "Are you saying this on your own, or have
others been telling you about me? " Pilate is unwilling to become
involved. "I am no Jew! . . . your own people and the chief priests . . .
have handed you over to me. What have you done? " Jesus replies
that his kingdom does not belong to this world. If it did, his
subjects would be fighting. Pilate is interested but puzzled; he has
not met this kind of king before. Jesus goes on, "I came into the
world. . . to testify to the truth. Anyone committed to the truth
hears my voice." "Truth! " says Pilate, "What does that mean? " dis-
playing the pagan agnostic's refusal to face reality.

C.   Pilate went back into the praetorium and summoned Jesus.
He asked him.

S.   "Are you the King of the Jews? "

C.   Jesus answered,

✠   "Are you saying this on your own,
or have others been telling you about me? "

S.   "I am no Jew! "
"It is your own people and the chief priests who have handed you over
to me.
What have you done? "

C.   Pilate retorted.

C.   Jesus answered:

✠ "My kingdom does not belong to this world.
If my kingdom were of this world,
   my subjects would be fighting
    to save me from being handed over to the Jews.
As it is, my kingdom is not here."

C. At this Pilate said to him,

S. "So, then, you are a king? "

C. Jesus replied:

✠ "It is you who say I am a king.
The reason I was born,
   the reason why I came into the world, is to testify to the truth.
Anyone committed to the truth hears my voice "

C. Said Pilate,

S. "Truth! "What does that mean? "

*Pilate goes back to the Jews, and declares that he finds no case
against Jesus. He asks contemptuously, "Do you want me to
release to you the king of the Jews? " The reply of the crowd is
an indignant roar: "We want Barabbas, not this one! "*

C. After this remark, Pilate went out again to the Jews and told them:

S. "Speaking for myself, I find no case against this man.
Recall your custom whereby I release to you someone at Páss-over time.
Do you want me to release to you the king of the Jews? "

C. They shouted back,

S. "We want Ba-ráb-bas, not this one! "

. (Ba-ráb-bas was an insurrectionist.)

*Pilate's next move is to have Jesus scourged. He is handed over
to the Roman soldiers who enjoy Jew-baiting. They make a crown
of thorns, put on him a cloak of royal purple, and jeer: "All hail,
King of the Jews! " Pilate again goes out to the Jews and shows
them Jesus, still wearing the crown of thorns: "Look at the man."
The chief priests are even more rabid than before for Jesus' death;
they shout, "Crucify him! Crucify him! " Pilate is so bewildered
by this hatred that he gives in. "Take him and crucify him yourselves, I find no case against him." The chief priests are suspicious about this reply. They have no right to crucify Jesus on
their own responsbility. They reply, "We have our law . . . he
must die because he made himself God's Son." Like most Romans, Pilate is very superstitious. This answer disturbs him.*

C.   Pilate's next move was to take Jesus and have him scourged.
The soldiers then wove a crown of thorns and fixed it on his head,
     throwing around his shoulders a cloak of royal purple.
Repeatedly they came up to him and said,
     slapping his face as they did so.

SS.   "All hail, King of the Jews! "

C.   Pilate went out a second time and said to the crowd:

S.   "Observe what I do.
I am going to bring him out to you to make you realize
     that I find no case [against him]."

C.   When Jesus came out wearing the crown of thorns and the purple cloak,
     Pilate said to them,

S.   "Look at the man! "

C.   As soon as the chief priests and the temple guards saw him they shouted,

SS.   "Crucify him! Crucify him! "

C.   Pilate said,

S.   "Take him and crucify him yourselves;
     I find no case against him."

C.   The Jews responded,

SS.   "We have our law,
     "and according to that law he must die
     because he made himself God's Son."

C.   When Pilate heard this kind of talk, he was more afraid than ever.

*Pilate goes back to the praetorium. In a tone of puzzled awe, he
asks, "Where do you come from? " Jesus makes no reply. Pilate
is surprised at this unusual behavior from a man in such danger.
He reminds Jesus, "I have the power to release you and the power to crucify you." Jesus answers, "You would have no power
over me whatever unless it were given you from above." Pilate
is now very anxious to avoid all responsibility for Jesus' death.*

C.   Going back into the praetorium, he said to Jesus,

S.   "Where do you come from? "

C.   Jesus would not give him any answer.
     Pilate asked him.

S. "Do you refuse to speak to me?
"Do you not know that I have the power to release you
   and the power to crucify you? "

C. Jesus answered:

✝ "You would have no power over me whatever
unless it were given you from above.
That is why he who handed me over to you
   is guilty of the greater sin."

When the chief priests realize that Pilate is softening, they shout:
"If you free this man, you are no 'Friend of Caesar.' " This threat
is frightening; if they forward such an accusation to Rome,
Pilate will be in great danger. Pilate must now give sentence. Once
more he says to the Jews, "Look at your King! " They give
the same answer as before — "Crucify him! " "What! Shall
I crucify your king? " The chief priests reply, "We have no
king but Caesar." The reply astonishes and delights Pilate, for
hitherto, the trouble with the Jews had always been that the
chief priests would never recognize that Caesar had any rights
over them. So Pilate gives in without further protest, and the
soldiers lead Jesus away to be crucified.

C. After this, Pilate was eager to release him, but the Jews shouted,

S. "If you free this man you are no 'Friend of Caesar.'
Anyone who makes himself a king becomes Caesar's rival."

C. Pilate heard what they were saying,
   then brought Jesus outside and took a seat on a judge's bench
      at the place called the Stone Pavement—Gáb-ba-tha in Hebrew.
   (It was the Preparation Day for Páss-over,
      and the hour was about noon.)
   He said to the Jews,

"Look at your king! "

At this they shouted,

"Away with him!
Away with him! Crucify him! "

Pilate exclaimed.

"What! Shall I crucify your king? "

"We have no king but Caesar."

The chief priests replied,
In the end, Pilate handed Jesus over to be crucified.

*Jesus is crucified, and over his head is placed an inscription in
Pilate's own words: "JESUS THE NAZOREAN, THE KING OF
THE JEWS." When the chief priests protest, Pilate has the last
word: "What I have written, I have written."*

C.   Jesus was led away, and carrying the cross by himself,
         went out to what is called the Place of the Skull (in Hebrew, Gól-go-tha).
      There they crucified him, and two others with him:
         one on either side, Jesus in the middle.
      Pilate had an inscription placed on the cross which read,
         JESUS THE NA-ZO-RÉ-AN
         THE KING OF THE JEWS

      This inscription, in Hebrew, Latin and Greek,
         was read by many of the Jews,
            since the place where Jesus was crucified was near the city.
      The chief priests of the Jews tried to tell Pilate,

SS.   "You should not have written, 'The King of the Jews.'
      Write instead, 'This man claimed to be king of the Jews.' "

C.   Pilate answered,

S.   "What I have written, I have written."

The soldiers throw dice for Jesus' clothes.

C.   After the soldiers had crucified Jesus
         they took his garments and divided them four ways,
            one for each soldier.
      There was also his tunic,
         but this tunic was woven in one piece from top to bottom and had
            no seam.
      They said to each other,

SS.   "We shouldn't tear it.
      Let's throw dice to see who gets it."

C.   (The purpose of this was to have the Scripture fulfilled:
         "They divided my garments among them;
            for my clothing they cast lots.")
      And this was what the soldiers did.

*Jesus, from the cross, sees his mother and the disciple whom
he loves: "Woman, there is your son . . . . There is your mother."
Jesus is now near death. He murmurs, "I am thirsty." They*

give him wine in a sponge. He says, "Now it is finished." Then
he bows his head, and dies. A longer pause.

Near the cross of Jesus there stood his mother,
    his mother's sister, Mary the wife of Cló-pas, and Mary Mág-da-lene.
Seeing his mother there with the disciple whom he loved,
    Jesus said to his mother,

"Woman, there is your son."

In turn he said to the disciple,

"There is your mother."

From that hour onward, the disciple took her into his care.
After that, Jesus realizing that everything was now finished,
    to bring the Scripture to fulfillment said,

"I am thirsty."

There was a jar there, full of common wine.
They stuck a sponge soaked in this wine on some hyssop and raised it
      to his lips.
When Jesus took the wine, he said,

"Now it is finished."

Then he bowed his head, and delivered over his spirit.

Since it was the Preparation Day
    the Jews did not want to have the bodies left on the cross
      during the sabbath,
    for that sabbath was a solemn feast day.
They asked Pilate that the legs be broken and the bodies be taken away.
Accordingly, the soldiers came and broke the legs of the men crucified
      with Jesus,
    first of one, then of the other.
When they came to Jesus and saw that he was already dead,
    they did not break his legs.
One of the soldiers thrust a lance into his side,
    and immediately blood and water flowed out.

(This testimony has been given by an eyewitness, and his testimony
    is true.
He tells what he knows is true, so that you may believe.)
These events took place for the fulfillment of Scripture:
    "Break none of his bones."
There is still another Scripture passage which says:
    They shall look on him whom they have pierced."

For the rest of the reading the tension is lowered. All is
finished. Jesus is dead. His friends take his body and lay it
in the tomb. A long pause before "This is the Gospel of the
Lord.

Afterward, Joseph of Ari-ma-thé-a,
> a disciple of Jesus (although a secret one for fear of the Jews),
> asked Pilate's permission to remove Jesus' body.

Pilate granted it, so they came and took the body away.
Ni-co-dé-mus (the man who had first come to Jesus at night) likewise
> came,
> bringing a mixture of myrrh and aloes which weighed about a hundred
> pounds.

They took Jesus' body, and in accordance with Jewish burial custom
> bound it up in wrappings of cloth with perfumed oils.

In the place where he had been crucified there was a garden,
> and in the garden a new tomb in which no one had ever been buried.

Because of the Jewish Preparation Day
> they buried Jesus there, for the tomb was close at hand.

This is the gospel of the Lord.

EASTER: THE RESURRECTION OF THE LORD
EASTER VIGIL

Nine readings are assigned to the Easter Vigil: seven from the Old Testament and two from the New. If circumstances demand in individual cases, the number of prescribed readings may be reduced. However, three selections from the Old Testament should be read before the Epistle and Gospel, although when necessary, two may be read. In any case, the reading from Exodus about the escape through the Red Sea (reading 3) should always be used.

FIRST READING

Long Form: Genesis 1, 1-2, 2 God saw all he had made, and indeed it was good.

The creation of the universe. Written in a formal, almost ritualistic manner which increases the sense of awe at the power and majesty of the Creator. Each section follows the same verbal pattern. "God said . . . And there was . . . God saw that it was good. Evening came, and morning followed. The first day . . ." Be conscious of this rhythmic pattern, which is repeated for each of the days of Creation.

After the seventh paragraph—the creation of the living creatures —the pattern changes with the creation of man. The last paragraph sums it all up: "seventh day . . . finished . . . rested the day. . . " And reaches its climax in the final words: "God looked at everything he had made, and he found it very good."

A reading from the book of Genesis

In the beginning, when God created the heavens and the earth,
　　the earth was a formless wasteland, and darkness covered the abyss,
　　while a mighty wind swept over the waters.

Then God said, "Let there be light," and there was light.
God saw how good the light was.
God then separated the light from the darkness.
God called the light "day," and the darkness he called "night."
Thus evening came, and morning followed—the first day.

Then God said, "Let there be a dome in the middle of the waters,
　　to separate one body of water from the other."
And so it happened: God made the dome,
　　and it separated the water above the dome from the water below it.
God called the dome "the sky."
Evening came, and morning followed—the second day.

Then God said, "Let the water under the sky be gathered
    into a single basin,
  so that the dry land may appear." And so it happened:
  the water under the sky was gathered into its basin, and the dry land
    appeared.
God called the dry land "the earth,"
  and the basin of the water he called "the sea."
God saw how good it was.

Then God said, "Let the earth bring forth vegetation:
  every kind of plant that bears seed
  and every kind of fruit tree on earth that bears fruit with its seed in it."
And so it happened: the earth brought forth every kind of plant that
    bears seed
  and every kind of fruit tree on earth that bears fruit with its seed in it.
God saw how good it was.
Evening came, and morning followed—the third day.

Then God said: "Let there be lights in the dome of the sky,
  to separate day from night.
Let them mark the fixed times, the days and the years,
  and serve as luminaries in the dome of the sky, to shed light upon the
    earth."
And so it happened: God made the two great lights,
  the greater one to govern the day, and the lesser one to govern the night;
  and he made the stars.
God set them in the dome of the sky, to shed light upon the earth,
  to govern the day and the night, and to separate the light from the
    darkness.
God saw how good it was.
Evening came, and morning followed—the fourth day.

Then God said, "Let the water teem with an abundance of living
    creatures,
  and on the earth let birds fly beneath the dome of the sky."
And so it happened: God created the great sea monsters
  and all kinds of swimming creatures with which the water teems,
  and all kinds of winged birds.
God saw how good it was, and God blessed them, saying,
  "Be fertile, multiply, and fill the water of the seas;
  and let the birds multiply on the earth."
Evening came, and morning followed—the fifth day.

Then God said, "Let the earth bring forth all kinds of living creatures:
  cattle, creeping things, and wild animals of all kinds."

And so it happened:
> God made all kinds of wild animals, all kinds of cattle,
> and all kinds of creeping things of the earth.

God saw how good it was.

Then God said: "Let us make man in our image, after our likeness.

Let them have dominion over the fish of the sea, the birds of the air,
> and the cattle, and over all the wild animals
> and all the creatures that crawl on the ground."

God created man in his image;
> in the divine image he created him;
> male and female he created them.

God blessed them, saying: "Be fertile and multiply;
> fill the earth and subdue it.

Have dominion over the fish of the sea, the birds of the air,
> and all the living things that move on the earth."

God also said: "See, I give you every seed-bearing plant
> > all over the earth
> and every tree that has seed-bearing fruit on it to be your food;
> and to all the animals of the land, all the birds of the air,
> and all the living creatures that crawl on the ground,
> I give all the green plants for food."

And so it happened.

God looked at everything he had made,
> and he found it very good.

Evening came, and morning followed—the sixth day.

Thus the heavens and the earth and all their array were completed.

Since on the seventh day God was finished with the work
> > he had been doing,
> he rested on the seventh day from all the work he had undertaken.

> This is the Word of the Lord.

*Short Form: Genesis 1. 26-31 God saw all he had made, and
indeed it was good.*

A reading from the book of Genesis

In the beginning, when God created the heavens and the earth,
> God said: "Let us make man in our image, after our likeness.

Let them have dominion over the fish of the sea, the birds of the air,
> and the cattle, and over all the wild animals
> and all the creatures that crawl on the ground."

God created man in his image;
> in the divine image he created him;
> male and female he created them.

God blessed them, saying: "Be fertile and multiply;
     fill the earth and subdue it.
Have dominion over the fish of the sea, the birds of the air,
     and all the living things that move on the earth."
God also said: "See, I give you every seed-bearing plant
     all over the earth
     and every tree that has seed-bearing fruit on it to be your food;
     and to all the animals of the land, all the birds of the air,
     and all the living creatures that crawl on the ground,
     I give all the green plants for food."
And so it happened.
God looked at everything he had made, and he found it very good.

     This is the Word of the Lord.

RESPONSORIAL PSALM

*Psalm 104, 1-2. 5-6. 10. 12. 13-14. 24. 35   After the reading the
psalmist sings or says the responsorial verse, and all repeat it. This
response is also repeated after each verse of the psalm.*

℟. Lord, send out your Spirit, and renew the face of the earth.

Bless the Lord, O my soul!
O Lord, my God, you are great indeed!
You are clothed with majesty and glory,
     robed in light as with a cloak.   ℟.

You fixed the earth upon its foundation,
     not to be moved forever;
With the ocean, as with a garment, you covered it;
     above the mountains the waters stood.   ℟.

You send forth springs into the watercourses
     that wind among the mountains.
Beside them the birds of heaven dwell;
     from among the branches they send forth their song.   ℟.

You water the mountains from your palace;
     the earth is replete with the fruit of your works.
You raise grass for the cattle,
     and vegetation for men's use,
Producing bread from the earth.   ℟.

How manifold are your works, O Lord!
   In wisdom you have wrought them all—
   the earth is full of your creatures.
Bless the Lord, O my soul! Alleluia.   ℟.

OR: RESPONSORIAL PSALM

*Psalm 33, 4-5. 6-7. 12-13. 20-22   After the reading the psalmist
sings or says the responsorial verse, and all repeat it. This response
is also repeated after each verse of the psalm.*

℟. The earth is full of the goodness of the Lord.

Upright is the world of the Lord,
   and all his works are trustworthy.
He loves justice and right;
   of the kindness of the Lord the earth is full.   ℟.

By the word of the Lord the heavens were made;
   by the breath of his mouth all their host.
He gathers the waters of the sea as in a flask;
   in cellars he confines the deep.   ℟.

Happy the nation whose God is the Lord,
   the people he has chosen for his own inheritance.
From heaven the Lord looks down;
   he sees all mankind.   ℟.

Our soul waits for the Lord,
   who is our help and our shield.
May your kindness, O Lord, be upon us
   who have put our hope in you.   ℟.

SECOND READING

Long Form: Genesis 22, 1-18 Abraham's Sacrifice of Isaac.

The testing of Abraham. Until late in life, Sarah, Abraham's wife, was childless, but in her old age she conceived, and bore a son, who was named Isaac. When Isaac grew to be a boy, God tested Abraham by commanding him to offer up his only son as a holocaust (a sacrifice entirely destroyed by fire). Indicate the drama and human pathos of this story—the broken-hearted father, who cannot bring himself to tell the boy what is happening, the growing fear of Isaac when he realizes that there is something unusual in the sacrifice, and the silent walk of father and son.

Straight narrative until Isaac is saved, but the reading should reveal the tension under the surface. Slight pause after "going forward," "wood on it," add altar." Slow and deliberate at the words: "Then he reached out and took the knife to slaughter his son." At this point comes the sudden reversal and the happy ending when Abraham is praised for not withholding from God even his beloved son. In the last paragraph, Abraham is blessed, and the moral of the story is strongly stressed in the last words, "All this because you obeyed my command."

A reading from the book of Genesis

God put A-bra-ham to the test. He called to him, "A-bra-ham! "
"Ready! " he replied.
Then God said: "Take your son I-saac,
    your only one, whom you love, and go to the land of Mo-ri-ah.
There you shall offer him up as a holocaust on a height that I will point
        out to you."
Early the next morning A-bra-ham saddled his donkey,
    took with him his son Isaac, and two of his servants as well,
    and with the wood that he had cut for the holocaust,
    set our for the place of which God had told him.

On the third day A-bra-ham got sight of the place from afar.
Then he said to his servants: "Both of you stay here with the donkey,
    while the boy and I go on over yonder.
We will worship and then come back to you."
Thereupon A-bra-ham took the wood for the holocaust
    and laid it on his son I-saac's shoulders,
    while he himself carried the fire and the knife.
As the two walked on together, I-saac spoke to his father A-bra-ham.

"Father! " he said. "Yes, son," he replied.

I-saac continued, "Here are the fire and the wood,
but where is the sheep for the holocaust? "

"Son," A-bra-ham answered, "God himself will provide the sheep
for the holocaust."

Then the two continued going forward.

When they came to the place of which God had told him,
A-bra-ham built an altar there and arranged the wood on it.

Next he tied up his son I-saac, and put him on top of the wood on the
altar.

Then he reached out and took the knife to slaughter his son.

But the Lord's messenger called to him from heaven, "A-bra-ham,
A-bra-ham! "

"Yes, Lord," he answered.

"Do not lay your hand on the boy," said the messenger.

"Do not do the least thing to him.

I know now how devoted you are to God,
since you did not withhold from me your own beloved son."

As A-bra-ham looked about, he spied a ram caught by its horns in the
thicket.

So he went and took the ram
and offered it up as a holocaust in place of his son.

A-bra-ham named the site Yáh-weh-yí-reh;
hence people now say, "On the mountain the Lord will see."

Again the Lord's messenger called to A-bra-ham from heaven and said:
"I swear by myself, declares the Lord,
that because you acted as you did in not withholding from me your
beloved son,
I will bless you abundantly and make your descendants
as countless as the stars of the sky and the sands of the seashore;
your descendants shall take possession of the gates of their enemies,
and in your descendants all the nations of the earth shall find blessing—
all this because you obeyed my command."

This is the Word of the Lord.

Short Form: Genesis 22, 1-2. 9. 10-13. 15-18 Abraham's Sacrifice of Isaac.

A reading from the book of Genesis

God put A-bra-ham to the test. He called to him, "A-bra-ham! "
"Ready! " he replied.
Then God said: "Take your son I-saác,
your only one, whom you love, and go to the land of Mo-rí-ah.

There you shall offer him up as a holocaust
   on a height that I will point out to you."

When they came to the place of which God had told him,
   A-bra-ham built an altar there and arranged the wood on it.
Then he reached out and took the knife to slaughter his son.
But the Lord's messenger called to him from heaven, "A-bra-ham,
      A-bra-ham! "
"Yes, Lord, " he answered.

"Do not lay your hand on the boy," said the messenger.
"Do not do the least thing to him.
I know now how devoted you are to God,
   since you did not withhold from me your own beloved son."
As A-bra-ham looked about, he spied a ram caught by its horns in the
   thicket.
So he went and took the ram and offered it up as a holocaust in place
      of his son.

Again the Lord's messenger called to A-bra-ham from heaven and said:
   "I swear by myself, declares the Lord,
      that because you acted as you did in not withholding from me your
         beloved son,
      I will bless you abundantly and make your descendants
      as countless as the stars of the sky and the sands of the seashore;
      your descendants shall take possession of the gates of their enemies,
      and in your descendants all the nations of the earth shall find blessing.
   —all this because you obeyed my command."

   This is the Word of the Lord.

RESPONSORIAL PSALM

Psalm 16, 5. 8. 9-10. 11   After the reading the psalmist sings or
says the responsorial verse, and all repeat it. This response is
also repeated after each verse of the psalm.

R̸. Keep me safe, O God; you are my hope.

O Lord, my allotted portion and my cup,
   you it is who hold fast my lot.
I set the Lord ever before me;
   with him at my right hand I shall not be disturbed.   R̸.

Therefore my heart is glad and my soul rejoices,
   my body, too, abides in confidence;
Because you will not abandon my soul to the nether world,
   nor will you suffer your faithful one to undergo corruption.   R̸.

You will show me the path to life,
 fullness of joys in your presence,
  the delights at your right hand forever.   ℞.

THIRD READING

*Exodus 14, 15-15, 1 Tell the sons of Israel to march on, to walk
through the sea on dry ground.*

*The saving of the Israelites at the crossing of the Red Sea.
Moses has led the Israelites out of Egypt, and they are encamped
by the Red Sea. They see the Egyptian chariots coming toward
them, and, in their panic, they turn on Moses, who cries to the
Lord for help. The story is intense and dramatic, reaching a triumphant conclusion when the Israelites look on their enemies
lying dead on the seashore.*

A reading from the book of Éx-o-dus

The Lord said to Moses, "Why are you crying out to me?
Tell the Is-ra-el-ites to go forward.
And you, lift up your staff and,
 with hand outstretched over the sea, split the sea in two.
 that the Is-ra-el-ites may pass through it on dry land.
But I will make the Egyptians so obstinate
 that they will go in after them.
Then I will receive glory through Pharaoh and all his army,
 his chariots and charioteers.
The Egyptians shall know that I am the Lord,
 when I receive glory through Pha-ra-oh and his chariots and charioteers."

The angel of God, who had been leading Israel's camp,
 now moved and went around behind them.
The column of cloud also, leaving the front,
 took up its place behind them,
 so that it came between the camp of the Egyptians and that of Israel.
But the cloud now became dark, and thus the night passed
 without the rival camps coming any closer together all night long.
Then Moses stretched out his hand over the sea,
 and the Lord swept the sea with a strong east wind throughout the
  night
 and so turned it into dry land.
When the water was thus divided,
 the Ís-ra-el-ites marched into the midst of the sea on dry land,
 with the water like a wall to their right and to their left.

The Egyptians followed in pursuit;
>   all Phá-ra-oh's horses and chariots and charioteers
>   went after them right into the midst of the sea.

In the night watch just before dawn
>   the Lord cast through the column of the fiery cloud
>>   upon the Egyptian force
>   a glance that threw it into a panic;
>   and he so clogged their chariot wheels that they could hardly drive.

With that the Egyptians sounded the retreat before Israel,
>   because the Lord was fighting for them against the Egyptians.

Then the Lord told Moses, "Stretch out your hand over the sea,
>   that the water may flow back upon the Egyptians,
>   upon their chariots and their charioteers."

So Moses stretched out his hand over the sea,
>   and at dawn the sea flowed back to its normal depth.

The Egyptians were fleeing head on toward the sea,
>   when the Lord hurled them into its midst.

As the water flowed back,
>   it covered the chariots and the charioteers of Phá-ra-oh's whole army
>   which had followed the Israelites into the sea.

Not a single one of them escaped.

But the Israelites had marched on dry land
>>   through the midst of the sea,
>   with the water like a wall to their right and to their left.

Thus the Lord saved Israel on that day from the power of the Egyptians.

When Israel saw the Egyptians lying dead on the seashore
>   and beheld the great power that the Lord had shown
>>   against the Egyptians,
>   they feared the Lord and believed in him and in his servant Moses.

Then Moses and the Israelites sang this song to the Lord:
>   I will sing to the Lord, for he is gloriously triumphant;
>   horse and chariot he has cast into the sea.

This is the Word of the Lord.

RESPONSORIAL PSALM

Exodus 15, 1-2. 3-4. 5-6. 17-18   After the reading the psalmist sings or says the responsorial verse, and all repeat it. This response is also repeated after each verse of the psalm.

℟. Let us sing to the Lord; he has covered himself in glory.

I will sing to the Lord, for he is gloriously triumphant;
   horse and chariot he has cast into the sea.
My strength and my courage is the Lord,
   and he has been my savior.
He is my God, I praise him;
   the God of my father, I extol him.   ℟.

The Lord is a warrior,
   Lord is his name!
Phá-ra-oh's chariots and army he hurled into the sea;
   the elite of his officers were submerged in the Red Sea.   ℟.

The flood waters covered them,
   they sank into the depths like a stone.
Your right hand, O Lord, magnificent in power,
   your right hand, O Lord, has shattered the enemy.   ℟.

You brought in the people you redeemed
   and planted them on the mountain of your inheritance.
The place where you made your seat, O Lord,
   the sanctuary, O Lord, which your hands established.
The Lord shall reign forever and ever.   ℟.

FOURTH READING

Isaiah 54, 5-14 But with everlasting love I have taken pity on you, says the Lord, your redeemer.

But with everlasting love I have taken pity on you, says the Lord, your redeemer.

The original prophecy was probably the work of one of the exiles in Babylon, thinking of Jerusalem in ruins. Here it is applied to the new Jerusalem, the Holy City, as she will be when the Messiah comes. Jerusalem is pictured as a wife forsaken by her husband but now restored to his love. Read as a poem of hope and consolation.

A reading from the book of the prophet I-sai-ah

He who has become your husband is your Maker;
> his name is the Lord of hosts;
Your redeemer is the Holy One of Israel,
> called God of all the earth.
The Lord calls you back,
> like a wife forsaken and grieved in spirit,
A wife married in youth and then cast off,
> says your God.
For a brief moment I abandoned you,
> but with great tenderness I will take you back.
In an outburst of wrath, for a moment
> I hid my face from you;
But with enduring love I take pity on you,
> says the Lord, your redeemer.
This is for me like the days of Noah,
> when I swore that the waters of Noah
> should never again deluge the earth;
So I have sworn not to be angry with you,
> or to rebuke you.
Though the mountains leave their place and the hills be shaken,
My love shall never leave you
> nor my covenant of peace be shaken,
> says the Lord, who has mercy on you.
O afflicted one, storm-battered and unconsoled,
> I lay your pavements in carnelians,
> and your foundations in sapphires;
I will make your battlements of rubies,
> your gates of carbuncles,

and all your walls of precious stones.
All your sons shall be taught by the Lord,
   and great shall be the peace of your children.
In justice shall you be established,
   far from the fear of oppression,
   where destruction cannot come near you.

   This is the Word of the Lord.

RESPONSORIAL PSALM

Psalm 30, 2. 4. 5-6. 11-12. 13 After the reading the psalmist sings
or says the responsorial verse, and all repeat it. This response is also
repeated after each verse of the psalm.

℟. I will praise you, Lord, for you have rescued me.

I will extol you, O Lord, for you drew me clear
   and did not let my enemies rejoice over me.
O Lord, you brought me up from the nether world;
   you preserved me from among those going down into the pit.   ℟.

Sing praise to the Lord, you his faithful ones,
   and give thanks to his holy name.
For his anger lasts but a moment;
   a lifetime, his good will.
At nightfall, weeping enters in,
   but with the dawn, rejoicing.   ℟.

Hear, O Lord, and have pity on me;
   O Lord, be my helper.
You changed my mourning into dancing;
   O Lord, my God, forever will I give you thanks.   ℟.

FIFTH READING

Isaiah 55, 1-11 Come to me and your soul will live. With you I
will make an everlasting covenant.

An invitation to those who have fallen away to come back to
the Lord. The tone is a tender pleading of God to his people.
Keep this tone throughout, and intensify the appeal at "Seek
the Lord while he may be found," to the end.

A reading from the book of the prophet I-sai-ah

Thus says the Lord:
All you who are thirsty,
   come to the water!

You who have no money,
   come, receive grain and eat;
Come, without paying and without cost,
   drink wine and milk!
Why spend your money for what is not bread;
   your wages for what fails to satisfy?
Heed me, and you shall eat well,
   you shall delight in rich fare.
Come to me heedfully,
   listen, that you may have life.
I will renew with you the everlasting covenant,
   the benefits assured to David.
As I made him a witness to the peoples,
   a leader and commander of nations,
So shall you summon a nation you knew not,
   and nations that knew you not shall run to you,
Because of the Lord, your God,
   the Holy One of Israel, who has glorified you.
Seek the Lord while he may be found,
   call him while he is near.
Let the scoundrel forsake his way,
   and the wicked man his thoughts;
Let him turn to the Lord for mercy;
   to our God, who is generous in forgiving.
For my thoughts are not your thoughts;
   nor are your ways my ways, says the Lord.
As high as the heavens are above the earth,
   so high are my ways above your ways
   and my thoughts above your thoughts .
For just as from the heavens
   the rain and snow come down
And do not return there
   till they have watered the earth,
   making it fertile and fruitful,
Giving seed to him who sows
   and bread to him who eats,
So shall my word be
   that goes forth from my mouth;
It shall not return to me void,
   but shall do my will,
   achieving the end for which I sent it.

   This is the Word of the Lord.

RESPONSORIAL PSALM

Isaiah 12, 2-3. 4. 5-6 After the reading the psalmist sings or says the responsorial verse, and all repeat it. This response is also repeated after each verse of the psalm.

℞. You will draw water joyfully from the springs of salvation.

God indeed is my savior;
  I am confident and unafraid.
My strength and my courage is the Lord,
  and he has been my savior.
With joy you will draw water
  at the fountain of salvation.   ℞.

Give thanks to the Lord, acclaim his name;
  among the nations make known his deeds,
  proclaim how exalted is his name.   ℞.

Sing praise to the Lord for his glorious achievement;
  let this be known throughout all the earth.
Shout with exultation, O city of Zion,
    for great in your midst
    is the Holy One of Israel!   ℞.

SIXTH READING

Baruch 3, 9-15. 32-34, 4 Walk in the way of God and you will live in peace for ever.

The prophet asks the people of Israel why they are now in exile. Because, he replies, they forsook God's wisdom. He goes on to the praise of wisdom and of those who seek her. If they are faithful to wisdom, they will live. And the consoling end is "Blessed are we, O Israel; for what pleases God is known to us!"

A reading from the book of the prophet Bá-ruch

Hear, O Israel, the commandments of life:
  listen, and know prudence!
How is it, Israel,
  that you are in the land of your foes,
  grown old in a foreign land,
Defiled with the dead,
  accounted with those destined for the nether world?
You have forsaken the fountain of wisdom!
  Had you walked in the way of God,
  you would have dwelt in enduring peace.

Learn where prudence is,
    where strength, where understanding;
That you may know also
    where are length of days, and life,
    where light of the eyes, and peace.

Who has found the place of wisdom,
    who has entered into her treasuries?
He who knows all things knows her;
    he has probed her by his knowledge—
He who established the earth for all time,
    and filled it with four-footed beasts;
He who dismisses the light, and it departs,
    calls it, and it obeys him trembling;
Before whom the stars at their posts
    shine and rejoice;
When he calls them, they answer, "Here we are! "
    shining with joy for their Maker.
Such is our God;
    no other is to be compared to him:
He has traced out all the way of understanding,
    and has given her to Jacob, his servant,
    to Israel, his beloved son.

Since then she has appeared on earth,
    and moved among men.
She is the book of the precepts of God,
    the law that endures forever;
All who cling to her will live,
    but those will die who forsake her.
Turn, O Jacob, and receive her:
    walk by her light toward splendor.
Give not your glory to another,
    your privileges to an alien race.
Blessed are we, O Israel;
    for what pleases God is known to us!

    This is the Word of the Lord.

RESPONSORIAL PSALM

*Psalm 19, 8. 9. 10. 11 After the reading the psalmist sings or says
the responsorial verse, and all repeat it. This response is also
repeated after each verse of the psalm.*

℟. Lord, you have the words of everlasting life.

The law of the Lord is perfect,
    refreshing the soul;
The decree of the Lord is trustworthy,
    giving wisdom to the simple.   ℟.

The precepts of the Lord are right,
    rejoicing the heart;
The command of the Lord is clear,
    enlightening the eye.   ℟.

The fear of the Lord is pure,
    enduring forever;
The ordinances of the Lord are true,
    all of them just.   ℟.

They are more precious than gold,
    than a heap of purest gold;
Sweeter also than syrup
    or honey from the comb.   ℟.

SEVENTH READING

*Ezekiel 36, 16-28 I shall pour clean water over you and I shall
give you a new heart.*

*God's people have offended him by their foul ways, and there-
fore he has scattered them as exiled among other nations. Now
he relents. Because of his name, he will bring them back to their
own land and cleanse them of their impurities. Start on a note
of indignation which turns to forgiveness at "I will prove the holiness of my great name . . . take you away . . . gather . . . bring
you back . . . clean water . . . give you a new heart . . . put my
spirit . . . shall live in the land . . . your fathers . . . my people
. . . your God."*

A reading from the book of the prophet E-zé-ki-el

Thus the word of the Lord came to me;
    Son of man, when the house of Israel lived in their land,
    they defiled it by their conduct and deeds.
In my sight their conduct was like the defilement of a menstruous woman.

Therefore I poured out my fury upon them
  [because of the blood which they poured out on the ground,
  and because they defiled it with idols].

I scattered them among the nations, dispersing them over foreign lands;
  according to their conduct and deeds I judged them.

But when they came among the nations [wherever they came],
  they served to profane my holy name,
  because it was said of them: "These are the people of the Lord,
  yet they had to leave their land."

So I have relented because of my holy name
  which the house of Israel profaned among the nations where they came.

Therefore say to the house of Israel: Thus says the Lord God:
  Not for your sakes do I act, house of Israel,
  but for the sake of my holy name,
  which you profaned among the nations to which you came.

I will prove the holiness of my great name,
  profaned among the nations, in whose midst you have profaned it.

Thus the nations shall know that I am the Lord, says the Lord God,
  when in their sight I prove my holiness through you.

For I will take you away from among the nations,
  gather you from all the foreign lands,
  and bring you back to your own land.

I will sprinkle clean water upon you to cleanse you
      from all your impurities,
    and from all your idols I will cleanse you.

I will give you a new heart and place a new spirit within you,
  taking from your bodies your stony hearts and giving you natural
  hearts.

I will put my spirit within you and make you live by my statutes,
  careful to observe my decrees.

You shall live in the land I gave your fathers;
  you shall be my people, and I will be your God.

  This is the Word of the Lord.

RESPONSORIAL PSALM

*Psalm 42, 3. 5; 43, 3. 4   After the reading the psalmist sings or says
the responsorial verse, and all repeat it. This response is also repeated
after each verse of the psalm.*

℟. Like a deer that longs for running streams,
      my soul longs for you, my God.

Athirst is my soul for God, the living God.
When shall I go and behold the face of God?   ℟.

I went with the throng
 and led them in procession to the house of God,
Amid loud cries of joy and thanksgiving,
 with the multitude keeping festival.   ℟.

Send forth your light and your fidelity;
 they shall lead me on
And bring me to your holy mountain,
 to your dwelling-place.   ℟.

Then will I go in to the altar of God,
 the God of my gladness and joy;
Then will I give you thanks upon the harp,
 O God, my God!   ℟.

*When baptism is celebrated, the Responsorial Psalm after Reading V
'Is 12, 2-3. 4. 5-6), page 139 may be used; or the following:*

Or: RESPONSORIAL PSALM

*Psalm 51, 12-13. 14-15. 18-19   After the reading the psalmist sings
or says responsorial verse, and all repeat it. This response is also
repeated after each verse of the psalm.*

℟. Create a clean heart in me, O God.

A clean heart create for me, O God,
 and a steadfast spirit renew within me.
Cast me not out from your presence,
 and your holy spirit take not from me.   ℟.

Give me back the joy of your salvation,
 and a willing spirit sustain in me.
I will teach transgressors your ways,
 and sinners shall return to you.   ℟.

For you are not pleased with sacrifices;
 should I offer a holocaust, you would not accept it.
My sacrifice, O God, is a contrite spirit;
 a heart contrite and humbled, O God, you will not spurn.   ℟.

EPISTLE

*Romans 6, 3-11   Christ, having been raised from the dead, will never
die again.*

*A difficult passage. The argument is that baptism is like the
death and resurrection of Christ. As we go down into and
under the water, the old self dies; as we emerge from the
water we rise as a new creature, freed from sin. Christ died
and rose from the dead, never to die again. So, too, after
death we will rise with Christ and live with him. A profound
passage which the lector must understand before he can read it
aloud.*

A reading from the letter of Paul to the Romans

Are you not aware that we who were baptized into Christ Jesus
  were baptized into his death?
Through baptism into his death we were buried with him,
  so that, just as Christ was raised from the dead by the glory of the
    Father,
  we too might live a new life.
If we have been united with him through likeness to his death,
  so shall we be through a like resurrection.
This we know: our old self was crucified with him
  so that the sinful body might be destroyed and we might be slaves
    to sin no longer.
A man who is dead has been freed from sin.
If we have died with Christ, we believe that we are also to live with him.
We know that Christ, once raised from the dead, will never die again;
  death has no more power over him.
His death was death to sin, once for all;
  his life is life for God.
In the same way, you must consider yourselves dead to sin
  but alive for God in Christ Jesus.

  This is the Word of the Lord.

RESPONSORIAL PSALM

After the epistle all rise, and the priest solemnly intones the alleluia,
which is repeated by all present.

Al - le   lu - ia.

The cantor sings the psalm and the people answer Alleluia. If necessary,
the cantor of the psalm may himself intone the alleluia.

Al - le - lu - ia,   Al - le - lu - ia,___   Al - le - lu - ia.

Give thanks to the Lord, for he is good,
  for his mercy endures forever.
Let the house of Israel say,
  "His mercy endures forever."   ℟.

The right hand of the Lord has struck with power;
  the right hand of the Lord is exalted.
I shall not die, but live,
  and declare the works of the Lord.   ℟.

The stone which the builders rejected
  has become the cornerstone.
By the Lord has this been done;
  It is wonderful in our eyes.   ℟.

GOSPEL

Luke 24, 1-12 Why look among the dead for someone who is alive.

*Luke's short account of the morning of Christ's resurrection. The
tone of this reading should express the atmosphere of the early
morning, the first bewilderment of the women when they find the
tomb empty, their terror at the words of the two men, the
incredulity of the Eleven.*

✠   A reading from the holy gospel according to Luke

On the first day of the week, at dawn,
    the women came to the tomb bringing the spices they had prepared.
They found the stone rolled back from the tomb;
    but when they entered the tomb,
    they did not find the body of the Lord Jesus.
While they were still at a loss what to think of this,
    two men in dazzling garments appeared beside them.
Terrified, the women bowed to the ground.
The men said to them:
"Why do you search for the living One among the dead?
He is not here; he has been raised up.
Remember what he said to you while he was still in Gál-i-lee—
    that the Son of Man must be delivered into the hands of sinful men,
    and be crucified, and on the third day rise again."
With this reminder, his words came back to them.

On their return from the tomb,
    they told all these things to the Eleven and the others.
The women were Mary of Mág-da-la, Jo-án-na,
    and Mary the mother of James.
The other women with them also told the apostles,
    but the story seemed like nonsense and they refused to believe them.
Peter, however, got up and ran to the tomb.
He stooped down but could see nothing but the wrappings.
So he went away full of amazement at what had occurred.

    This is the gospel of the Lord.

EASTER SUNDAY

FIRST READING

Acts 10, 34. 37-43   We have eaten and drunk with him after his resurrection from the dead.

The passage is part of Peter's address to Cornelius, the centurion, and his household. In the early days of Christianity, Peter and the other apostles were concerned with testifying that after his crucifixion Jesus had risen from the dead. They knew he had risen because they had seen him; he had eaten with them and spoken to them. Read as a simple account of one who was a witness to what he describes.

A reading from the Acts of the Apostles

Peter addressed the people in these words;
  "I take it you know what has been reported all over Judea
    about Jesus of Ná-za-reth, beginning in Gá-li-lee with the baptism
        John preached;
      of the way God anointed him with the Holy Spirit and power.
He went about doing good works and healing all who were
        in the grip of the devil,
    and God was with him.
We are witnesses to all that he did in the land of the Jews and in Je-rú-sa-lem.
They killed him finally, 'hanging him on a tree,'
    only to have God raise him up on the third day
        and grant that he be seen,
    not by all, but only by such witnesses as had been chosen beforehand
        by God—
    by us who ate and drank with him after he rose from the dead.
He commissioned us to preach to the people
    and to bear witness that he is the one set apart by God
    as judge of the living and the dead.
To him all the prophets testify, saying that everyone who believes in him
    has forgiveness of sins through his name."

  This is the Word of the Lord.

RESPONSORIAL PSALM

Psalm 118, 1-2. 16-17. 22-23   After the reading the psalmist sings or says the responsorial verse, and all repeat it.   This response is also repeated after each verse of the psalm.

Common response:

Al - le - lu - ia   al - le - lu - ia.

Or:

℞. This is the day the Lord has made; let us rejoice and be glad.

Give thanks to the Lord, for he is good,
    for his mercy endures forever.
Let the house of Israel say,
    "His mercy endures forever."   ℞.

"The right hand of the Lord has struck with power;
    the right hand of the Lord is exalted.
I shall not die, but live,
    and declare the works of the Lord.   ℞.

The stone which the builders rejected
    has become the cornerstone.
By the Lord has this been done;
    it is wonderful in our eyes.   ℞.

SECOND READING

Colossians 3, 1-4   Look for the things that are in heaven, where Christ is.

By baptism, you have died to sin and been born again in Christ. Do not, therefore, concern yourselves any longer with earthly trifles, but rather think of heaven.   When Christ appears at the second coming, you will be with him in glory.   Read as straight argument.

A reading from the letter of Paul to the Co-lós-si-ans

Since you have been raised up in company with Christ,
    set your heart on what pertains to higher realms
    where Christ is seated at God's right hand.
Be intent on things above rather than on things of earth.

After all, you have died! Your life is hidden now with Christ in God.
When Christ our life appears, then you shall appear with him in glory.

This is the Word of the Lord.

Or:
1 Corinthians 5, 6-8 Throw away the old yeast, that you may be new dough.

*Paul is rebuking the Corinthian converts because they are too
pleased with themselves. He urges them to get rid of the old
yeast (their former imperfections) and make fresh dough
without yeast (unleavened bread which should be eaten during
the Feast of the Passover). Christ the Paschal Lamb has been
sacrificed; we must celebrate the feast not with old, but with new,
pure, unleavened bread. The sense of the passage is clear,
but for the modern hearer the metaphorical use of yeast and
unleavened bread may cause difficulties. Slight over-emphasis
on "yeast," "dough," "unleavened" will help to clarify.*

A reading from the first letter of Paul to the Cor-ín-thi-ans

Do you not know that a little yeast has its effect all through the dough?
Get rid of the old yeast to make of yourselves fresh dough,
> unleavened loaves, as it were;
> Christ our Páss-over has been sacrificed.

Let us celebrate the feast not with the old yeast, that of corruption and
> wickedness,
> but with the unleavened bread of sincerity and truth.

This is the Word of the Lord.

SEQUENCE *(Prose Text)*

To the Paschal Victim let Christians offer a sacrifice of praise.
The Lamb redeemed the sheep. Christ, sinless, reconciled sinners to
> the Father.
Death and life were locked together in a unique struggle.
Life's captain died; now he reigns, never more to die.
Tell us, Mary, "What did you see on the way? "
"I saw the tomb of the now living Christ.
I saw the glory of Christ, now risen.
"I saw angels who gave witness; the cloths too which once had covered
> head and limbs.
"Christ my hope has arisen. He will go before his own into Gá-li-lee."
We know that Christ has indeed risen from the dead.
Do you, conqueror and king, have mercy on us. Amen. Alleluia.

Or (Poetic Text)

Christians, to the Paschal Victim
   Offer your thankful praises!
A Lamb the sheep redeems: Christ,
    who only is sinless,
    Reconciles sinners to the Father.
Death and life have contended in that combat stupendous:
    The Prince of life, who died, reigns immortal.

Speak, Mary, declaring
   What you saw, wayfaring.
"The tomb of Christ, who is living,
    The glory of Jesus' resurrection;
    Bright angels attesting,
    The shroud and napkin resting.
Yes, Christ my hope is arisen:
    To Gá-li-lee he goes before you."

Christ indeed from death is risen, our new life obtaining.
Have mercy, victor King, ever reigning!
Amen. Alleluia.

GOSPEL

*The cantor sings the alleluia and the people repeat it; the cantor then
sings the verse and the people repeat the alleluia. Otherwise the alleluia
may be omitted. Reference: 1 Corinthians 5, 7-8.*

Al - le-lu - ia, al - le - lu - ia, al - le - lu - ia.___

Christ has be-come our pas-chal sa - cri-fice; let us feast with joy in the Lord.

John 20, 1-9 The teaching of scripture is that he must rise from the dead.

Be conscious of the vivid details of this account. It is still dark when Mary Magdalene comes to the tomb. When she sees that the stone has been moved away, she runs to Peter and the other disciple and tells them with a sense of great shock: "The Lord . . . taken from the tomb! . . . put him! " Peter and the other disciple go to see at once, running side by side.". . . the other disciple outran Peter . . . He did not enter . . . peer in. Simon Peter entered the tomb . . . observed the wrappings . . . cloth . head . . . rolled up in a place by itself. The other disciple went in. He saw and believed.

✠ A reading from the holy gospel according to John

Early in the morning on the first day of the week,
   while it was still dark, Mary Mág-da-lene came to the tomb.
She saw that the stone had been moved away,
   so she ran off to Simon Peter and the other disciple
   (the one Jesus loved) and told them,
   "The Lord has been taken from the tomb!
We don't know where they have put him! "
At that, Peter and the other disciple started out
      on their way toward the tomb.
They were running side by side,
   but then the other disciple outran Peter and reached the tomb first.
He did not enter but bent down to peer in,
   and saw the wrappings lying on the ground.
Presently, Simon Peter came along behind him and entered the tomb.
He observed the wrappings on the ground
   and saw the piece of cloth which had covered the head
      not lying with the wrappings,
   but rolled up in a place by itself.
Then the disciple who had arrived first at the tomb went in.
He saw and believed.
(Remember, as yet they did not understand the Scripture that Jesus had
      to rise from the dead.)

   This is the gospel of the Lord.

SECOND SUNDAY OF EASTER

FIRST READING

*Acts 5, 12-16   The numbers of men and women who came to believe in
the Lord increased steadily.*

*In the Sundays of Easter Season the first reading is taken from
the Acts of the Apostles which tell of the establishment of the
Church; the second reading is from the Book of Revelation—
John's mystical visions of heaven and things to come; the gospel
readings are all from John's gospel.*

A simple note of the first gradual spread of the faith.

A reading from the Acts of the Apostles

Through the hands of the apostles,
  many signs and wonders occurred among the people.
By mutual agreement they used to meet in Solomon's Portico.
No one else dared to join them,
  despite the fact that the people held them in great esteem.
Nevertheless more and more believers,
  men and women in great numbers,
  were continually added to the Lord.
The people carried the sick into the streets
  and laid them on cots and mattresses,
  so that when Peter passed by
  at least his shadow might fall on one or another of them.
Crowds from the towns around Jerusalem would gather, too,
  bringing their sick and those who were troubled by
    unclean spirits,
  all of whom were cured.

This is the Word of the Lord.

RESPONSORIAL PSALM

*Psalm 118, 2-4. 22-24. 25-27 After the reading the psalmist sings or says
the responsorial verse, and all repeat it. This response is also repeated
after each verse of the psalm.*

Common response:

Al - le - lu - ia   al - le - lu - ia.

Or:

℞. Give thanks to the Lord for he is good,
    his love is everlasting.

Let the house of Israel say,
  "His mercy endures forever."
Let the house of Á-a-ron say,
  "His mercy endures forever "
Let those who fear the Lord say,
  "His mercy endures forever."   ℞.

The stone which the builders rejected
  has become the cornerstone.
By the Lord has this been done;
  it is wonderful in our eyes.
This is the day the Lord has made;
  let us be glad and rejoice in it.   ℞.

O Lord, grant salvation!
  O Lord, grant prosperity!
Blessed is he who comes in the name of the Lord;
  we bless you from the house of the Lord.
The Lord is God, and he has given us light.   ℞.

SECOND READING

Revelation 1, 9-11. 12-13. 17-19   I was dead and now I am to live for ever and ever.

The first of John's visions. Readings from the Book of Revelation demand a special tone and style to convey the sense of mystery, for visions of this kind are a setting forth in symbols of matters too deep to be expressed in words. Read slowly and solemnly to convey the impression that we too are being allowed glimpses of things normally beyond human experience. At the same time stress the sights and sounds of the visions. Emphasize particularly the final words.

A reading from the book of Revelation

I, John, your brother, who share with you the distress
    and the kingly reign and the endurance we have in Jesus,
    found myself on the island called Pát-mos
    because I proclaimed God's word and bore witness to Jesus.
On the Lord's day I was caught up in ecstasy,
    and I heard behind me a piercing voice
    like the sound of a trumpet, which said,
    "Write on a scroll what you now see.
I turned around to see
    whose voice it was that spoke to me.
When I did so I saw seven lampstands of gold,
    and among the lampstands One like a Son of Man
    wearing an ankle-length robe, with a sash of gold about his breast.

When I caught sight of him
    I fell down at his feet as though dead.
He touched me with his right hand and said:
    "There is nothing to fear.
I am the First and the Last and the One who lives.
Once I was dead but now I live—forever and ever.
I hold the keys of death and the nether world.
Write down, therefore, whatever you see in visions—
    what you see now and will see in time to come.

This is the Word of the Lord.

GOSPEL

The cantor sings the alleluia and the people repeat it; the cantor then sings the verse and the people repeat the alleluia. Otherwise the alleluia may be omitted. Reference: John 20, 29.

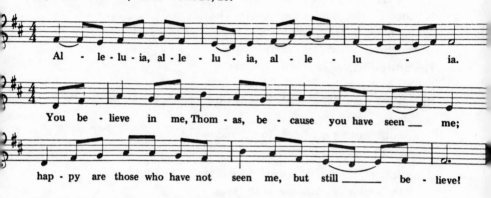

Al - le - lu - ia, al - le - lu - ia, al - le - lu - ia.

You be - lieve in me, Thom - as, be - cause you have seen ___ me;

hap - py are those who have not seen me, but still _____ be - lieve!

John 20, 19-31   After eight days Jesus came in and stood among them.

The night after his resurrection, Jesus appears to his disciples. He breathes on them so that they may receive the Holy Spirit, and he gives them power to forgive sins, or retain them. Thomas, who is absent, refuses to believe their reports that have indeed seen the Lord. A week later, Jesus again appears and Thomas is convinced by the evidence of his senses. The lector should read this passage as straight narrative, but emphasize the words of Jesus throughout, with special note of significance given to the gentle rebuke of Thomas.

✠   A reading from the holy gospel according to John

On the evening of that first day of the week,
    even though the disciples had locked the doors of the place
    where they were for fear of the Jews,
    Jesus came and stood before them.
"Peace be with you," he said.
When he had said this,
    he showed them his hands and his side.
At the sight of the Lord the disciples rejoiced.
"Peace be with you," he said again.
"As the Father has sent me,
    so I send you."
Then he breathed on them and said:
    "Receive the Holy Spirit.

If you forgive men's sins,
    they are forgiven them;
    if you hold them bound,
    they are held bound."
It happened that one of the Twelve, Thomas
    (the name means "Twin"),
    was absent when Jesus came.
The other disciples kept telling him:
    "We have seen the Lord! "
His answer was, "I'll never believe it without probing the nailprints
    in his hands,
    without putting my finger in the nailmarks
    and my hand into his side."

A week later, the disciples were once more in the room,
    and this time Thomas was with them.
Despite the locked doors, Jesus came and stood before them.
"Peace be with you," he said;
    then, to Thomas: "Take your finger and examine my hands.
Put your hand into my side.
Do not persist in your unbelief, but believe! "
Thomas said in response, "My Lord and my God! "
Jesus then said to him:
    "You became a believer because you saw me.
Blest are they who have not seen and have believed."

Jesus performed many other signs as well—
    signs not recorded here—
    in the presence of his disciples.
But these have been recorded to help you believe
    that Jesus is the Mes-si-ah, the Son of God,
    so that through this faith you may have life in his name.

    This is the gospel of the Lord.

THIRD SUNDAY OF EASTER

FIRST READING

Acts 5, 27-32. 40-41 We are witnesses to all this, we and the Holy Spirit whom God has given to those who obey him.

In the earliest days of the faith Peter had cured a cripple. As a result he and John were brought before the Sanhedrin—the Great Council of the Jews—and forbidden to preach that Jesus had been raised from the dead. They did not obey and were again arrested. Active persecution of the new Church now begins. Read the whole episode in Acts as preparation.

A reading from the Acts of the Apostles

The high priest began the interrogation of the apostles in this way:
    "We gave you strict orders not to teach about that name,
    yet you have filled Je-rú-sa-lem with your teaching
    and are determined to make us responsible for that
        man's blood."
To this, Peter and the apostles replied:
    "Better for us to obey God than men!
The God of our fathers has raised up Jesus whom you put to death,
    hanging him on a tree.
He whom God has exalted at his right hand as ruler and savior
    is to bring repentance to Israel and forgiveness of sins.
We testify to this.
    So too does the Holy Spirit,
    whom God has given to those that obey him."
The Sán-hed-rin ordered the apostles
    not to speak again about the name of Jesus,
    and afterward dismissed them.
The apostles for their part left the Sán-hed-rin full of joy
    that they had been judged worthy of ill—treatment for the
        sake of the Name.

    This is the Word of the Lord.

RESPONSORIAL PSALM

Psalm 30, 2. 4. 5-6. 11-12. 13   After the reading the psalmist sings or says the responsorial verse, and all repeat it.   This response is also repeated after each verse of the psalm.

Al - le - lu - ia   al - le - lu - ia.

Or:

℟. I will praise you, Lord, for you have rescued me.

I will extol you, O Lord, for you drew me clear
    and did not let my enemies rejoice over me,
O Lord, you brought me up from the nether world;
    you preserved me from among those going
    down into the pit.   ℟.

Sing praise to the Lord, you his faithful ones,
    and give thanks to his holy name.
For his anger lasts but a moment;
    a lifetime, his good will.
At nightfall, weeping enters in,
    but with the dawn, rejoicing.   ℟.

Hear, O Lord, and have pity on me;
    O Lord, be my helper.
You changed my mourning into dancing;
    O Lord, my God, forever will I give you thanks.   ℟.

SECOND READING

Revelation 5, 11-14   The Lamb that was sacrificed is worthy to be given power, wealth, glory, and blessing.

Part of the vision of the Scroll and the Lamb. See note on last Sunday's second reading.

A reading from the book of Revelation

I, John, had a vision,
    and I heard the voices of many angels
    who surrounded the throne
    and the living creatures and the elders.

They were countless in number,
  thousands and tens of thousands, and they all cried out:
"Worthy is the Lamb that was slain
  to receive power and riches, wisdom and strength,
  honor and glory and praise! "
Then I heard the voices of every creature
  in heaven and on earth and under the earth and in the sea;
  everything in the universe cried aloud:
  "To the One seated on the throne, and to the Lamb,
  be praise and honor, glory and might,
  forever and ever! "
The four living creatures answered "Amen,"
  and the elders fell down and worshiped.

  This is the Word of the Lord.

GOSPEL

*The cantor sings the alleluia and the people repeat it; the cantor then
sings the verse and the people repeat the alleluia. Otherwise the alleluia
may be omitted.*

Al - le - lu - ia, al - le - lu - ia, al - le - lu - ia.

My sheep ___ lis - ten to my voice, says the Lord; I

know them __ and __ they __ fol - low me.

*Long Form: John 21, 1-19 Jesus stepped forward, took the bread
and gave it to them, and did the same with the fish.*

*The last recorded appearance of the risen Christ, which requires
special sensitive reading to bring out the details of the story and
the full significance of Jesus' three fold question to Peter.*

✠ A reading from the holy gospel according to John

At the sea of Ti-bé-ri-as Jesus showed himself to the disciples [once again].
This is how the appearance took place.

Assembled were Simon Peter, Thomas ("the Twin"),
  Na-thán-a-el (from Cana in Gál-i-lee), Zé-be-dee's sons, and
    two other disciples.
Simon Peter said to them, "I am going out to fish."
  "We will join you," they replied,
    and went off to get into their boat.
All through the night they caught nothing.
Just after daybreak Jesus was standing on the shore,
  though none of the disciples knew it was Jesus.
He said to them,
  "Children, have you caught anything to eat? "
"Not a thing," they answered.
"Cast your net off to the starboard side," he suggested,
  "and you will find something."
So they made a cast,
  and took so many fish they could not haul the net in.
Then the disciple Jesus loved cried out to Peter,
  "It is the Lord! "
On hearing it was the Lord, Simon Peter threw on some clothes—
  he was stripped—and jumped into the water.

Meanwhile the other disciples came in the boat,
  towing the net full of fish.
Actually they were not far from land—
  no more than a hundred yards.

When they landed, they saw a charcoal fire there
  with a fish laid on it and some bread.
"Bring some of the fish you just caught," Jesus told them.
Simon Peter went aboard and hauled ashore the net
  loaded with sizable fish—one hundred fifty-three of them!
In spite of the great number, the net was not torn.

"Come and eat your meal," Jesus told them.
Not one of the disciples presumed to inquire "Who are you? "
  for they knew it was the Lord.
Jesus came over, took the bread and gave it to them,
  and did the same with the fish.
This marked the third time that Jesus appeared to the disciples
  after being raised from the dead.

When they had eaten their meal, Jesus
  said to Simon Peter,

"Simon, son of John, do you love me more than these? "
"Yes, Lord," Peter said, "you know that I love you."
At which Jesus said, " Feed my lambs."
A second time he put his question, "Simon, son of John,
    do you love me? "
"Yes, Lord," Peter said, "you know that I love you."
    Jesus replied, "Tend my sheep."

A third time Jesus asked him,
    "Simon, son of John, do you love me? "
Peter was hurt because he had asked a third time,
    "Do you love me? "
So he said to him::
    "Lord, you know everything. You know well that I love you."
Jesus told him, "Feed my sheep.
    "I tell you solemnly:
    as a young man
    you fastened your belt
    and went about as you pleased;
    but when you are older
    you will stretch out your hands,
    and another will tie you fast
    and carry you off against your will."
(What he said indicated the sort of death
    by which Peter was to glorify God.)
When Jesus had finished speaking
    he said to him, "Follow me."

    This is the gospel of the Lord.

*Short Form: John 21, 1-14 Jesus stepped forward, took the bread
and gave it to them, and did the same with the fish.*

✠   A reading from the holy gospel according to John

At the sea of Ti-bé-ri-as Jesus showed himself to the
    disciples once again.
This is how the appearance took place.
Assembled were Simon Peter, Thomas ("the Twin"),
    Na-thán-a-el (from Cana in Gál-i-lee), Zé-be-dee's sons
    and two other disciples.

Simon Peter said to them, "I am going out to fish."
"We will join you," they replied,
   and went off to get into their boat.
All through the night they caught nothing.

Just after daybreak Jesus was standing on the shore,
   though none of the disciples knew it was Jesus.
He said to them,
   "Children, have you caught anything to eat? "
"Not a thing," they answered.
"Cast your net off to the starboard side," he suggested,
   "and you will find something."
So they made a cast,
   and took so many fish they could not haul the net in.
Then the disciple Jesus loved cried out to Peter,
   "It is the Lord! "
On hearing it was the Lord, Simon Peter threw on some clothes—
   he was stripped—and jumped into the water.

Meanwhile the other disciples came in the boat,
   towing the net full of fish.
Actually they were not far from land—
   no more than a hundred yards.

When they landed, they saw a charcoal fire there
   with a fish laid on it and some bread.
"Bring some of the fish you just caught," Jesus told them.
Simon Peter went aboard and hauled ashore the net
   loaded with sizable fish—one hundred fifty-three of them!
In spite of the great number, the net was not torn.

"Come and eat your meal," Jesus told them.
Not one of the disciples presumed to inquire "Who are you? "
   for they knew it was the Lord.
Jesus came over, took the bread and gave it to them,
   and did the same with the fish.
This marked the third time that Jesus appeared to the disciples
   after being raised from the dead.

   This is the gospel of the Lord.

FOURTH SUNDAY OF EASTER

Acts 13, 14. 43-52   Many became believers.

*Paul came to Antioch in Pisidia on his first missionary journey.
On the sabbath he went into the local Jewish synagogue and, as
was customary when a visitor appeared, he was invited to address
the congregation. Paul would then speak of Jesus and his resurrection.
The message usually aroused much controversy. When as here, the
Jews rejected it, Paul turned to the Gentiles from whom he usually
had a good reception. Bring out the violence of the opposition and
the vigor of Paul's retort. Prepare by studying the whole chapter
which includes also Paul's manner of introducing Jesus and his
teaching for the first time.*

A reading from the Acts of the Apostles

Paul and Bár-na-bas travelled on from Pér-ga and came to
     Án-ti-och in Pi-sí-di-a.
On the sabbath day they entered the synagogue and sat down.
Many Jews and devout Jewish converts followed Paul and Bár-na-bas,
     who spoke to them and urged them
     to hold fast to the grace of God.

The following sabbath, almost the entire city gathered to
     hear the word of God.
When the Jews saw the crowds,
     they became very jealous
     and countered with violent abuse whatever Paul said.

Paul and Bár-na-bas spoke out fearlessly, nonetheless:
     "The word of God has to be declared to you first of all;
     but since you reject it
     and thus convict yourselves as unworthy of everlasting life,
     we now turn to the Gentiles.
For thus were we instructed by the Lord:
     'I have made you a light to the nations,
     a means of salvation to the ends of the earth.' "
The Gentiles were delighted when they heard this
     and responded to the word of the Lord with praise.
All who were destined for life everlasting believed in it.
Thus the word of the Lord was carried throughout
     that area.

But some of the Jews stirred up their influential women sympathizers
     and the leading men of the town, and in that way
     got a persecution started against Paul and Bár-na-bas.

The Jews finally expelled them from their territory.
So the two shook the dust from their feet in protest
   and went on to Iconium.
The disciples could not but be filled with joy and the Holy Spirit.

   This is the Word of the Lord.

RESPONSORIAL PSALM

*Psalm 100, 1-2. 3. 5   After the reading the psalmist sings or says the
responsorial verse, and all repeat it. This response is also repeated
after each verse of the psalm.*

Common response:

Al - le - lu - ia   al - le - lu - ia.

Or:

℟. We are his people: the sheep of his flock.

Sing joyfully to the Lord, all you lands;
   serve the Lord with gladness;
   come before him with joyful song.   ℟.

Know that the Lord is God;
   he made us, his we are;
   his people, the flock he tends.   ℟.

The Lord is good:
   his kindness endures forever,
   and his faithfulness, to all generations.   ℟.

SECOND READING

Revelation 7, 9. 14-17   The Lamb who is at the throne will be their
shepherd and will lead them to springs of living water.

John's vision of the last judgment when all the saints who have
stood fast under great persecution are brought before the Throne
in glory and pass into the joy of the beatific vision.   An ecstatic
vision.

A reading from the book of Revelation

I, John, saw before me a huge crowd which no one could count
    from every nation and race, people and tongue.
They stood before the throne and the Lamb,
    dressed in long white robes
    and holding palm branches in their hands.

Then one of the elders said to me:
    "These are the ones who have survived
    the great period of trial;
    they have washed their robes
    and made them white in the blood of the Lamb.

"It was this that brought them before God's throne:
    day and night they minister to him in his temple;
    he who sits on the throne will give them shelter.
Never again shall they know hunger or thirst,
    nor shall the sun or its heat beat down on them,
    for the Lamb on the throne will shepherd them.
He will lead them to springs of life-giving water,
    and God will wipe every tear from their eyes."

    This is the Word of the Lord.

GOSPEL

The cantor sings the alleluia and the people repeat it; the cantor then
sings the verse and the people repeat the alleluia. Otherwise the alleluia
may be omitted. Reference: John 10, 14.

Al - le - lu - ia, al - le - lu - ia, al - le - lu - ia.

I __ am the good shep-herd says the Lord; I __ know __ my

sheep __ and __ mine know __ me.

John 10, 27-30 I give my sheep eternal life.

Jesus is the Good Shepherd who cares for his sheep. Effective
reading of this very simple passage needs a slow pace and the
exact use of emphasis.

✠ A reading from the holy gospel according to John

Jesus said:
 "My sheep hear my voice.
I know them,
    and they follow me.
I give them eternal life,
    and they shall never perish.
No one shall snatch them out of my hand.
My Father is greater than all, in what he has given me,
    and there is no snatching out of his hand.
The Father and I are one."

    This is the gospel of the Lord.

FIFTH SUNDAY OF EASTER

FIRST READING

*Acts 14, 21-27   They assembled the church and gave an account of all
that God had done with them.*

*A straight report at the end of the first missionary journey of
Paul and Barnabas. Bring out the importance of the final sentence,
for although Paul preached first to his own countrymen, his real
mission was to the Gentiles.*

A reading from the Acts of the Apostles

After Paul and Bár-na-bas had proclaimed
  the good news in Derbe and made numerous disciples,
    they retraced their steps to Lýs-tra and I-cón-i-um first, then to
      Án-ti-och.
They gave their disciples reassurances,
  and encouraged them to persevere in the faith with this instruction:
  "We must undergo many trials
  if we are to enter into the reign of God."
In each church they installed elders and, with prayer and fasting,
  commended them to the Lord in whom they had put their faith.

Then they passed through Pi-síd-i-a and come to Pám-phi.
After preaching the message in Pér-ga, they went down to At-tál-i-a.
From there they sailed back to An-ti-och
  where they had first been commended to the favor of God
  for the task they had now completed.
On their arrival, they called the congregation together
  and related all that God had helped them accomplish,
  and how he had opened the door of faith to the Gentiles.

  This is the Word of the Lord.

RESPONSORIAL PSALM

Psalm 145, 8-9. 10-11. 12-13   After the reading the psalmist sings or says the responsorial verse, and all repeat it. This response is also repeated after each verse of the psalm.

Al - le - lu - ia   al - le - lu - ia.

Or:

℞. I will praise your name for ever, my king and my God.

The Lord is gracious and merciful,
  slow to anger and of great kindness.
The Lord is good to all
  and compassionate toward all his works.   ℞.

Let all your works give you thanks, O Lord,
  and let your faithful ones bless you.
Let them discourse of the glory of your kingdom
  and speak of your might.   ℞.

Let them make known to men your might
  and the glorious splendor of your kingdom.
Your kingdom is a kingdom for all ages,
  and your dominion endures through all generations.   ℞.

SECOND READING

Revelation 21, 1-5   He will wipe away all the tears from their eyes.

See note on page 154. The last judgement has been made and John sees the vision of the New Jerusalem—that is, the Church in glory—as the Bride of Christ, the Lamb of God. The meaning of this vision is conveyed to the reader in the depths and by the rhythm of the words.

A reading from the book of Revelation

I, John, saw new heavens and a new earth.
The former heavens and the former earth had passed away,
   and the sea was no longer.
I also saw a new Jerusalem, the holy city,
   coming down out of heaven from God,
   beautiful as a bride prepared to meet her husband.
I heard a loud voice from the throne cry out:
   "This is God's dwelling among men.
He shall dwell with them and they shall be his people,
   and he shall be their God who is always with them.
He shall wipe every tear from their eyes,
   and there shall be no more death or mourning,
   crying out or pain, for the former world has passed away."

The One who sat on the throne said to me,
   "See, I make all things new! "

   This is the Word of the Lord.

GOSPEL

The cantor sings the alleluia and the people repeat it; the cantor then sings the verse and the people repeat the alleluia. Otherwise the alleluia may be omitted. Reference: John 13, 34.

Al - le - lu - ia, al - le - lu - ia, al - le - lu - ia.

I __ give you a new ___ com - mand - ment: love one an -

oth - er as I have loved you.

John 13, 31-33. 34-35 I give you a new commandment: love one another.

At the last supper Jesus sups with his disciples but Judas the traitor is among them. Only when Judas has left can Jesus speak his farewell message with freedom. As so often in this gospel, the recurring message is "love one another."

✠   A reading from the holy gospel according to John

Once Judas had left [the cenacle], Jesus said:
  "Now is the Son of Man glorified
  and God is glorified in him.
  [If God has been glorified in him,]
  God will, in turn, glorify him in himself,
  and will glorify him soon.
My children, I am not to be with you much longer.
I give you a new commandment:
  Love one another.
Such as my love has been for you,
  so must your love be for each other.
This is how all will know you for my disciples:
  your love for one another."
    This is the gospel of the Lord.

SIXTH SUNDAY OF EASTER

FIRST READING

*Acts 15, 1-2. 22-29 It seemed right to the Holy Spirit and to us not
to burden you beyond what is essential.*

*In the early years of the Church, there was bitter controversy
because some of the Jewish converts insisted that all converts
from outside must accept the Mosaic Law and especially the
rite of circumcision, which was repugnant to Greeks and Romans.
Paul, as apostle to the Gentiles, was strongly for freedom from
this demand. The dispute came to a head when Paul had returned
to Antioch after his first missionary journey. As recorded in this
reading, the matter was debated at Jerusalem, and it was agreed
that pagan converts should be required only to observe the
restrictions noted in the last sentence. Nevertheless the controversy
lasted through Paul's ministry and the 'Judaizers' caused much
trouble in the various churches he had founded. Read as an
interesting record, which shows that the Fathers of the Church
opposed excessive and unnecessary regulations.*

A reading from the Acts of the Apostles

Some men came down to Án-ti-och from Ju-dé-a
    and began to teach the brothers:
      "Unless you are circumcised according to Mosaic practice,
        you cannot be saved."
This created dissension and much controversy between them and
        and Paul and Bár-na-bas.
Finally it was decided that Paul, Bár-na-bas, and some others
    should go up to see the apostles and prés-by-ters in Jerusalem
    about this question.

It was resolved by the apostles and the prés-by-ters,
    in agreement with the whole Jerusalem church,
    that representatives be chosen from among their number
    and sent to Án-ti-och along with Paul and Bár-na-bas.
Those chosen were leading men of the community,
    Judas, known as Bar-sáb-bas, and Sí-las.
They were to deliver this letter:
      "The apostles and the prés-by-ters, your brothers,
    send greetings to the brothers of Gentile origin
    in An-ti-och, Syria and Ci-lí-ci-a.
We have heard that some of our number without any
      instructions from us
    have upset you with their discussions and disturbed your
      peace of mind.

Therefore we have unanimously resolved to choose representatives
  and send them to you, along with our beloved Bár-na-bas
    and Paul,
  who have dedicated themselves to the cause of our Lord Jesus Christ.
Those whom we are sending you are Judas and Silas,
  who will convey this message by word of mouth:
'It is the decision of the Holy Spirit, and ours too,
not to lay on you any burden
beyond that which is strictly necessary,
namely, to abstain from meat sacrificed to idols, from blood,
  from the meat of strangled animals, and from illicit sexual union.
You will be well advised to avoid these things.

Farewell.' "

This is the Word of the Lord.

RESPONSORIAL PSALM

*Psalm 67, 2-3. 5. 6. 8 After the reading the psalmist sings or says the
responsorial verse, and all repeat it. This response is also repeated
after each verse of the psalm.*

Al - le - lu - ia al - le - lu - ia.

Or:

℟. O God, let all the nations praise you!

May God have pity on us and bless us;
  may he let his face shine upon us.
So may your way be known upon earth;
  among all nations, your salvation. ℟.

May the nations be glad and exult
  because you rule the peoples in equity;
  the nations on the earth you guide. ℟.

May the peoples praise you, O God;
  may all the peoples praise you!
May God bless us,
  and may all the ends of the earth fear him! ℟.

SECOND READING

*Revelation 21, 10-14. 22-23   He showed me the holy city coming down
out of heaven.*

*Continuation from Last Sunday of the vision of the New Jerusalem.
Bring out the magnificence of the sight, especially the images of
radiance.*

A reading from the book of Revelation

The angel carried me away in spirit
　　to the top of a very high mountain
　　and showed me the holy city Jerusalem
　　coming down out of heaven from God.
It gleamed with the splendor of God.
The city had the radiance of a precious jewel
　　that sparkled like a diamond.
Its wall, massive and high, had twelve gates
　　at which twelve angels were stationed.
Twelve names were written on the gates,
　　the names of the twelve tribes of Israel.
There were three gates facing east, three north,
　　three south, and three west.
The wall of the city had twelve courses of stones as its foundation,
　　on which were written the names of the twelve apostles of the Lamb.

I saw no temple in the city.
The Lord, God the Almighty, is its temple—he and the Lamb.
The city had no need of sun or moon,
　　for the glory of God gave it light, and its lamp was the Lamb.

　　This is the Word of the Lord.

GOSPEL

*The cantor sings the alleluia and the people repeat it; the cantor then
sings the verse and the people repeat the alleluia. Otherwise the alleluia
may be omitted. Reference: John 14, 23.*

Al - le - lu - ia, al - le - lu - ia, al - le - lu - ia.

If __ an - y - one loves me he will hold to my words, and my

Fa - ther will love him and we __ will come __ to him.

*John 14, 23-29 The Holy Spirit will teach you everything and remind
you of all I have said to you.*

*From Jesus' farewell words to his disciples at the last supper. He
tells them of the coming of the Holy Spirit. The key words of the
message are 'love' and 'peace'.*

✠ A reading from the holy gospel according to John

Jesus said to his disciples:
  "Anyone who loves me
  will be true to my word,
  and my Father will love him;
  we will come to him
  and make our dwelling place with him always.
He who does not love me does not keep my words.
Yet the word you hear is not mine;
  it comes from the Father who sent me.
This much have I told you while I was still with you;
  the Paraclete, the Holy Spirit
  whom the Father will send in my name,
  will instruct you in everything,
  and remind you of all that I told you.
'Peace' is my farewell to you,
  my peace is my gift to you;
  I do not give it to you as the world gives peace.
Do not be distressed or fearful.

You have heard me say,
  'I go away for a while, and I come back to you.'
If you truly loved me
  you would rejoice to have me go to the Father,
  for the Father is greater than I.
I tell you this now, before it takes place,
  so that when it takes place you may believe.

  This is the gospel of the Lord.

ASCENSION

FIRST READING

Acts 1, 1-11 Why are you standing here looking into the sky? Jesus has been taken into heaven.

This reading is in three parts. The first is the explanatory prologue which links the Acts of the Apostles with Luke's Gospel (also addressed to Theophilus), and summarizes events in the forty days after the crucifixion. The second part shows that the Apostles had recognized that Jesus was indeed the Messiah, but were still hoping that he would bring about a political restoration of the Jews. Jesus replies that their business is to be his witness in Judea, in Samaria and to the ends of the earth. He is taken from them. In the last paragraph they are consoled by the message that Jesus will one day come back to them. Read as straight narration.

The beginning of the Acts of the Apostles

In my first account, The-ó-phi-lus,
  I dealt with all that Jesus did and taught
  until the day he was taken up to heaven,
  having first instructed the apostles he had chosen through the Holy
    Spirit.
In the time after his suffering he showed them in many convincing ways
    that he was alive, appearing to them over the course of forty days
    and speaking to them about the reign of God.
On one occasion when he met with them,
    he told them not to leave Je-rú-sa-lem:
  "Wait, rather, for the fulfillment of my Father's promise,
    of which you have heard me speak.
John baptized with water,
    but within a few days you will be baptized with the Holy Spirit."

While they were with him they asked,
  "Lord, are you going to restore the rule to Israel now? "
His answer was: "The exact time it is not yours to know.
The Father has reserved that to himself.
You will receive power when the Holy Spirit comes down on you;
    then you are to be my witnesses in Je-rú-sa-lem,
    throughout Judea and Sa-má-ri-a
    yes, even to the ends of the earth."
No sooner had he said this than he was lifted up before their eyes
    in a cloud which took him from their sight.

They were still gazing up into the heavens
   when two men dressed in white stood beside them.
"Men of Gá-li-lee," they said,
   "why do you stand here looking up at the skies?
This Jesus who has been taken from you
   will return, just as you saw him go up into the heavens."

   This is the Word of the Lord.

RESPONSORIAL PSALM

*Psalm 47, 2-3. 6-7. 8-9 After the reading the psalmist sings or says
the responsorial verse, and all repeat it. This response is also repeated
after each verse of the psalm.*

Common response:

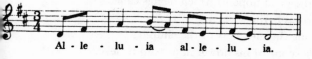

Al - le - lu - ia   al - le - lu - ia.

Or:

℟. God mounts his throne to shouts of joy;
   a blare of trumpets for the Lord.

All you peoples, clap your hands,
   shout to God with cries of gladness,
For the Lord, the Most High, the awesome,
   is the great king over all the earth.   ℟.

God mounts his throne amid shouts of joy;
   the Lord, amid trumpet blasts.
Sing praise to God, sing praise;
   sing praise to our king, sing praise.   ℟.

For king of all the earth is God;
   sing hymns of praise.
God reigns over the nations,
   God sits upon his holy throne.   ℟.

SECOND READING

Ephesians 1, 17-23   He made Jesus to sit at his right hand in heaven.

*Paul prays that God the Father will show the Ephesians what
belief in Christ really means. He is a manifestation of the
same power which God showed when he raised Christ from the
dead and seated him in heaven, high above every kind of spiritual
and earthly power. Read in a mood of exaltation.*

A reading from the letter of Paul to the E-phé-si-ans

May the God of our Lord Jesus Christ, the Father of glory,
   grant you a spirit of wisdom and insight to know him clearly.
May he enlighten your innermost vision
   that you may know the great hope to which he has called you,
   the wealth of his glorious heritage
   to be distributed among the members of the church,
   and the immeasurable scope of his power in us who believe.
It is like the strength he showed in raising Christ from the dead
   and seating him at his right hand in heaven,
   high above every principality, power, virtue and domination,
   and every name that can be given in this age or the age to come.
He has put all things under Christ's feet
   and has made him thus exalted, head of the church, which is his body:
   the fullness of him who fills the universe in all its parts.
   This is the Word of the Lord.

GOSPEL

*The cantor sings the alleluia and the people repeat it; the cantor then
sings the verse and the people repeat the alleluia. Otherwise the alleluia
may be omitted. Reference: Matthew 28, 19. 20.*

Al - le - lu - ia, al - le - lu - ia, al - le - lu - ia.

Go and teach all peo - ple my gos - pel. I am with you

al - ways, un - til the end of the world.

*Luke 24, 46-53 He blessed them, withdrew from them, and was
carried up to heaven.*

*Read as the closing words—and the happy ending—of the story
of Jesus' life on earth.*

✠   The conclusion of the holy gospel according to Luke

Jesus said to the Eleven: "Thus it is written
    that the Mes-sí-ah must suffer and rise from the dead
        on the third day.
In his name, penance for the remission of sins
    is to be preached to the nations, beginning at Jerusalem.
You are witnesses of all this.
See, I send down upon you the promise of my Father.
Remain here in the city until you are clothed with power from
        on high."

He then led thèm out near Béth-a-ny,
    and with hands upraised, blessed them.
As he blessed, he left them, and was taken up to heaven.
They fell down to do him reverence,
    then returned to Jerusalem filled with joy.
There they were to be found in the temple
    constantly, speaking the praises of God.

    This is the gospel of the Lord.

SEVENTH SUNDAY OF EASTER

FIRST READING

*Acts 7, 55-60 I can see the heavens thrown open and the Son of Man
standing at the right hand of God.*

*Stephen, one of the first deacons, of the new Church, was
charged before the Sanhedrin with blaspheming against Moses
and God. He spoke at length, showing how the leaders of the
people had always opposed the Holy Spirit; and he denounced
his accusers as betrayers and murderers of Christ. The words
caused an uproar. Express the fury of this dramatic moment
in the history of the Church, and convey the thought that as
a result of the martyrdom of Stephen, Saul was converted to
become the Apostle Paul.*

A reading from the Acts of the Apostles

Stephen, filled with the Holy Spirit,
> looked to the sky above and saw the glory of God,
> and Jesus standing at God's right hand.

"Look! " he exclaimed, "I see an opening in the sky,
> and the Son of Man standing at God's right hand."

The onlookers were shouting aloud,
> holding their hands over their ears as they did so.

Then they rushed at him as one man,
> dragged him out of the city, and began to stone him.

The witnesses meanwhile were piling their cloaks
> at the feet of a young man named Saul.

As Stephen was being stoned he could be heard praying,
> "Lord Jesus, receive my spirit."

He fell to his knees and cried out in a loud voice,
> "Lord, do not hold this sin against them."

And with that he died.

> This is the Word of the Lord.

RESPONSORIAL PSALM

Psalm 97, 1-2. 6-7. 9   After the reading the psalmist sings or says the responsorial verse, and all repeat it. This response is also repeated after each verse of the psalm.

Common response:

Al - le - lu - ia   al - le - lu - ia.

Or:

℟. The Lord is king, the most high over all the earth.

The Lord is king; let the earth rejoice;
   let the many isles be glad.
Justice and judgment are the foundation of his throne.   ℟.

The heavens proclaim his justice,
   and all peoples see his glory.
All gods are prostrate before him.   ℟.

You, O Lord, are the Most High over all the earth,
   exalted far above all gods.   ℟.

SECOND READING

Revelation 22, 12-14. 16-17. 20 Come, Lord Jesus!

*From the closing words of John's vision. The key words are
'come,' 'coming soon;' and end on this note.*

A reading from the book of Revelation

I, John, heard a voice saying to me:
  "Remember, I am coming soon!
I bring with me the reward
  that will be given to each man as his conduct deserves.
I am the Alpha and the Omega, the First and the Last,
  the Beginning and the End!
Happy are they who wash their robes
  so as to have free access to the tree of life
  and enter the city through its gates!

"It is I, Jesus, who have sent my angel to give you this testimony
  about the churches.
I am the Root and Offspring of David,
  the Morning Star shining bright."

The Spirit and the Bride say, "Come! "
  Let him who hears answer, "Come! "
Let him who is thirsty come forward; let all who desire it
  accept the gift of life-giving water.

The One who gives this testimony says,
  "Yes, I am coming soon! "
Amen! Come, Lord Jesus!

  This is the Word of the Lord.

GOSPEL

*The cantor sings the alleluia and the people repeat it; the cantor then
sings the verse and the people repeat the alleluia. Otherwise the alleluia
may be omitted. Reference: John 14, 18.*

Al - le - lu - ia, al - le - lu - ia, al - le - lu - ia.

The _ Lord said: _ I will not leave _ you or - phans.

I will come back to you, — and — your hearts — will re - joice.

John 17, 20-26 Father, may they be one in us!

*The closing words of Jesus' prayer to his Father just before he
goes out to his betrayal. He prays for the whole world that
through faith in the Father and the Son all may be united.
Show the significance of the key words 'believe,' 'world,' 'one,'
'love,' and end with the suggestion that now Jesus has completed
his mission.*

✝ A reading from the holy gospel according to John

Jesus looked up to heaven and said:
   "I do not pray for my disciples alone.
I pray also for those who will believe in me through their word,
   that all may be one as you, Father, are in me, and I in you;
   I pray that they may be one in us,
      that the world may believe that you sent me.
I have given them the glory you gave me
   that they may be one, as we are one—
I living in them, you living in me—
that their unity may be complete.
So shall the world know that you sent me,
   and that you loved them as you loved me.
Father,
   all those you gave me
   I would have in my company
   where I am,
   to see this glory of mine
   which is your gift to me,
   because of the love you bore me before the world began.
Just Father,
   the world has not known you,
   but I have known you;
   and these men have known that you sent me.
To them I have revealed your name,
   and I will continue to reveal it
   so that your love for me may live in them,
   and I may live in them."

      This is the gospel of the Lord.

PENTECOST VIGIL

FIRST READING

*Genesis 11, 1-9　It was named Babel because there the Lord confused
the language of the whole earth.*

*The passage is the last of the pre-history anecdotes—an explana-
tion of the variety of languages spoken by mankind and of the
misunderstandings that follow. By contrast, after the gift of
tongues on the day of Pentecost, men from many lands can all
understand what the apostles are saying. Straight narrative
leading up to the explanation at the end.*

A reading from the book of Genesis

At that time the whole world spoke the same language,
　　using the same words.
While men were migrating in the east,
　　they came upon a valley in the land of Shí-nar and settled there.
They said to one another, "Come, let us mold bricks and harden them
　　　with fire."
They used bricks for stone, and bitumen for mortar.
Then they said, "Come, let us build ourselves a city
　　and a tower with its top in the sky,
　　and so make a name for ourselves;
　　otherwise we shall be scattered all over the earth."

The Lord came down to see the city and the tower
　　that the men had built.
Then the Lord said: "If now, while they are one people,
　　all speaking the same language,
　　they have started to do this, nothing will later stop them
　　from doing whatever they presume to do.
Let us then go down and there confuse their language,
　　so that one will not understand what another says."
Thus the Lord scattered them from there all over the earth,
　　and they stopped building the city.
That is why it was called Babel,
　　because there the Lord confused the speech of all the world.
It was from that place that he scattered them all over the earth.

　　This is the Word of the Lord.

Or:

*Exodus 19, 3-8. 16-20   The Lord God appeared before all the people
on Mount Sinai.*

*According to one tradition, the Jewish Feast of Pentecost
commemorated the giving of the Law to Moses on Mount
Sinai. This passage tells how Moses is summoned by God
to come up the mountain. The reading is in two parts. In
the first, God renews his promise to make the house of Jacob
his special people. The second part describes how God comes
down to the top of the mountain.*

A reading from the book of Éx-o-dus

Moses went up the mountain to God.
Then the Lord called to him and said,
   "Thus shall you say to the house of Jacob; tell the Ís-ra-el-ites:
   You have seen for yourselves how I treated the Egyptians
   and how I bore you up on eagle wings and brought you here to myself.
Therefore, if you hearken to my voice and keep my covenant,
   you shall be my special possession, dearer to me than all other people,
   though all the earth is mine.
You shall be to me a kingdom of priests, a holy nation.
That is what you must tell the Ís-ra-el-ites."
So Moses went and summoned the elders of the people.
When he set before them all that the Lord had ordered him
    to tell them,
   the people all answered together,
   "Everything the Lord has said, we will do."

On the morning of the third day there were peals of thunder and lightning,
   and a heavy cloud over the mountain,
   and a very loud trumpet blast, so that all the people in the camp
    trembled.
But Moses led the people out of the camp to meet God,
   and they stationed themselves at the foot of the mountain.
Mount Sí-nai was all wrapped in smoke,
   for the Lord came down upon it in fire.
The smoke rose from it as though from a furnace,
   and the whole mountain trembled violently.
The trumpet blast grew louder and louder,
   while Moses was speaking and God answering him with thunder.

When the Lord came down to the top of Mount Sí-nai,
   he summoned Moses to the top of the mountain.

   This is the Word of the Lord.

Or:

Ezekiel 37, 1-14   Dry bones of Israel, I shall put my spirit in you, and you will live.

This vision was given to Ezekiel in Babylon. It reveals that the exiled people of Israel, scattered and dead like dry bones strewn about the desert, will be restored to life by the Lord, and settled once more in their own land.

A reading from the book of the prophet E-zé-ki-el

The hand of the Lord came upon me,
   and he led me out in the spirit of the Lord
   and set me in the center of the plain,
   which was now filled with bones.
He made me walk among them in every direction
   so that I saw how many they were on the surface of the plain.
How dry they were!
He asked me: Son of man, can these bones come to life?
"Lord God," I answered, "you alone know that."
Then he said to me: Prophesy over these bones, and say to them:
   Dry bones, hear the word of the Lord!
Thus says the Lord God to these bones:
   See!   I will bring spirit into you, that you may come to life.
I will put sinews upon you, make flesh grow over you,
   cover you with skin, and put spirit in you
   so that you may come to life and know that I am the Lord.
I prophesied as I had been told,
   and even as I was prophesying I heard a noise;
   it was a rattling as the bones came together, bone joining bone.
I saw the sinews and the flesh come upon them,
   and the skin cover them, but there was no spirit in them.
Then he said to me: Prophesy to the spirit,
   prophesy, son of man, and say to the spirit:
   Thus says the Lord God:
   From the four winds come, O spirit,
   and breathe into these slain that they may come to life.
I prophesied as he told me, and the spirit came into them;
   they came alive and stood upright, a vast army.
Then he said to me: Son of man,
   these bones are the whole house of Israel.
They have been saying, "Our bones are dried up,
   our hope is lost, and we are cut off."
Therefore, prophesy and say to them:

Thus says the Lord God:

O my people, I will open your graves and have you rise from them,
and bring you back to the land of Israel.

Then you shall know that I am the Lord,
    when I open your graves and have you rise from them, O my people!

I will put my spirit in you that you my live,
    and I will settle you upon your land;
        thus you shall know that I am the Lord.

I have promised, and I will do it, says the Lord.

This is the Word of the Lord.

Or:

Joel 3, 1-5   I will pour out my spirit on all mankind.

*The short book of Joel is a vision of the day of the Lord, when
he will restore his people and pass judgment on the nations.
Peter quoted this passage in his first words to the people on the
day of Pentecost. (2:17-20).*

*The reading calls for a tone of pentecostal enthusiasm, every
phrase uttered with full power.*

A reading from the book of the prophet Joel

Thus says the Lord:
    I will pour out
        my spirit upon all mankind.

Your sons and daughters shall prophesy,
    your old men shall dream dreams,
        your young men shall see visions;

Even upon the servants and the handmaids,
    in those days, I will pour out my spirit.

And I will work wonders in the heavens and on the earth,
    blood, fire, and columns of smoke;

The sun will be turned to darkness,
    and the moon to blood,

At the coming of the Day of the Lord,
    the great and terrible day.

Then everyone shall be rescued
    who calls on the name of the Lord;

For on Mount Zion there shall be a remnant,
    as the Lord has said,

And in Jer-ú-sa-lem survivors
    whom the Lord shall call.

This is the Word of the Lord.

RESPONSORIAL PSALM

*Psalm 104, 1-2. 24. 35. 27-28. 29. 30 After the reading the psalmist sings
or says the responsorial verse, and all repeat it. This response is also
repeated after each verse of the psalm.*

Common response:

Al - le - lu - ia   al - le - lu - ia.

Or.

℟.   Lord, send out your Spirit, and renew the face of the earth.

Bless the Lord, O my soul!
O Lord, my God, you are great indeed!
You are clothed with majesty and glory,
    robed in light as with a cloak.   ℟.

How manifold are your works, O Lord!
In wisdom you have wrought them all—
    the earth is full of your creatures;
    Bless the Lord, O my soul!   Alleluia.   ℟.

Creatures all look to you
    to give them food in due time.
When you give it to them, they gather it;
    when you open your hand, they are filled with good things.   ℟.

If you take away their breath, they perish
    and return to their dust.
When you send forth your spirit, they are created,
    and you renew the face of the earth.   ℟.

SECOND READING

Romans 8, 22-27　The Spirit himself pleads for us in a way that could never be put into words.

A difficult passage, especially since it is taken out of its context. The message is that the world of God's creatures has been damaged by man's sin, but with the aid of the Spirit, we hope to be saved.

At the same time, Creation will be released from the sinful bondage under which man has placed it. We cannot pray unaided, but the Spirit within prays for us, and God knows what we mean to say. Read in a tone of subdued hope.

A reading from the letter of Paul to the Romans

We know that all creation groans and is in agony even until now.
Not only that, but we ourselves, although we have the Spirit as first fruits,
　　groan inwardly while we await the redemption of our bodies.
In hope we were saved.
But hope is not hope if its object is seen;
　　how is it possible for one to hope for what he sees?
And hoping for what we cannot see
　　means awaiting it with patient endurance.

The Spirit too helps us in our weakness,
　　for we do not know how to pray as we ought;
　　but the Spirit himself makes intercession for us
　　with groanings which cannot be expressed in speech.
He who searches hearts knows what the Spirit means,
　　for the Spirit intercedes for the saints as God himself wills.

　　This is the Word of the Lord.

GOSPEL

The cantor sings the alleluia and the people repeat it; the cantor then sings the verse and the people repeat the alleluia. Otherwise the alleluia may be omitted.

Al-le - lu - ia, al - le - lu - ia, al - le - lu - ia.

Come, — Ho - ly Spir - it, fill the hearts of your faith - ful; and

kin - dle in them the ___ fire of your love.

John 7, 37-39   From his breast shall flow fountains of living waters.

John records that Jesus went up privately to Jerusalem to the Feast of the Booths; he did not appear in public until the feast was almost over, when his words caused much controversy. Christ's words in this gospel reading echo not only a passage in Isaiah (Is 55: 1): "All you who are thirsty, come to the water," but his own words to the Samaritan woman as well, "Whoever drinks the water I give him will never be thirsty; no, the water I give shall become a fountain within him, leaping up to provide eternal life."(John 4: 14)

Read with a note of appeal, as those who come to Christ will receive the Holy Spirit—if only they will come.

✠ A reading from the holy gospel according to John

On the last and greatest day of the festival, Jesus stood up and cried out:
    "If anyone thirsts, let him come to me;
    Let him drink who believes in me.
    Scripture has it:
    'From within him rivers of living water shall flow.' "
(Here he was referring to the Spirit,
    whom those that came to believe in him were to receive.
There was, of course, no Spirit as yet,
    since Jesus had not yet been glorified.)

    This is the gospel of the Lord.

PENTECOST

FIRST READING

Acts 2, 1-11   They were all filled with the Holy Spirit, and began to speak in different languages.

The Feast of Pentecost (called also Whitsunday) is the climax of the Easter celebration. It commemorates the coming of the Holy Spirit and the beginning of the Christian Church.

At the Last Supper, on the night before he died on the cross, Jesus promised that he would ask the Father to send them an advocate (the Greek word is Paraclete)—the Holy Spirit— to guide them to all truth. Jesus was crucified during the Jewish Feast of the Passover. The Feast of Pentecost (the Greek word for fiftieth) was held fifty days after the Passover and celebrated the end of the grain harvest. Mary, the Mother of Jesus, and the disciples, being devout Jews, were in Jerusalem for the Feast.

A reading from the Acts of the Apostles

When the day of Pentecost came it found the brethren gathered in
    one place.
Suddenly from up in the sky there came a noise
    like a strong, driving wind
  which was heard all through the house where they were seated.
Tongues as of fire appeared which parted
    and came to rest on each of them.
All were filled with the Holy Spirit.
They began to express themselves in foreign tongues
    and make bold proclamation as the Spirit prompted them.

Staying in Jer-ú-sa-lem at the time
    were devout Jews of every nation under heaven.
These heard the sound, and assembled in a large crowd.
They were much confused
    because each one heard these men speaking his own language.
The whole occurrence astonished them.
They asked in utter amazement,
    "Are not all of these men who are speaking Ga-li-lé-ans?
How is it that each of us hears them in his native tongue?
We are Pár-thi-ans, Medes, and É-la-mites.
We live in Me-so-po-tá-mi-a, Ju-dé-a and Cap-pa-dó-cia,
    Pón-tus, the province of Asia, Phrý-gi-a and Pam-phý-li-a,
    Egypt, and the regions of Libya around Cyrene.

There are even visitors from Rome—
   all Jews, or those who have come over to Judaism;
   Cretans and Arabs too.
Yet each of us hears them speaking in his own tongue
   about the marvels God has accomplished."

   This is the Word of the Lord.

RESPONSORIAL PSALM

*Psalm 104, 1. 24. 29-30. 31. 34   After the reading the psalmist sings or says
the responsorial verse, and all repeat it.   This response is also repeated
after each verse of the psalm.*

Common response:

Al - le - lu - ia   al - le - lu - ia.

Or:

℟.   Lord, send out your Spirit, and renew the face of the earth.

Bless the Lord, O my soul!
O Lord, my God, you are great indeed!
How manifold are your works, O Lord!
   the earth is full of your creatures.   ℟.

If you take away their breath, they perish and return to their dust.
When you send forth your spirit, they are created,
   and you renew the face of the earth.   ℟.

May the glory of the Lord endure forever;
   may the Lord be glad in his works!
Pleasing to him be my theme;
   I will be glad in the Lord.   ℟.

SECOND READING

*1 Corinthians 12, 3-7. 12-13   In one Spirit we were all baptized, making
one body.*

*The Holy Spirit works in each of us in different ways for the com-
mon good. Each is a different member (part of the body as a whole),
making up one body which is Christ. Read in a tone of exalted explanation.*

A reading from the first letter of Paul to the Cor-ín-thi-ans

No one can say: "Jesus is Lord," except in the Holy Spirit.

There are different gifts but the same Spirit;
   there are different ministries but the same Lord;
   there are different works but the same God
   who accomplishes all of them in every one.
To each person the manifestation of the Spirit is given for the common
    good.

The body is one and has many members,
   but all the members, many though they are, are one body;
   and so it is with Christ.
It was in one Spirit that all of us,
   whether Jew or Greek, slave or free, were baptized into one body.
All of us have been given to drink of the one Spirit.

   This is the Word of the Lord.

SEQUENCE *(Prose Text)*

Come, Holy Spirit, and from heaven direct on man the rays of your
    light.
Come, Father of the poor; come, giver of God's gifts;
   come, light of men's hearts.

Kindly Paraclete, in your gracious visits to man's soul
   you bring relief and consolation.
If it is weary with toil, you bring it ease;
   in the heat of temptation, your grace cools it;
   if sorrowful, your words console it.

Light most blessed, shine on the hearts of your faithful—
   even into their darkest corners;
   for without your aid man can do nothing good,
   and everything is sinful.

Wash clean the sinful soul,
   rain down your grace on the parched soul and heal the injured soul.
Soften the hard heart, cherish and warm the ice-cold heart,
   and give direction to the wayward.

Give your seven holy gifts to your faithful, for their trust is in you.
Give them reward for their virtuous acts;
   give them a death that ensures salvation;
   give them unending bliss. Amen. Alleluia.

Or (Poetic Text)

Come, Holy Spirit, come!
And from your celestial home
　Shed a ray of light divine!

Come, Father of the poor!
Come, source of all our store!
Come, within our bosoms shine!

You, of comforters the best;
　You, the soul's most welcome guest;
　Sweet refreshment here below;

In our labor, rest most sweet;
　Grateful coolness in the heat;
　Solace in the midst of woe.

O most blessed Light divine,
　Shine within these hearts of yours,
　And our inmost being fill!

Where you are not, man has naught,
　Nothing good in deed or thought,
　Nothing free from taint of ill.

Heal our wounds, our strength renew;
　On our dryness pour your dew;
　Wash the stains of guilt away:

Bend the stubborn heart and will;
　Melt the frozen, warm the chill;
　Guide the steps that go astray.

On the faithful, who adore
　And confess you, evermore
　In your sev'nfold gift descend;

Give them virtue's sure reward;
　Give them your salvation, Lord;
　Give them joys that never end. Amen.
Alleluia.

GOSPEL

The cantor sings the alleluia and the people repeat it; the cantor then sings the verse and the people repeat the alleluia. Otherwise the alleluia may be omitted.

Al - le - lu - ia, al - le - lu - ia, al - le - lu - ia.

Come, — Ho - ly Spir - it, fill the hearts of your faith - ful; and

kin - dle in them the ___ fire of your love.

John 20, 19-23 As the Father, sent me, so I send you: Receive the Holy Spirit.

The words of Jesus to his chosen disciples on the first evening after his resurrection. He gives them power to forgive or to hold men bound for their sins. A solemn reading.

✠ A reading from the holy gospel according to John

On the evening of that first day of the week,
   even though the disciples had locked the doors of the place where they
      were for fear of the Jews,
   Jesus came and stood before them.
"Peace be with you," he said.
When he had said this, he showed them his hands and his side.
At the sight of the Lord the disciples rejoiced.
"Peace be with you," he said again.
"As the Father has sent me,
   so I send you."
Then he breathed on them and said:
   "Receive the Holy Spirit.
If you forgive men's sins,
   they are forgiven them;
   if you hold them bound,
   they are held bound."

   This is the gospel of the Lord.

SECOND SUNDAY OF THE YEAR

FIRST READING

Isaiah 62, 1-5   As the bridegroom rejoices in his bride, so will your God rejoice in you.

A prophecy from the last part of the Book of Isaiah, written after the return of the exiles from Babylon: The Lord will once more take delight in Jerusalem. The tone is hopeful enthusiasm, with slight emphasis on the words that stress the future joy of God's city.

For Zion's sake I will not be silent,
    for Jerusalem's sake I will not be quiet,
      Until her vindication shines forth like the dawn
      and her victory like a burning torch.

Nations shall behold your vindication,
    and all kings your glory;
      You shall be called by a new name
      pronounced by the mouth of the Lord.
You shall be a glorious crown in the hand of the Lord,
    a royal diadem held by your God.
No more shall men call you "Forsaken,"
    or your land "Desolate,"
      But you shall be called "My Delight,"
      and your land "Espoused."
For the Lord delights in you,
    and makes your land his spouse.
As a young man marries a virgin,
    your Builder shall marry you;
      And as a bridegroom rejoices in his bride,
      so shall your God rejoice in you.

This is the Word of the Lord.

RESPONSORIAL PSALM

Psalm 96, 1-2. 2-3. 7-8. 9-10 After the reading the psalmist sings or says the responsorial verse, and all repeat it. This response is also repeated after each verse of the psalm.

Common response:

We praise you, O Lord, for all your works are won - der - ful.

For other common responses see page 441.

Or:

℟. Proclaim his marvelous deeds to all the nations.

Sing to the Lord a new song;
  sing to the Lord, all you lands.
Sing to the Lord; bless his name. ℟.

Announce his salvation, day after day.
  Tell his glory among the nations;
  Among all peoples, his wondrous deeds. ℟.

Give to the Lord, you families of nations,
  give to the Lord glory and praise;
  give to the Lord the glory due his name! ℟.

Worship the Lord in holy attire.
Tremble before him, all the earth;
  Say among the nations: The Lord is king.
He governs the peoples with equity. ℟.

SECOND READING

1 Corinthians 12, 4-11   One and the same Spirit distributes different gifts as he chooses.

Paul has been urging the Corinthians to cease from rivalries and factions. We should never, says he, be jealous because someone else has gifts that we lack. The Holy Spirit gives each one his own special gift so that each makes a different contribution to the common good. Read as vigorous argument.

A reading from the first letter of Paul to the Cor-in-thi-ans

There are different gifts but the same Spirit;
   there are different ministries but the same Lord;
   there are different works but the same God
   who accomplishes all of them in everyone.
To each person the manifestation of the Spirit is given for
    the common good.
To one the Spirit gives wisdom in discourse,
   to another the power to express knowledge.
Through the Spirit one receives faith;
   by the same Spirit another is given the gift of healing,
   and still another miraculous powers.
Prophecy is given to one,
   to another power to distinguish one spirit from another.
One receives the gift of tongues,
   another that of interpreting the tongues.
But it is one and the same Spirit who produces all these gifts,
   distributing them to each as he wills.

   This is the Word of the Lord.

GOSPEL

*The cantor sings the alleluia and the people repeat it; the cantor then
sings the verse and the people repeat the alleluia. Otherwise the alleluia
may be omitted.*

Al - le - lu - ia.

Speak, O Lord, your ser - vant is lis - ten - ing; you __

have the words of ev-er - last - ing life.

For other alleluia verses see pages 437, 438 and 439.

John 2, 1-12   The first of the signs given by Jesus was at Cana in Galilee.

*A very human story. The words that pass between Jesus and his
mother need careful reading, in the present translation, Jesus'
reply may seem brusque and unfriendly. Today a man would
not normally address his mother as "woman". A more modern
version would be: "Mother, don't press me to do something.
I am not ready yet to come out into the open. Besides, it is not
our concern." But Mary knows that her Son will do what she asks,
and so she tells the servants to do whatever Jesus orders them. Bring
out this close relationship between Mother and Son. The word
translated "drinking awhile" in the Greek means "are drunk".
Village weddings were boisterous. Read with sympathetic understanding.*

✠ A reading from the holy gospel according to John

There was a wedding at Cana in Gál-i-lee,
    and the mother of Jesus was there.
Jesus and his disciples had likewise been invited to the celebration.
At a certain point the wine ran out,
    and Jesus' mother told him,
    "Thay have no more wine."
Jesus replied, "Woman, how does this concern of yours involve me?
My hour has not yet come."

His mother instructed those waiting on table,
     "Do whatever he tells you."
As prescribed for Jewish ceremonial washings,
     there were at hand six stone water jars,
     each one holding fifteen to twenty-five gallons.
"Fill those jars with water," Jesus ordered,
     at which they filled them to the brim.
"Now," he said, "draw some out and take it to the waiter in charge."
They did as he instructed them.
The waiter in charge tasted the water made wine,
     without knowing where it had come from;
     only the waiters knew, since they had drawn the water.
Then the waiter in charge called the groom over
     and remarked to him:
     "People usually serve the choice wine first;
     then when the guests have been drinking awhile,
          a lesser vintage.
What you have done is keep the choice wine until now."
Jesus performed this first of his signs at Cana in Gál-i-lee.
Thus did he reveal his glory, and his disciples believed in him.

After this he went down to Cap-ér-na-um,
     along with his mother and brothers [and his disciples]
     but they stayed there only a few days.

     This is the gospel of the Lord.

THIRD SUNDAY OF THE YEAR

FIRST READING

Nehemiah 8, 2-4. 5-6. 8-10   They read from the book of Law and they understood what was read.

When the Jews returned from Babylon to Jerusalem they found chaos. Even the Law of Moses was unknown. The reading records how Ezra summoned the people and read the Law to them. Thereafter the Jews became a separated people. Bring out the drama of this decisive event in history, which was thus a kind of forecast of Jesus' appearance in the synagogue at Nazareth (today's gospel),— also a decisive event in history.

A reading from the book of Ne-hem-í-ah

Éz-ra the priest brought the law before the assembly,
   which consisted of men, women,
     and those children old enough to understand.
Standing at one end of the open place that was before the Water Gate,
   he read out of the book from daybreak till midday,
     in the presence of the men, the women,
   and those children old enough to understand;
   and all the people listened attentively to the book of the law.
Éz-ra the scribe stood on a wooden platform
   that had been made for the occasion.
Éz-ra opened the scroll
   so that all the people might see it
   (for he was standing higher up than any of the people);
   and, as he opened it, all the people rose.
Éz-ra blessed the Lord, the great God,
   and all the people, their hands raised high, answered,
     "Amen, amen! "
Then they bowed down and prostrated themselves before the Lord,
   their faces to the ground.
Éz-ra read plainly from the book of the law of God,
   interpreting it so that all could understand what was read.
Then [Ne-hem-í-ah, that is, His Excellency, and] Éz-ra the priest scribe
   [and the Levites who were instructing the people]
   said to all the people:
"Today is holy to the Lord your God.
Do not be sad, and do not weep"—
   for all the people were weeping as they heard the words of the law.

He said further. "Go, eat rich foods and drink sweet drinks,
  and allot portions to those who had nothing prepared;
  for today is holy to our Lord.
Do not be saddened this day,
  for rejoicing in the Lord must be your strength! "

  This is the Word of the Lord.

RESPONSORIAL PSALM

Psalm 19, 8. 9. 10. 15   After the reading the psalmist sings or says the
responsorial verse, and all repeat it.   This response is also repeated
after each verse of the psalm.

Common response:

We   praise you, O Lord, for   all   your works are   won - der - ful.

For other common responses see page 441.

Or:

℟. Your words, Lord, are spirit and life.

The law of the Lord is perfect,
  refreshing the soul;
The decree of the Lord is trustworthy,
  giving wisdom to the simple.   ℟.

The precepts of the Lord are right,
  rejoicing the heart;
The command of the Lord is clear,
  enlightening the eye.   ℟.

The fear of the Lord is pure,
  enduring forever;
The ordinances of the Lord are true,
  all of them just.   ℟.

Let the words of my mouth and the thought of my heart
  find favor before you,
O Lord, my rock and my redeemer.   ℟.

SECOND READING

*Long Form: 1 Corinthians 12, 12-30   Together you are Christ's body,
but each of you is a different part of it.*

*Continuation from last Sunday. Paul elaborates the idea of the
special gifts of the individual into the image of the Church as the
Body of Christ, made up of many individual parts. Develop the
argument point by point so that everyone can follow. Pause after
"share its joy", before you continue "You, then, are the Body of
Christ", which is directed to your congregation.*

A reading from the first letter of Paul to the Cor-ín-thi-ans

The body is one and has many members,
  but all the members, many though they are, are one body;
  and so it is with Christ.
It was in one Spírit that all of us, whether Jew or Greek,
  slave or free, were baptized into one body.
All of us have been given to drink of the one Spirit.
Now the body is not one member, it is many.
If the foot should say,
  "Because I am not a hand I do not belong to the body,"
  would it then no longer belong to the body?
If the ear should say,
  "Because I am not an eye I do not belong to the body,"
  would it then no longer belong to the body?
If the body were all eye, what would happen to our hearing?
If it were all ear, what would happen to our smelling?
As it is, God has set each member of the body
  in the place he wanted it to be.
If all the members were alike, where would the body be?
There are, indeed, many different members, but one body.
The eye cannot say to the hand, "I do not need you,"
  any more than the head can say to the feet, "I do not need you."
Even those members of the body which seem less important
  are in fact indispensable.
We honor the members we consider less honorable
  by clothing them with greater care,
    thus bestowing on the less presentable
    a propriety which the more presentable already have.
God has so constructed the body
  as to give greater honor to the lowly members,
    that there may be no dissension in the body,
    but that all the members may be concerned for one another.

If one member suffers, all the members suffer with it;
 if one member is honored, all the members share its joy.

You, then, are the body of Christ.

Every one of you is a member of it.

Furthermore, God has set up in the church first apostles,
 second prophets, third teachers, then miracle workers,
 healers, assistants, administrators, and those who speak in tongues.

Are all apostles?   Are all prophets?

Are all teachers?   Do all work miracles
 or have the gift of healing?

Do all speak in tongues,
 all have the gift of interpretation of tongues?

This is the Word of the Lord.

*Short Form: 1 Corinthians 12, 12-14. 27 Together you are Christ's body,
but each of you is a different part of it.*

A reading from the first letter of Paul to the Cor-in-thi-ans

The body is one and has many members,
 but all the members, many though they are, are one body;
 and so it is with Christ.

It was in one Spirit that all of us,
 whether Jew or Greek, slave or free,
 were baptized into one body.

All of us have been given to drink of the one Spirit.

Now the body is not one member, it is many.

You then, are the body of Christ.

Every one of you is a member of it.

This is the Word of the Lord.

GOSPEL

*The cantor sings the alleluia and the people repeat it; the cantor then
sings the verse and the people repeat the alleluia. Otherwise the alleluia
may be omitted. Reference: Luke 4, 18-19.*

Al - le - lu - ia.

The Lord sent me to bring Good News to the poor, and free - dom to pri - son-e

Luke 1, 1-4; 4, 14-21   The scriptures were fulfilled on this day.

The gospel reading is in two parts; the first part shows the purpose of Luke's gospel, given in its short preface; the second gives Jesus' opening words in the synagogue at Nazareth. The key phrase is in the last sentence.

✝ The beginning of the holy gospel according to Luke

Many have undertaken to compile a narrative of the events
   which have been fulfilled in our midst,
     precisely as those events were transmitted to us
     by the original eye witnesses and ministers of the word.
I too have carefully traced the whole sequence of events from
     the beginning,
     and have decided to set it in writing for you, Theo-phi-lus,
     so that Your Excellency may see how reliable the instruction
     was that you received.

Jesus returned in the power of the Spirit to Gál-i-lee,
   and his reputation spread throughout the region.
He was teaching in their synagogues, and all were loud
   in his praise.

He came to Ná-za-reth where he had been reared,
   and entering the synagogue on the sabbath
     as he was in the habit of doing, he stood up to do the reading.
When the book of the prophet I-sai-ah was handed him,
   he unrolled the scroll and found the passage where it was written:
   "The spirit of the Lord is upon me;
   therefore he has anointed me.
He has sent me to bring glad tidings to the poor,
   to proclaim liberty to captives,
Recovery of sight to the blind
   and release to prisoners,
   To announce a year of favor from the Lord."

Rolling up the scroll he gave it back to the assistant and sat down.
All in the synagogue had their eyes fixed on him.
Then he began by saying to them,
"Today this Scripture passage is fulfilled in your hearing."

This is the gospel of the Lord.

FOURTH SUNDAY OF THE YEAR

FIRST READING

Jeremiah 1, 4-5. 17-19 I have appointed you as a prophet to the nations.

When Jeremiah first received the divine call, he was timid but the Lord promised him strength. Then he was told to declare the punishment that was coming to Jerusalem and that the Lord would make him strong always. Read with power.

A reading from the book of the prophet Je-re-mí-ah

In the days of Jo-sí-ah the word of the Lord came to me thus:
   Before I formed you in the womb I knew you,
   before you were born I dedicated you,
   a prophet to the nations I appointed you.

But do you gird your loins;
   stand up and tell them
   all that I command you.
Be not crushed on their account,
   as though I would leave you crushed before them;
   For it is I this day
   who have made you a fortified city,
   A pillar of iron, a wall of brass,
   against the whole land:
Against Judah's kings and princes,
   against its priests and people.
They will fight against you, but not prevail over you,
   for I am with you to deliver you, says the Lord.

   This is the Word of the Lord.

RESPONSORIAL PSALM

Psalm 71, 1-2. 3-4. 5-6. 15-17 After the reading the psalmist sings or says the
responsorial verse, and all repeat it. This response is also repeated after
each verse of the psalm.

Common response:

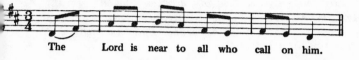

The   Lord is near to all who   call on him.

For other common responses see page 441.

Or:

℟. I will sing of your salvation.

In you, O Lord, I take refuge;
   let me never be put to shame.
In your justice rescue me, and deliver me;
   incline your ear to me, and save me.   ℟.

Be my rock of refuge,
   a stronghold to give me safety,
   for you are my rock and my fortress.
O my God, rescue me from the hand of the wicked.   ℟.

For you are my hope, O Lord;
   my trust, O God, from my youth.
On you I depend from birth;
   from my mother's womb you are my strength.   ℟.

My mouth shall declare your justice,
   day by day your salvation.
O God, you have taught me from my youth,
   and till the present I proclaim your wondrous deeds.   ℟.

SECOND READING

*Long Form: 1 Corinthians 12, 31-13, 13   There are three things that
last: faith, hope and love; and the greatest of these is love.*

*Continuation from last Sunday. Love is greater than all other
gifts. Read this most famous passage slowly, especially when
you come to "Love is patient", and pause slightly after each
quality of love, which, naturally, is the key word. End on a high
note at "the greatest of these is love."*

A reading from the first letter of Paul to the Cor-ín-thi-ans

Set your hearts on the greater gifts.

Now I will show you the way which surpasses all the others.
If I speak with human tongues and angelic as well,
   but do not have love,
   I am a noisy gong, a clanging cymbal.
If I have the gift of prophecy and,
   with full knowledge, comprehend all mysteries,
   if I have faith great enough to move mountains,
   but have not love, I am nothing.
If I give everything I have to feed the poor
   and hand over my body to be burned,
   but have not love, I gain nothing.

Love is patient; love is kind.
Love is not jealous, it does not put on airs,
   it is not snobbish.
Love is never rude, it is not self-seeking,
   it is not prone to anger; neither does it brood over injuries.
Love does not rejoice in what is wrong
   but rejoices with the truth.
There is no limit to love's forebearance,
   to its trust, its hope, its power to endure.

Love never fails. Prophecies will cease,
   tongues will be silent, knowledge will pass away.
Our knowledge is imperfect and our prophesying is imperfect.
When the perfect comes, the imperfect will pass away.
When I was a child I used to talk like a child,
   think like a child, reason like a child.
When I became a man I put childish ways aside.
Now we see indistinctly, as in a mirror;
   then we shall see face to face.
My knowledge is imperfect now;

then I shall know even as I am known.

There are in the end three things that last: faith, hope, and love, and the greatest of these is love.

This is the Word of the Lord.

Short Form: 1 Corinthians 13, 4-13 There are three things that last: faith, hope and love; and the greatest of these is love.

A reading from the first letter of Paul to the Cor-in-thi-ans

Love is patient; love is kind.

Love is not jealous, it does not put on airs,
  it is not snobbish.

Love is never rude, it is not self-seeking,
  it is not prone to anger; neither does it brood over injuries.

Love does not rejoice in what is wrong
  but rejoices with the truth.

There is no limit to love's forbearance,
  to its trust, its hope, its power to endure.

Love never fails. Prophecies will cease,
  tongues will be silent, knowledge will pass away.

Our knowledge is imperfect and our prophesying is imperfect.

When the perfect comes, the imperfect will pass away.

When I was a child I used to talk like a child,
  think like a child, reason like a child.

When I became a man I put childish ways aside.

Now we see indistinctly, as in a mirror;
  then we shall see face to face.

My knowledge is imperfect now;
  then I shall know even as I am known.

There are in the end three things that last: faith, hope, and love,
  and the greatest of these is love.

This is the Word of the Lord.

GOSPEL

The cantor sings the alleluia and the people repeat it; the cantor then sings the verse and the people repeat the alleluia. Otherwise the alleluia may be omitted.

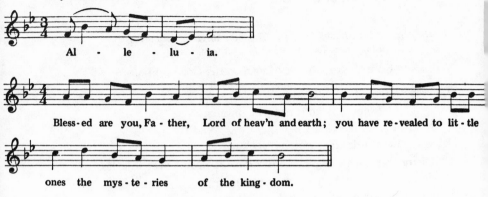

Al - le - lu - ia.

Bless-ed are you, Fa - ther,   Lord of heav'n and earth;   you have re - vealed to lit - tle

ones the mys - te - ries   of the king - dom.

For other alleluia verses see pages 437, 438 and 439.

Luke 4, 21-30   Jesus, like Elijah and Elisha, was not sent only to the Jews.

Continuation from last Sunday. Jesus' words in the synagogue at Nazareth. Bring out the latent hostility of Jesus' fellow townsmen, so quickly aroused when he seems to be criticizing them.

✠ A reading from the holy gospel according to Luke

Jesus began speaking in the synagogue:
　　"Today this Scripture passage is fulfilled in your hearing."
All who were present spoke favorably of him;
　　they marveled at the appealing discourse
　　which came from his lips.
They also asked, "Is not this Joseph's son? "

He said to them, "You will doubtless quote me the proverb,
　　'Physician, heal yourself,' and say,
　　'Do here in your own country
　　the things we have heard you have done in Ca-pér-na-um.'
But in fact," he went on,
　　"no prophet gains acceptance in his native place.
Indeed, let me remind you,
　　there were many widows in Israel in the days of E-lí-jah
　　　when the heavens remained closed for three and a half years
　　　and a great famine spread over the land.
It was to none of these that E-lí-jah was sent,
　　but to a widow of Za-réph-tah near Si-don.

Recall, too, the many lepers in Israel in the time of
  E-lí-sha the prophet;
 yet not one was cured except Ná-am-an the Syrian."

At these words the whole audience in the synagogue
  was filled with indignation.
They rose up and expelled him from the town,
  leading him to the brow of the hill on which it was built,
  and intending to hurl him over the edge.
But he went straight through their midst and walked away.

 This is the gospel of the Lord.

FIFTH SUNDAY OF THE YEAR

FIRST READING

Isaiah 6, 1-2. 3-8   Here am I!   Send me.

The call of Isaiah.   As with other accounts of the presence of God, read this passage with the sense of awe and ecstacy felt by Isaiah as he realises his fearful but exalted destiny; and end on a note of inspired to resolve to accept the call.

A reading from the book of the prophet I-sai-ah

In the year King Uz-zi-ah died,
   I saw the Lord seated on a high and lofty throne,
   with the train of his garment filling the temple.
Seraphim were stationed above.

"Holy, holy, holy is the Lord of hosts! "
   they cried one to the other.
"All the earth is filled with his glory! "
At the sound of that cry, the frame of the door shook
   and the house was filled with smoke.

Then I said, "Woe is me, I am doomed!
For I am a man of unclean lips,
   living among a people of unclean lips;
   yet my eyes have seen the King, the Lord of hosts! "
Then one of the seraphim flew to me,
   holding an ember which he had taken with tongs from the altar.

He touched my mouth with it.
   "See," he said, "now that this has touched your lips,
   your wickedness is removed, your sin purged."

Then I heard the voice of the Lord saying,
   "Whom shall I send?   Who will go for us? "
"Here I am, " I said; "send me! "

   This is the Word of the Lord.

RESPONSORIAL PSALM

Psalm 138, 1-2. 2-3. 4-5. 7-8   After the reading the psalmist sings or says the responsorial verse, and all repeat it. This response is also repeated after each verse of the psalm.

Common response:

We   praise you, O Lord, for   all   your works are   won - der - ful.

For other common responses see page 441.

Or:

℟. In the sight of the angels I will sing your praises, Lord.

I will give thanks to you, O Lord, with all my heart,
   [for you have heard the words of my mouth;]
   in the presence of the angels I will sing your praise;
  I will worship at your holy temple
  and give thanks to your name.   ℟.

Because of your kindness and your truth;
  for you have made great above all things
  your name and your promise.
When I called, you answered me;
  you built up strength within me.   ℟.

All the kings of the earth shall give thanks to you, O Lord,
  when they hear the words of your mouth;
And they shall sing of the ways of the Lord:
  "Great is the glory of the Lord."   ℟.

Your right hand saves me.
The Lord will complete what he has done for me;
  Your kindness, O Lord, endures forever;
  forsake not the work of your hands.   ℟.

SECOND READING

*Long Form: 1 Corinthians 15, 1-11   I preach what they preach, and
this is what you believe.*

*Paul's account of the appearance of the risen Jesus, as related
to him by Peter and other eye witnesses. This is the earliest
account of the resurrection still existing. As preparation, study
also the other accounts of Paul's encounter with the risen Christ
on the Damascus road in Acts 9: 1-19; 22: 3-16; 26: 2-18;
Galatians 1: 11-19 (read on the Tenth Sunday of this Cycle).
Read as Paul's own claim to be regarded one of the apostles.*

A reading from the first letter of Paul to the Cor-ín-thi-ans

Brothers, I want to remind you of the gospel I preached to you,
   which you received and in which you stand firm.
You are being saved by it at this very moment
   if you retain it as I preached it to you.
Otherwise you have believed in vain.
I handed on to you first of all what I myself received,
   that Christ died for our sins in accordance with the Scriptures;
   that he was buried and, in accordance with the Scriptures,
   rose on the third day;
   that he was seen by Céph-as, then by the Twelve.
After that he was seen by five hundred brothers at once,
   most of whom are still alive,
   although some have fallen asleep.
Next he was seen by James; then by all the apostles.
Last of all he was seen by me,
   as one born out of the normal course.
I am the least of the apostles;
   in fact, because I persecuted the church of God,
   I do not even deserve the name.
But by God's favor I am what I am.
This favor of his to me has not proved fruitless.
Indeed, I have worked harder than all the others,
   not on my own but through the favor of God.
In any case, whether it be I or they,
   this is what we preach and this is what you believed.

   This is the Word of the Lord.

Short Form: 1 Corinthians 15, 3-8. 11 I preach what they preach,
and this is what you believe.

A reading from the first letter of Paul to the Cor-ín-thi-ans

Brothers, I handed on to you first of all what I myself received,
   that Christ died for our sins in accordance with the Scriptures;
   that he was buried and, in accordance with the Scriptures,
   rose on the third day;
   that he was seen by Céph-as, then by the Twelve.
After that he was seen by five hundred brothers at once,
   most of whom are still alive,
   although some have fallen asleep.
Next he was seen by James; then by all the apostles.
Last of all he was seen by me,
   as one born out of the normal course.
In any case, whether it be I or they,
   this is what we preach and this is what you believed.

   This is the Word of the Lord.

GOSPEL

The cantor sings the alleluia and the people repeat it; the cantor then
sings the verse and the people repeat the alleluia. Otherwise the alleluia
may be omitted.

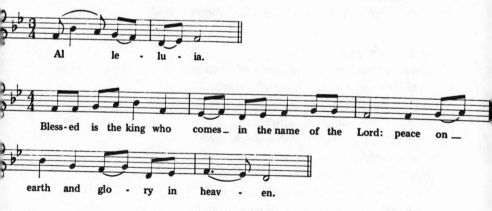

Al le - lu - ia.

Bless-ed is the king who comes_ in the name of the Lord: peace on _

earth and glo - ry in heav - en.

For other alleluia verses see pages 437, 438 and 439.

Luke 5, 1-11   They left everything and followed him.

One of several accounts of how Peter, James and John were
called to be followers of Jesus. Read with conviction as if you
had heard it at first hand from someone who was present.

✠   A reading from the holy gospel according to Luke

As the crowd pressed in on Jesus to hear the word of God,
    he saw two boats moored by the side of the lake;
    the fishermen had disembarked and were washing their nets.
He got into one of the boats, the one belonging to Simon,
    and asked him to pull out a short distance from the shore;
    then, remaining seated, he continued to teach the crowds from
        the boat.
When he had finished speaking he said to Simon,
    "Put out into deep water and lower your nets for a catch."
Simon answered, "Master, we have been hard at it all night long
    and have caught nothing;
    but if you say so, I will lower the nets."
Upon doing this they caught such a great number of fish
    that their nets were at the breaking point.
They signaled to their mates in the other boat
    to come and help them.
These came and together they filled the two boats
    until they nearly sank.

At the sight of this,
    Simon Peter fell at the knees of Jesus saying,
    "Leave me, Lord. I am a sinful man."
For indeed, amazement at the catch they had made
    seized him and all his shipmates,
    as well as James and John, Zé-be-dee's sons,
    who were partners with Simon.
Jesus said to Simon, "Do not be afraid.
From now on you will be catching men."
With that they brought their boats to land,
    left everything, and became his followers.

    This is the gospel of the Lord.

SIXTH SUNDAY OF THE YEAR

FIRST READING

Jeremiah 17, 5-8   Unhappy is he who trusts in man; happy the man
who trusts in the Lord.

Jeremiah lived in Jerusalem during the last years before the
city was destroyed by the Babylonians. He warned the people
in vain of the destruction that was coming on them for their
idolatry and faithlessness. Read as a stern threat. Contrast
the first part "Cursed is the man. . . " with the second "Blessed
is the man. . ."

A reading from the book of the prophet Je-re-mí-ah

Thus says the Lord:
Cursed is the man who trusts in human beings,
   who seeks his strength in flesh,
   whose heart turns away from the Lord.
He is like a barren bush in the desert
   that enjoys no change of season,
But stands in a lava waste,
   a salt and empty earth.
Blessed is the man who trusts in the Lord,
   whose hope is the Lord.
He is like a tree planted beside the waters
   that stretches out its roots to the stream:
It fears not the heat when it comes,
   its leaves stay green;
In the year of drought it shows no distress,
   but still bears fruit.

   This is the Word of the Lord.

RESPONSORIAL PSALM

*Psalm 1, 1-2. 3. 4. 6 After the reading the psalmist sings or says the
responsorial verse, and all repeat it. This response is also repeated
after each verse of the psalm.*

Common response:

We praise you, O Lord, for all your works are won-der-ful.

For other common responses see page 441.

Or:

℟. Happy are they who hope in the Lord.

Happy the man who follows not
    the counsel of the wicked
Nor walks in the way of sinners,
    nor sits in the company of the insolent,
But delights in the law of the Lord
    and meditates on his law day and night.   ℟.

He is like a tree
    planted near running water,
That yields its fruit in due season,
    and whose leaves never fade.
[Whatever he does, prospers.]   ℟.

Not so the wicked, not so;
    they are like chaff which the wind drives away.
For the Lord watches over the way of the just,
    but the way of the wicked vanishes.   ℟.

SECOND READING

1 Corinthians 15, 12. 16-20 If Christ is not raised from the dead, your faith is in vain.

Continuation from last Sunday. Many Greeks in Paul's time believed that the soul was immortal but rejected the possibility of a resurrection of the body from the dead; this belief was also held by some of the Corinthian converts. Here, as always, Paul declares that the bodily resurrection of Jesus from the dead is the central fact of Christianity. A vigorous attack on a deadly heresy, ending on a strong declaration of faith.

A reading from the first letter of Paul to the Cor-ín-thi-ans

If Christ is preached as raised from the dead,
> how is it that some of you say
> there is no resurrection of the dead? :
If the dead are not raised,
> then Christ was not raised;
> and if Christ was not raised, your faith is worthless.
You are still in your sins,
> and those who have fallen asleep in Christ
> are the deadest of the dead.
If our hopes in Christ are limited to this life only,
> we are the most pitiable of men.

But as it is, Christ has been raised from the dead,
> the first fruits of those who have fallen asleep.

This is the Word of the Lord.

GOSPEL

The cantor sings the alleluia and the people repeat it; the cantor then sings the verse and the people repeat the alleluia. Otherwise the alleluia may be omitted.

Al - le - lu - ia.

The word of God be - came a man and lived a - mong us.

He en - a - bled those who ac - cept - ed him to be-come the chil-dren of God.

For other alleluia verses see pages 437, 438 and 439.

Luke 6, 17. 20-26   Happy are the poor; their reward will be great.

From Luke's account of the Sermon on the Mount (which is much shorter than that given in Matthew 5: 3-7:28). Jesus continually attacked the complacent notion that prosperity in this world was a sign of God's favor. His followers would rather be blessed for their poverty and sufferings; his enemies would be cursed for their riches and comfort. Stress especially the contrast and the difference between the true and the false prophets.

✠   A reading from the holy gospel according to Luke

When Jesus came down the mountain,
   he stopped at a level stretch
   where there were many of his disciples;
   a large crowd of people was with them
   from all Ju-dé-a and Jerusalem and the coast of Tý-re and Sí-don.
Then, raising his eyes to his disciples, he said:
   "Blest are you poor; the reign of God is yours.
Blest are you who hunger; you shall be filled.
Blest are you who are weeping; you shall laugh.

   "Blest shall you be when men hate you,
   when they ostracize you and insult you
   and proscribe your name as evil because of the Son of Man.
On the day they do so, rejoice and exult,
   for your reward shall be great in heaven.
Thus it was that their fathers treated the prophets.
"But woe to you rich, for your consolation is now.
Woe to you who are full; you shall go hungry.
Woe to you who laugh now; you shall weep in your grief.
"Woe to you when all speak well of you.
Their fathers treated the false prophets in just this way."

   This is the gospel of the Lord.

SEVENTH SUNDAY OF THE YEAR

FIRST READING

1 Samuel 26, 2. 7-9. 12-13. 22-23   The Lord has put you in my power,
but I will not raise my hand against you.

David the great king, in his earlier years was the chief captain of
King Saul; but Saul became jealous and suspicious, and tried to
kill David who fled and became an outlaw.   The few verses selected
for this reading record an occasion when David spared Saul's life.
Read as a dramatic story of unusual chivalry.

A reading from the first book of Samuel

Saul went off down to the desert of Zíph
   with three thousand picked men of Israel,
   to search for David in the desert of Zíph.
So David and A-bísh-ai went among Saul's soldiers by night
   and found Saul lying asleep within the barricade,
   with his spear thrust into the ground at his head
   and Áb-ner and his men sleeping around him.

A-bísh-ai whispered to David:
   "God has delivered your enemy into your grasp this day.
Let me nail him to the ground with one thrust of the spear;
   I will not need a second thrust! "
But David said to A-bísh-ai, "Do not harm him,
   for who can lay hands on the Lord's anointed and remain
     unpunished?
So David took the spear and the water jug from their place at
     Saul's head,
   and they got away without anyone's seeing or knowing or
     awakening.
All remained asleep,
   because the Lord had put them into a deep slumber.

Going across to an opposite slope,
   David stood on a remote hilltop
   at a great distance from Áb-ner, son of Nér, and the troops.
He said: "Here is the king's spear.
Let an attendant come over to get it.
The Lord will reward each man for his justice and faithfulness.
Today, though the Lord delivered you into my grasp,
   I would not harm the Lord's anointed."

This is the Word of the Lord.

RESPONSORIAL PSALM

Psalm 103, 1-2. 3-4. 10. 12-13 After the reading the psalmist sings or says
the responsorial verse, and all repeat it. This response is also repeated
after each verse of the psalm.

Common response:

Al - le - lu - ia.

For other common responses see page 441.

Or:

℞. The Lord is kind and merciful.

Bless the Lord, O my soul;
    and all my being, bless his holy name.
Bless the Lord, O my soul,
    and forget not all his benefits.   ℞.

He pardons all your iniquities,
    he heals all your ills.
He redeems your life from destruction,
    he crowns you with kindness and compassion.   ℞.

Merciful and gracious is the Lord,
    slow to anger and abounding in kindness.
Not according to our sins does he deal with us,
    nor does he requite us according to our crimes.   ℞.

As far as the east is from the west,
    so far has he put our transgressions from us.
As a father has compassion on his children,
    so the Lord has compassion on those who fear him.   ℞.

SECOND READING

*1 Corinthians 15, 45-49 Just as we have carried the earthly image, we
must carry the heavenly image.*

*In Paul's theology there are two Adams; the first was Adam of the
book of Genesis, the first physical man, created by God, from whom
all human beings are descended; the second Adam is Jesus Christ
who became man and by his resurrection from the dead, became the
source of true spiritual life to all who believe in him. Present Paul's
arguments slowly and deliberately, clause by clause.*

A reading from the first letter of Paul to the Cor-ín-thi-ans

Scripture has it that Adam, the first man, became a living soul;
   the last Adam has become a life-giving spirit.
Take note, the spiritual was not first;
   first came the natural and after that the spiritual.
The first man was of earth, formed from dust,
   the second is from heaven.
Earthly men are like the man of earth,
   heavenly men are like the man of heaven.
Just as we resemble the man from the earth,
   so shall we bear the likeness of the man from heaven.

   This is the Word of the Lord.

GOSPEL

*The cantor sings the alleluia and the people repeat it; the cantor then
sings the verse and the people repeat the alleluia. Otherwise the alleluia
may be omitted.*

Al - le - lu - ia.

Your words, O Lord, __ are __ spir - it and life, __

you have the words of ev - er - last - ing life.

For other alleluia verses see pages 437, 438 and 439.

Luke 6, 27-38   Be merciful as your Father is merciful.

Continuation from last Sunday; further passages from the Sermon on the Mount . Jesus commands his followers to substitute love for legal justice; you shall love your enemies impartially as God loves good and evil alike.   Read with authority, as commands which must be obeyed without question.

✛   A reading from the holy gospel according to Luke

Jesus said to his disciples:
   "To you who hear me, I say:
   Love your enemies, do good to those who hate you;
   bless those who curse you and pray for those who maltreat you.
When someone slaps you on one cheek,
   turn and give him the other;
When someone takes your coat,
   let him have your shirt as well.
Give to all who beg from you.
When a man takes what is yours, do not demand it back.
Do to others what you would have them do to you.
If you love those who love you,
   what credit is that to you?
Even sinners love those who love them.
If you do good to those who do good to you,
   how can you claim any credit?
Sinners do as much.
If you lend to those from whom you expect repayment,
   what merit is there in it for you?
Even sinners lend to sinners,
   expecting to be repaid in full.

"Love your enemy and do good;
   lend without expecting repayment.
Then will your recompense be great.
You will rightly be called sons of the Most High,
   since he himself is good to the ungrateful and the wicked.

"Be compassionate, as your Father is compassionate.
Do not judge, and you will not be judged.
Do not condemn, and you will not be condemned.
Pardon, and you shall be pardoned.
Give, and it shall be given to you.
Good measure pressed down, shaken together, running over,
   will they pour into the fold of your garment.
For the measure you measure with will be measured back to you."

   This is the gospel of the Lord.

EIGHTH SUNDAY OF THE YEAR

FIRST READING

Sirach 27, 4-7 Do not praise a man before he has spoken.

A man's true nature is shown in what he says. Pronounce each of the four judgments separately with a distinct pause after each.

A reading from the book of Sí-rach

When a sieve is shaken, the husks appear;
   so do a man's faults when he speaks.
As the test of what the potter molds is in the furnace,
   so in his conversation is the test of a man.
The fruit of a tree shows the care it has had;
   so too does a man's speech disclose the bent of his mind.
Praise no man before he speaks,
   for it is then that men are tested.

   This is the Word of the Lord.

RESPONSORIAL PSALM

Psalm 92, 2-3. 13-14. 15-16 After the reading the psalmist sings or says the responsorial verse and all repeat it. This response is also repeated after each verse of the psalm.

Common response:

We praise you, O Lord, for all your works are won-der-ful.

For other common responses see page 441.

Or:

℟. Lord, it is good to give thanks to you.

It is good to give thanks to the Lord,
   to sing praise to your name, Most High,
To proclaim your kindness at dawn
   and your faithfulness throughout the night.   ℟.

The just man shall flourish like the palm tree,
  like a cedar of Lebanon shall he grow.
They that are planted in the house of the Lord
  shall flourish in the courts of our God.　℟.

They shall bear fruit even in old age;
  vigorous and sturdy shall they be,
Declaring how just is the Lord,
  my Rock, in whom there is no wrong.　℟.

SECOND READING

1 Corinthians 15, 54-58　Victory has been given to us through Jesus Christ.

*Continuation from last Sunday. Paul.'s final words on the life
to come. The reading is part exaltation, part theological instruction.
Paul's teaching on sin and death is that if Adam—man—had never
sinned, there would have been no death. Christ by his victory over
death and sin frees us from sin and brings us immortal life. Begin
on a note of triumph down to "where is your sting." Then lower
the tone as Paul passes from triumph to instruction.*

A reading from the first letter of Paul to the Cor-ín-thi-ans

When the corruptible frame takes on incorruptibility
  and the mortal immortality,
    then will the saying of Scripture be fulfilled:
    "Death is swallowed up in victory."
"O death, where is your victory?　O death, where is your sting? "
The sting of death is sin,
  and sin gets its power from the law.
But thanks be to God who has given us the victory
  through our Lord Jesus Christ.
Be steadfast and persevering, my beloved brothers,
  fully engaged in the work of the Lord.
You know that your toil is not in vain
  when it is done in the Lord.

  This is the Word of the Lord.

GOSPEL

*The cantor sings the alleluia and the people repeat it; the cantor then
sings the verse and the people repeat the alleluia. Otherwise the alleluia
may be omitted.*

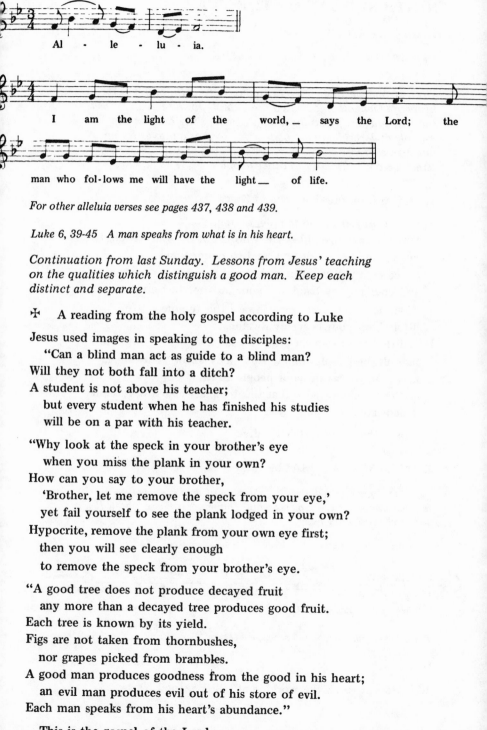

Al - le - lu - ia.

I am the light of the world, — says the Lord; the man who fol-lows me will have the light — of life.

For other alleluia verses see pages 437, 438 and 439.

Luke 6, 39-45   A man speaks from what is in his heart.

Continuation from last Sunday. Lessons from Jesus' teaching on the qualities which distinguish a good man. Keep each distinct and separate.

☩   A reading from the holy gospel according to Luke

Jesus used images in speaking to the disciples:
    "Can a blind man act as guide to a blind man?
Will they not both fall into a ditch?
A student is not above his teacher;
    but every student when he has finished his studies
    will be on a par with his teacher.

"Why look at the speck in your brother's eye
    when you miss the plank in your own?
How can you say to your brother,
    'Brother, let me remove the speck from your eye,'
    yet fail yourself to see the plank lodged in your own?
Hypocrite, remove the plank from your own eye first;
    then you will see clearly enough
    to remove the speck from your brother's eye.

"A good tree does not produce decayed fruit
    any more than a decayed tree produces good fruit.
Each tree is known by its yield.
Figs are not taken from thornbushes,
    nor grapes picked from brambles.
A good man produces goodness from the good in his heart;
    an evil man produces evil out of his store of evil.
Each man speaks from his heart's abundance."

    This is the gospel of the Lord.

NINTH SUNDAY OF THE YEAR

FIRST READING

1 Kings 8, 41-43 When the stranger comes, hear him.

*Words from the great prayer offered by King Solomon before
his people when he dedicated the Temple to the Lord. He asks
that the prayer of a stranger who worships the Lord in the
Temple at Jerusalem may be heard. Read as a prayer for an
unusual, extraordinary favor, for Solomon and the people of
Israel were not friendly to other peoples.*

A reading from the first book of Kings

Solomon prayed in the temple, saying,
   "To the foreigner, likewise, who is not of your people Israel,
   but comes from a distant land to honor you
   (since men will learn of your great name
   and your mighty hand and your outstretched arm),
   when he comes and prays toward this temple,
   listen from your heavenly dwelling.
Do all that the foreigner asks of you,
   that all the peoples of the earth may know your name,
   may fear you as do your people Israel,
   and may acknowledge that this temple which I have built
   is dedicated to your honor.

   This is the Word of the Lord.

RESPONSORIAL PSALM

*Psalm 117, 1. 2 After the reading the psalmist sings or says
the responsorial verse, and all repeat it. This response is also repeated
after each verse of the psalm.*

Common response:

We   praise you, O Lord, for   all   your works are   won - der - ful.

For other common responses see page 441.

Or:

℟.   Go out to all the world, and tell the Good News.

Praise the Lord, all you nations;
  glorify him, all you peoples!
For steadfast is his kindness toward us,
  and the fidelity of the Lord endures forever. ℟.

SECOND READING

Galatians 1, 1-2. 6-10 If I tried to please man, I could not be a servant
of Christ.

Most lectors find difficulty in readings from Paul's letter to the
Galatians because so much personal and scriptural history lies
behind it. There is even dispute among scholars whether the
'Galatians' lived in northern or southern Asia Minor.

In his early manhood Paul(then called Saul), was an orthodox
Jew, educated in the learning of the Pharisees. After this conversion
his special mission was to the Gentiles—non-Jews and pagans, to
whom he declared that on becoming a Christian a man was freed
from the sins of his old life. Later, the new Galatian churches were
visited by Jewish Christians who, preached that every new Christian
must accept the Jewish law and all its ritual observances, including
circumcision. They also said that Paul lacked the authority of a
true apostle of Christ. This bitter controversy between Paul and
the Judaizers is mentioned again and again in his letters; it lasted
until he was sent as a prisoner to Rome.

In the present reading from the first verses of the letter, Paul begins
with a vigorous declaration of his apostleship. Then he goes on to
rebuke those who had listened to the Judaizers. The tone is angry,
indignant rebuttal.

The beginning of the letter of Paul to the Gal-á-ti-ans

Paul, an apostle sent not by men or by any man,
  but by Jesus Christ and God his Father
  who raised him from the dead—
  I and my brothers who are with me,
  send greetings to the churches in Gal-á-ti-a.

I am amazed that you are so soon deserting him
  who called you in accord with his gracious design in Christ,
  and are going over to another gospel.
But there is no other.
Some who wish to alter the gospel of Christ
  must have confused you.

For if even we or an angel from heaven
  should preach to you a gospel
  not in accord with the one we delivered to you,
  let a curse be upon him!
I repeat what I have just said:
  if anyone preaches a gospel to you
  other than the one you received, let a curse be upon him!

Whom would you say I am trying to please at this point—
  men or God?
Is this how I seek to ingratiate myself with men?
If I were trying to win man's approval,
  I would surely not be serving Christ!

  This is the Word of the Lord.

GOSPEL

*The cantor sings the alleluia and the people repeat it; the cantor then
sings the verse and the people repeat the alleluia. Otherwise the alleluia
may be omitted.*

Al - le - lu - ia.

O - pen our hearts, _ O _ Lord, _ to lis - ten to the words of your Son.

For other alleluia verses see pages 437, 438 and 439.

Luke 7, 1-10   Nowhere in Israel have I found as much faith.

*The centurion was captain of a company of soldiers in the Roman
army of occupation. It was not common for a Roman officer to
show friendliness to the Jews. Stress Jesus' admiration for the
humility and the faith of the centurion.*

✠   A reading from the holy gospel according to Luke

When Jesus had finished his discourse in the hearing of the people,
    he entered Ca-pér-na-um.
A centurion had a servant he held in high regard,
    who was at that moment sick to the point of death.
When he heard about Jesus
    he sent some Jewish elders to him,
    asking him to come and save the life of his servant.
Upon approaching Jesus they petitioned him earnestly.
"He deserves this favor from you," they said,
    "because he loves our people,
    and even built our synagogue for us."
Jesus set out with them.
When he was only a short distance from the house,
    the centurion sent friends to tell him:
    "Sir, do not trouble yourself,
    for I am not worthy to have you enter my house.
That is why I did not presume to come to you myself.
Just give the order and my servant will be cured.
I too am a man who knows the meaning of an order,
    having soldiers under my command.
I say to one, 'On your way,' and off he goes;
    to another, 'Come here,' and he comes;
    to my slave, 'Do this,' and he does it."
Jesus showed amazement on hearing this,
    and turned to the crowd which was following him to say,
    "I tell you, I have never found so much faith among the Israelites."
When the deputation returned to the house,
    they found the servant in perfect health.

    This is the gospel of the Lord.

TENTH SUNDAY OF THE YEAR

FIRST READING

1 Kings 17, 17-24   Look, said Elijah, your son is living.

*One of several stories of the prophet Elijah. During the great
drought he had saved the lives of a widow of Sidon and her
son by causing the last of the oil and the flour to be miraculously
replenished day after day. Today's reading is the sequel—how
Elijah restored the boy to life and gave him back to his mother.
Straight story telling.*

A reading from the first book of Kings

The son of the mistress of the house fell sick,
   and his sickness grew more severe until he stopped breathing.
So she said to E-lí-jah,
   "Why have you done this to me, O man of God?
Have you come to me to call attention to my guilt
   and to kill my son? "
"Give me your son," E-lí-jah said to her.
Taking him from her lap, he carried him to the upper room
   where he was staying, and laid him on his own bed.
He called out to the Lord:
   "O Lord, my God, will you afflict even the widow
   with whom I am staying by killing her son? "
Then he stretched himself out upon the child three times
   and called out to the Lord:
   "O Lord, my God, let the life breath return to the body of
      this child."
The Lord heard the prayer of E-lí-jah;
   the life breath returned to the child's body and he revived.
Taking the child, E-lí-jah brought him down into the house
   from the upper room and gave him to his mother.
"See! " E-lí-jah said to her,
   "your son is alive."
"Now indeed I know that you are a man of God,"
   the woman replied to E-lí-jah.
"The word of the Lord comes truly from your mouth."

   This is the Word of the Lord.

RESPONSORIAL PSALM:

*Psalm 30, 2. 4. 5-6. 11. 12. 13 After the reading the psalmist sings or says
the responsorial verse and the people repeat it. This response is also
repeated after each verse of the psalm.*

Common response:

We   praise you, O Lord, for   all   your works are   won - der - ful.

For other common responses see page 441.

Or:

℟.   I will praise you, Lord, for you have rescued me.

I will extol you, O Lord, for you drew me clear
  and did not let my enemies rejoice over me.
O Lord, you brought me up from the nether world;
  you preserved me from among those going down into the pit.   ℟.

Sing praise to the Lord, you his faithful ones,
  and give thanks to his holy name.
For his anger lasts but a moment;
  a lifetime, his good will.
At nightfall, weeping enters in,
  but with the dawn, rejoicing.   ℟.

Hear, O Lord, and have pity on me;
  O Lord, be my helper.
You changed my mourning into dancing;
  O Lord, my God, forever will I give you thanks.   ℟.

SECOND READING

Galatians 1, 11-19   God has revealed his Son in me, that I might preach the good news about him to the pagans.

Continuation from last Sunday. Paul justifies his claim to be regarded as one of the Apostles by recalling his former life as a strict Jew and by his special call by Jesus Christ himself. Read Paul's defense of his mission with vigor.

A reading from the letter of Paul to the Gal-á-tians

I assure you, brothers,
    the gospel I proclaimed to you is no mere human invention.
I did not receive it from any man,
    nor was I schooled in it.
It came by revelation from Jesus Christ.
You have heard, I know,
    the story of my former way of life in Judaism.
You know that I went to extremes
    in persecuting the Church of God and tried to destroy it;
    I made progress in Jewish observances
    far beyond most of my contemporaries,
    in my excess of zeal to live out all the traditions of my ancestors.

But the time came when he who had set me apart
    before I was born and called me by his favor
    chose to reveal his Son through me,
    that I might spread among the Gentiles
    the good tidings concerning him.
Immediately, without seeking human advisers or even going to Jerusalem,
    to see those who were apostles before me,
    I went off to Arabia;
    later I returned to Dam-ás-cus.
Three years after that I went up to Jerusalem
    to get to know Céph-as,
    with whom I stayed fifteen days.
I did not meet any other apostles
    except James, the brother of the Lord.

    This is the Word of the Lord.

GOSPEL

The cantor sings the alleluia and the people repeat it; the cantor then sings the verse and the people repeat the alleluia. Otherwise the alleluia may be omitted.

Al - le - lu - ia.

My sheep ____ lis - ten to my voice, says the Lord; I

know them ___ and ___ they ___ fol - low me.

For other alleluia verses see pages 437, 438 and 439.

Luke 7, 11-17 Young man, I say to you, arise.

Continuation from last Sunday. Straight story telling. Stress especially Jesus' sympathy for the sorrowing mother and the amazement of the crowd.

✠　A reading from the holy gospel according to Luke

Jesus went to a town called Ná-im,
　　and his disciples and a large crowd accompanied him.
As he approached the gate of the town
　　a dead man was being carried out,
　　the only son of a widowed mother.
A considerable crowd of townsfolk were with her.
The Lord was moved with pity upon seeing her and said to her,
　　"Do not cry."
Then he stepped forward and touched the litter;
　　at this, the bearers halted.
He said, "Young man, I bid you get up."
The dead man sat up and began to speak.
Then Jesus gave him back to his mother.
Fear seized them all and they began to praise God.
"A great prophet has risen among us," they said;
　　and, "God has visited his people."
This was the report that spread about him
　　throughout Judea and the surrounding country.

　　This is the gospel of the Lord.

ELEVENTH SUNDAY OF THE YEAR

FIRST READING

2 Samuel 12, 7-10. 13   The Lord God forgave your sin; you will not die.

For the full story, read Chapters 11:1 - 26; 12:1 - 25. Nathan the prophet denounces King David for his great sin in committing adultery with the wife of Uriah the Hittite, one of his officers, whom he has caused to be killed in battle. The reading will be clearer if verses 1-6 are first added as a comment. In reading, give strong emphasis to David's genuine sorrow in the words "I have sinned against the Lord,", and bring out that David is forgiven because of his penitence.

A reading from the second book of Samuel

Ná-than said to David: "Thus says the Lord God of Israel:
   'I anointed you king of Israel.
I rescued you from the hand of Saul.
I gave you your lord's house and your lord's wives for your own.
I gave you the house of Israel and of Jú-dah.
And if this were not enough, I could count up for you still more.
Why have you spurned the Lord and done evil in his sight?
You have cut down U-rí-ah the Hít-tite with the sword;
   you took his wife as your own,
      and him you killed with the sword of the Ám-mon-ites.
Now, therefore, the sword shall never depart from your house,
   because you have despised me
      and have taken the wife of U-rí-ah to be your wife.' "
Then David said to Ná-than, "I have sinned against the Lord."
Ná-than answered David:
   "The Lord on his part has forgiven your sin: you shall not die."

This is the Word of our Lord.

RESPONSORIAL PSALM

*Psalm 32, 1-2. 5. 7. 11 After the reading the psalmist sings or says the
responsorial verse and all repeat it. This response is also repeated
after each verse of the psalm.*

Common response:

We — praise you, O Lord, for all your works are won - der - ful.

For other common responses see page 441.

Or:

℞. Lord, forgive the wrong I have done.

Happy is he whose fault is taken away,
  whose sin is covered.
Happy the man to whom the Lord imputes not guilt,
  in whose spirit there is no guile. ℞.

I acknowledged my sin to you,
  my guilt I covered not.
I said, "I confess my faults to the Lord,"
  and you took away the guilt of my sin. ℞.

You are my shelter; from distress you will preserve me;
  with glad cries of freedom you will ring me round. ℞.

Be glad in the Lord and rejoice, you just;
  exult, all you upright of heart. ℞.

SECOND READING

*Galatians 2, 16. 19-21   I live now, not with my own life but with the
life of Christ who lives in me.*

*Turn back to the note on Reading II for the Ninth Sunday. The
Judaizers claimed that salvation came through the Law of Moses.
Paul counters that it was not the Law but Christ's death on the
cross that redeem us. The same vigorous tone as Last Sunday.*

A reading from the letter of Paul to the Gal-á-ti-ans

Knowing that a man is not justified by legal observance
   but by faith in Jesus Christ,
   we too have believed in him
   in order to be justified by faith in Christ,
   not by observance of the law;
   for by works of the law no one will be justified.
It was through the law that I died to the law,
   to live for God.
I have been crucified with Christ,
   and the life I live now is not my own;
   Christ is living in me.
I still live my human life,
   but it is a life of faith in the Son of God,
   who loved me and gave himself for me.
I will not treat God's gracious gift as pointless.
If justice is available through the law,
   then Christ died to no purpose!

This is the Word of the Lord.

GOSPEL

*The cantor sings the alleluia and the people repeat it; the cantor then
sings the verse and the people repeat the alleluia. Otherwise the alleluia
may be omitted.*

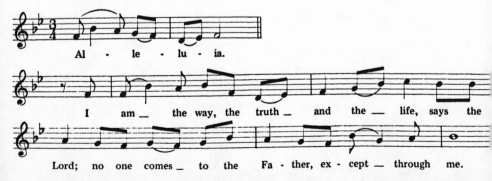

Al - le - lu - ia.

I am — the way, the truth — and the — life, says the

Lord; no one comes — to the Fa - ther, ex - cept — through me.

For other alleluia verses see pages 437, 438 and 439.

Long Form: Luke 7, 36—8, 3 *Her many sins were forgiven her, because she has shown great love.*

Bring out the drama in this story: the sorrow of the woman, the contempt of the Pharisee, followed by Jesus' rebuke for such lack of understanding, charity and good manners as a host. Conclude by stressing this demonstration of Jesus' absolute authority in his final words to the woman.

✠ A reading from the holy gospel according to Luke

There was a certain Pharisee who invited Jesus to dine with him.
Jesus went to the Pharisee's home and reclined to eat.
A woman known in the town to be a sinner
   learned that he was dining in the Pharisee's home.
She brought in a vase of perfumed oil and stood behind him at his feet,
   weeping so that her tears fell upon his feet.
Then she wiped them with her hair,
   kissing them and perfuming them with the oil.
When his host, the Pharisee, saw this, he said to himself,
   "If this man were a prophet, he would know
   who and what sort of woman this is that touches him—
   that she is a sinner."
In answer to his thoughts, Jesus said to him,
   "Sí-mon, I have something to propose to you."
"Teacher," he said, "speak."

"Two men owed money to a certain moneylender;
   one owed a total of five hundred coins, the other fifty.
Since neither was able to repay, he wrote off both debts.
Which of them was more grateful to him? "
Sí-mon answered, "He, I presume, to whom he remitted the larger sum."
Jesus said to him, "You are right."

Turning then to the woman, he said to Sí-mon:
   "You see this woman?
I came to your home and you provided me with no water for my feet.
She has washed my feet with her tears
   and wiped them with her hair.
You gave me no kiss,
   but she has not ceased kissing my feet since I entered.
You did not anoint my head with oil,
   but she has anointed my feet with perfume.

I tell you, that is why her many sins are forgiven—
  because of her great love.
Little is forgiven the one whose love is small."
He said to her then, "Your sins are forgiven,"
  at which his fellow guests began to ask among themselves,
  "Who is this that he even forgives sins? "
Meanwhile he said to the woman,
  "Your faith has been your salvation.
Go now in peace."

After this he journeyed through towns and villages
  preaching and proclaiming the good news of the kingdom of God.
The Twelve accompanied him,
  and also some women who had been cured of evil spirits and maladies:
  Mary called the Mág-da-lene, from whom seven devils had gone out,
  Jo-án-na, the wife of Herod's steward Chú-za,
  Su-sán-na, and many others who were assisting them out of their means.

  This is the gospel of the Lord.

*Short Form: Luke 7, 36-50 Her many sins were forgiven her, because
she has shown great love.*

✠   A reading from the holy gospel according to Luke

There was a certain Pharisee who invited Jesus to dine with him.
Jesus went to the Pharisee's home and reclined to eat.
A woman known in the town to be a sinner
  learned that he was dining in the Pharisee's home.
She brought in a vase of perfumed oil and stood behind him at his feet,
  weeping so that her tears fell upon his feet.
Then she wiped them with her hair,
  kissing them and perfuming them with the oil.
When his host, the Pharisee, saw this, he said to himself,
  "If this man were a prophet, he would know
  who and what sort of woman this is that touches him—
  that she is a sinner."
In answer to his thoughts, Jesus said to him,
  "Sí-mon, I have something to propose to you."
"Teacher," he said, "speak."

"Two men owed money to a certain moneylender;
  one owed a total of five hundred coins, the other fifty.

Since neither was able to repay, he wrote off both debts.

Which of them was more grateful to him? "

Sí-mon answered, "He, I presume, to whom he remitted the larger sum."

Jesus said to him, "You are right."

Turning then to the woman, he said to Sí-mon:

"You see this woman?

I came to your home and you provided me with no water for my feet.

She has washed my feet with her tears

and wiped them with her hair.

You gave me no kiss,

but she has not ceased kissing my feet since I entered.

You did not anoint my head with oil,

but she has anointed my feet with perfume.

I tell you, that is why her many sins are forgiven—

because of her great love.

Little is forgiven the one whose love is small."

He said to her then, "Your sins are forgiven,"

at which his fellow guests began to ask among themselves,

"Who is this that he even forgives sins? "

Meanwhile he said to the woman,

"Your faith has been your salvation.

Go now in peace."

This is the gospel of the Lord.

TWELFTH SUNDAY OF THE YEAR

FIRST READING

Zechariah 12, 10-11   They will look on the one, whom they have pierced.

*Verses from one of the messianic prophecies in the later chapters
of Zechariah, naturally interpreted as a reference to the crucifixion
of Christ. Read it as such. The reference to the mourning in
Jerusalem in the last sentence probably refers to the lamentation
over the death of king Josiah who was killed in battle against an
Egyptian army.*

A reading from the book of the prophet Ze-char-i-ah

I will pour out on the house of David
   and on the inhabitants of Je-rú-sa-lem a spirit of grace and petition;
   and they shall look on him whom they have thrust through,
   and they shall mourn for him as one mourns for an only son,
   and they shall grieve over him as one grieves over a first-born.

On that day the mourning in Je-rú-sa-lem shall be as great
   as the mourning of Há-dad-rím-mon in the plain of Me-gíd-do.

   This is the Word of the Lord.

RESPONSORIAL PSALM

*Psalm 63, 2. 3-4. 5-6. 8-9   After the reading the psalmist sings or says the
responsorial verse and all repeat it. This response is also repeated
after each verse of the psalm.*

Common response:

The   Lord is near to all who   call on   him.

For other common responses see page 441.

Or:

℞. My soul is thirsting for you, O Lord my God.

O God, you are my God whom I seek;
   for you my flesh pines and my soul thirsts
   like the earth, parched, lifeless and without water.   ℞.

Thus have I gazed toward you in the sanctuary
  to see your power and your glory,
For your kindness is a greater good than life;
  my lips shall glorify you. ℟.

Thus will I bless you while I live;
  lifting up my hands, I will call upon your name.
As with the riches of a banquet shall my soul be satisfied,
  and with exultant lips my mouth shall praise you. ℟.

You are my help,
  and in the shadow of your wings I shout for joy.
My soul clings fast to you;
  your right hand upholds me. ℟.

SECOND READING

Galatians 3, 26-29   You who have been baptized have put on Christ.

*Continuation from last Sunday. The Judaizers had declared
that since salvation was promised to the descendants of Abraham,
the original ancestor of the Jewish people, everyone who wished
to be saved must first become a Jew. Paul reverses the claim;
anyone who is baptized a Christian thereby inherits all that was
promised to Abraham and his descendants.*

A reading from the letter of Paul to the Gal-á-ti-ans

Each one of you is a son of God
  because of your faith in Christ Jesus.
All of you who have been baptized into Christ
  have clothed yourselves with him.
There does not exist among you Jew or Greek,
  slave or freeman, male or female.
All are one in Christ Jesus.
Furthermore, if you belong to Christ
  you are the descendants of Á-bra-ham,
    which means you inherit all that was promised.

  This is the Word of the Lord.

GOSPEL

*The cantor sings the alleluia and the people repeat it; the cantor then
sings the verse and the people repeat the alleluia. Otherwise the alleluia
may be omitted.*

Al - le - lu - ia.

If an - y - one loves me, he will hold to my words, and my

Fa - ther will love him and — we — will come — to him.

For other alleluia verses see pages 437, 438 and 439.

Luke 9, 18-24   You are the Messiah sent by God. It is necessary for
the Son of Man to suffer much.

This incident is related also in the gospels of Matthew and Mark,
but in each account the emphasis somewhat differs. In this reading
the significance is that Jesus having evoked from Peter the decla-
ration that he is the Messiah, commands his disciples to keep it
secret. He then forwarns them of his own sufferings and underlines
the lesson that the Christian must expect to suffer for Christ's sake.

✠   A reading from the holy gospel according to Luke

One day when Jesus was praying in seclusion
  and his disciples were with him,
  he put the question to them,
  "Who do the crowds say that I am? "
"John the Baptizer," they replied, "and some say E-lí-jah,
  while others claim
  that one of the prophets of old has returned from the dead."
"But you—who do you say that I am? " he asked them.
Peter said in reply, "The Messiah of God."
He strictly forbade them to tell this to anyone.
"The Son of Man," he said, "must first endure many sufferings,
  be rejected by the elders, the high priests and the scribes,
  and be put to death, and then be raised up on the third day."

Jesus said to all:
  "Whoever wishes to be my follower must deny his very self,
  take up his cross each day, and follow in my steps.
Whoever would save his life will lose it,
  and whoever loses his life for my sake will save it."

  This is the gospel of the Lord.

THIRTEENTH SUNDAY OF THE YEAR

FIRST READING

1 Kings 19, 16. 19-21   Elisha rose and followed Elijah and became his servant.

The calling of Elisha by the Prophet Elijah is read here as a comment on today's gospel. When Elijah threw his cloak over Elisha, it was a sign that Elijah appointed him to be his successor. Read as an example of instant obedience to a divine call.

A reading from the first book of Kings

The Lord said to E-lí-jah:

"You shall anoint Elí-sha, son of Sháp-hat of A-bel-me-hó-lah,
   as prophet to succeed you."

E-lí-jah set out, and came upon Elí-sha, son of Shá-phat,
   as he was plowing with twelve yoke of oxen;
   he was following the twelfth.
E-lí-jah went over to him and threw his cloak over him.
Elí-sha left the oxen, ran after E-lí-jah, and said,
   "Please, let me kiss my father and mother goodbye,
   and I will follow you."
"Go back! " E-lí-jah answered.
"Have I done anything to you? "
Elí-sha left him and, taking the yoke of oxen, slaughtered them;
   he used the plowing equipment for fuel to boil their flesh,
   and gave it to his people to eat.
Then he left and followed E-lí-jah as his attendant.

   This is the Word of the Lord.

RESPONSORIAL PSALM

*Psalm 16, 1-2. 5. 7-8. 9-10. 11   After the reading the psalmist sings or says
the responsorial verse and all repeat it. This response is also repeated
after each verse of the psalm.*

Common response:

Hear   us,   O Lord, and   save   us.

For other common responses see page 441.

Or:

℟. You are my inheritance, O Lord.

Keep me, O God, for in you I take refuge;
   I say to the Lord, "My Lord are you.
O Lord, my allotted portion and my cup,
   you it is who hold fast my lot.   ℟.

I bless the Lord who counsels me;
   even in the night my heart exhorts me.
I set the Lord ever before me;
   with him at my right hand I shall not be disturbed.   ℟.

Therefore my heart is glad and my soul rejoices,
   my body, too, abides in confidence;
Because you will not abandon my soul to the nether world,
   nor will you suffer your faithful one to undergo corruption.   ℟.

You will show me the path to life,
   fullness of joys in your presence,
   the delights at your right hand forever.   ℟.

SECOND READING

Galatians 5, 1. 13-18   My brothers, you were called to freedom.

*Continuation of the argument from last Sunday. The old Law, Paul
declares, bound men by its rites; Christ gives them freedom. But
freedom does not mean license but rather love for others, If you
live in the spirit of Christ, you will not yield to the 'flesh'— i.e.,
man's baser cravings. There is perpetual tension between 'flesh' and
spirit; but the spirit frees us from the bond of the law. Express the
argument clearly and forcibly. The key words are 'freedom', 'flesh',
'spirit'.*

A reading from the letter of Paul to the Gal-á-ti-ans

It was for liberty that Christ freed us.
So stand firm,
  and do not take on yourselves the yoke of slavery a second time!

My brothers, remember that you have been called to live in freedom
  —but not a freedom that gives free rein to the flesh.
Out of love, place yourselves at one another's service.
The whole law has found its fulfillment in this one saying:
  "You shall love your neighbor as yourself."
If you go on biting and tearing one another to pieces, take care!
You will end up in mutual destruction!

My point is that you should live in accord with the spirit
  and you will not yield to the cravings of the flesh.
The flesh lusts against the spirit
  and the spirit against the flesh;
  the two are directly opposed.
This is why you do not do what your will intends.
If you are guided by the spirit, you are not under the law.

  This is the Word of the Lord.

GOSPEL

The cantor sings the alleluia and the people repeat it; the cantor then sings the verse and the people repeat the alleluia. Otherwise the alleluia may be omitted.

Al - le - lu - ia.

I call you my friends, — says the Lord, for I have made known to you all that the Fa - ther has told _____ me.

For other alleluia verses see pages 437, 438 and 439.

*Luke 9, 51-62   Jesus resolutely set his face toward Jerusalem.   I will
follow you wherever you will go.*

*A short collection of Jesus' words on various occasions.   Keep them
separate as memorable sayings, with a pause after each.*

✟ A reading from the holy gospel according to Luke

As the time approached when Jesus was to be taken from this world,
    he firmly resolved to proceed toward Jerusalem,
    and sent messengers on ahead of him.
These entered a Samaritan town to prepare for his passing through,
    but the Samaritans would not welcome him
    because he was on his way to Jerusalem.
When his disciples James and John saw this, they said,
    "Lord, would you not have us call down fire from heaven to
      destroy them? "
He turned toward them only to reprimand them.
Then they set off for another town.

As they were making their way along, someone said to him,
    "I will be your follower where ever you go."
Jesus said to him, "The foxes have lairs,
    the birds of the sky have nests,
    but the Son of Man has nowhere to lay his head."
To another he said, "Come after me."
The man replied, "Let me bury my father first."
Jesus said to him, "Let the dead bury their dead;
    come away and proclaim the kingdom of God."
Yet another said to him, "I will be your follower, Lord,
    but first let me take leave of my people at home."
Jesus answered him,
    "Whoever puts his hand to the plow but keeps looking back
    is unfit for the reign of God."

    This is the gospel of the Lord.

FOURTEENTH SUNDAY OF THE YEAR

FIRST READING

Isaiah 66, 10-14   I will send toward Jerusalem peace like a river.

From the last chapter of Isaiah, a glad vision of the new Jerusalem when the Lord's enemies have been destroyed and all mankind worships before him. The key word is 'rejoice', repeated in the last sentence.

A reading from the book of the prophet I-saí-ah

Rejoice with Jerusalem and be glad because of her,
   all you who love her;
Exult, exult with her,
   all you who were mourning over her!
Oh, that you may suck fully
   of the milk of her comfort,
That you may nurse with delight
   at her abundant breasts!
For thus says the Lord:
   Lo, I will spread prosperity over her like a river,
   and the wealth of the nations like an overflowing torrent.
As nurslings, you shall be carried in her arms, and fondled in her lap;
   As a mother comforts her son,
   so will I comfort you;
   in Jerusalem you shall find your comfort.
When you see this, your heart shall rejoice,
   and your bodies flourish like the grass;
   The Lord's power shall be known to his servants.

   This is the Word of the Lord.

RESPONSORIAL PSALM

Psalm 66, 1-3. 4-5. 6-7. 16. 20   After the reading the psalmist sings or says the responsorial verse and all repeat it. This response is also repeated after each verse of the psalm.

Common response:

We   praise you, O Lord, for   all   your works are   won - der - ful.

For other common responses see page 441.

Or:

℟. Let all the earth cry out to God with joy.

Shout joyfully to God, all you on earth,
 sing praise to the glory of his name;
 proclaim his glorious praise.
Say to God, "How tremendous are your deeds! "   ℟.

"Let all on earth worship and sing praise to you,
 sing praise to your name! "
Come and see the works of God,
 his tremendous deeds among men.   ℟.

He has changed the sea into dry land;
 through the river they passed on foot;
 therefore let us rejoice in him.
He rules by his might forever.   ℟.

Hear now, all you who fear God, while I declare
 what he has done for me.
Blessed be God who refused me not
 my prayer or his kindness!   ℟.

SECOND READING

Galatians 6, 14-18   The marks I carry on my body are those of Jesus Christ.

*The end of the letter. Paul has had enough of the controversy.
Only the cross of Christ counts. Outward signs, such as circumcision, mean nothing; he has his own outward signs—the scars
of the scourgings he has endured for Jesus. Read in the tone
of one who is very sure of himself and of his faith.*

A reading from the letter of Paul to the Gal-á-tians

May I never boast of anything but the cross of our Lord Jesus Christ!

Through it, the world has been crucified to me and I to the world.

It means nothing whether one is circumcised or not.
All that matters is that one is created anew.

Peace and mercy on all who follow this rule of life,
    and on the Israel of God.

Henceforth, let no man trouble me,
    for I bear the brand marks of Jesus in my body.

Brothers, may the favor of our Lord Jesus Christ be with
        your spirit. Amen.

This is the Word of the Lord.

GOSPEL

*The cantor sings the alleluia and the people repeat it; the cantor then
sings the verse and the people repeat the alleluia. Otherwise the alleluia
may be omitted.*

Al - le - lu - ia.

May the Fa - ther of our Lord, __ Je - sus Christ, __ en - light - en the

eyes of our hearts that we might see how great __ is the hope to which we are called.

For other alleluia verses see pages 437, 438 and 439.

Long Form: Luke 10, 1-12. 17-20   Your peace will rest upon him.

*Jesus sends seventy-two of his disciples to preach the good news.
He gives them detailed instructions for their mission. Convey
the feeling of urgency: the harvest is ready for reaping but there
are not enough reapers. Be on your way. The kingdom of God
is near. When the mission has been completed, the seventy-two
return to report on their success. The reading climaxes on the
ultimate reward.*

✠   A reading from the holy gospel according to Luke

The Lord appointed a further seventy-two
     and sent them in pairs before him
     to every town and place he intended to visit.
He said to them:
     "The harvest is rich but the workers are few;
     therefore ask the harvest-master to send workers to his harvest.
Be on your way, and remember:
     I am sending you as lambs in the midst of wolves.
Do not carry a walking staff or traveling bag;
     wear no sandals and greet no one along the way.
On entering any house, first say, 'Peace to this house.'
If there is a peaceable man there,
     your peace will rest on him;
     if not, it will come back to you.
Stay in the one house eating and drinking what they have,
     for the laborer is worth his wage.
Do not move from house to house.

"Into whatever city you go, after they welcome you,
     eat what they set before you, and cure the sick there.
Say to them, 'The reign of God is at hand.'
If the people of any town you enter do not welcome you,
     go into its streets and say,
     'We shake the dust of this town from our feet
     as testimony against you.
But know that the reign of God is near.'
I assure you, on that day
     the fate of Sodom will be less severe than that of such a town."

The seventy-two returned in jubilation saying,
"Master, even the demons are subject to us in your name."
He said in reply:"I watched Satan fall from the sky like lightning.
See what I have done;
I have given you power to tread on snakes and scorpions
and all the forces of the enemy,
and nothing shall ever injure you.
Nevertheless, do not rejoice so much
in the fact that the devils are subject to you
as that your names are inscribed in heaven."

This is the gospel of the Lord.

Short Form: Luke 10, 1-9 Your peace will rest upon him.

✠ A reading from the holy gospel according to Luke

The Lord appointed a further seventy-two
and sent them in pairs before him
to every town and place he intended to visit.
He said to them:
"The harvest is rich but the workers are few;
therefore ask the harvest-master to send workers to his harvest.
Be on your way, and remember:
I am sending you as lambs in the midst of wolves.
Do not carry a walking staff or traveling bag;
wear no sandals and greet no one along the way.
On entering any house, first say, 'Peace to this house.'
If there is a peaceable man there,
your peace will rest on him;
if not, it will come back to you.
Stay in the one house eating and drinking what they have,
for the laborer is worth his wage.
Do not move from house to house.

"Into whatever city you go, after they welcome you,
eat what they set before you,
and cure the sick there.
Say to them, 'The reign of God is at hand.' "

This is the gospel of the Lord.

FIFTEENTH SUNDAY OF THE YEAR

FIRST READING

Deuteronomy 30, 10-14 Let the instruction of the Lord God be near you.

*Moses is instructing the people of Israel in the Law, setting
before them the blessings and the curses. After this reading,
Moses goes on to declare that if they keep the commandments,
they will prosper; if they disobey, they will perish. A sombre
but unemotional presentation of God's will.*

A reading from the book of Deu-ter-ón-o-my

Moses said to the people:
   "If only you heed the voice of the Lord, your God,
   and keep his commandments and statutes
   that are written in this book of the law,
   when you return to the Lord, your God,
   with all your heart and all your soul.

"For this command which I enjoin on you today
   is not too mysterious and remote for you.
It is not up in the sky, that you should say,
   'Who will go up in the sky to get it for us
   and tell us of it, that we may carry it out? "
Nor is it across the sea, that you should say,
   'Who will cross the sea to get it for us
   and tell us of it, that we may carry it out? '
No, it is something very near to you,
   already in your mouths and in your hearts;
   you have only to carry it out."

   This is the Word of the Lord.

RESPONSORIAL PSALM

*Psalm 69, 14. 17. 30-31. 33-34. 36. 37 After the reading the psalmist sings
or says the responsorial verse and all repeat it. This response is also repeated
after each verse of the psalm.*

Common response:

The   Lord is near to all who   call on him.

For other common responses see page 441.

Or:

℟. Turn to the Lord in your need, and you will live.

I pray to you, O Lord,
   for the time of your favor, O God!
In your great kindness answer me
   with your constant help.
Answer me, O Lord, for bounteous is your kindness:
   in your great mercy turn toward me.   ℟.

I am afflicted and in pain;
   let your saving help, O God, protect me.
I will praise the name of God in song,
   and I will glorify him with thanksgiving.   ℟.

"See, you lowly ones, and be glad;
   you who seek God, may your hearts be merry!
For the Lord hears the poor,
   and his own who are in bonds he spurns not."   ℟.

For God will save Zí-on
   and rebuild the cities of Jú-dah.
The descendants of his servants shall inherit it,
   and those who love his name shall inhabit it.   ℟.

SECOND READING

Colossians 1, 15-20 In him were created all things.

In this letter Paul is concerned with the divine nature of Christ the Son. The passage is an early hymn to Christ. Try to make your hearers aware of its similarity to some of the clauses of the Nicene Creed.

A reading from the letter of Paul to the Col-ós-si-ans

Christ Jesus is the image of the invisible God, the first-born of all creatures.
In him everything in heaven and on earth was created,
   things visible and invisible,
   whether thrones or dominations, principalities or powers;
all were created through him, and for him.
He is before all else that is.
In him everything continues in being.
It is he who is head of the body, the church;
   he who is the beginning, the first-born of the dead,
   so that primacy may be his in everything.
It pleased God to make absolute fullness reside in him
   and, by means of him, to reconcile everything in his person,
   everything, I say, both on earth and in the heavens,
   making peace through the blood of his cross.

This is the Word of the Lord.

GOSPEL

The cantor sings the alleluia and the people repeat it; the cantor then sings the verse and the people repeat the alleluia. Otherwise the alleluia may be omitted.

Al - le - lu - ia.

Your word, __ O Lord, __ is __ truth; make us ho - ly in __ the tru

For other alleluia verses see pages 437, 438 and 439.

Luke 10, 25-37 Who is my neighbor?

*A reader needs skill and careful preparation to bring out the
many significances in the parable of the Good Samaritan. The
lawyer hopes to trap Jesus and to show off his own superior
knowledge of the scriptures by Asking A Difficult Question.
Instead of replying, Jesus asks the lawyer to answer his own
question. The lawyer then asks another and more difficult:
who is my neighbor? In the opinion of an orthodox Jew, the
only answer can be that a man's neighbor is a fellow Jew who
keeps the whole law; and Jesus is far from orthodox. Again
Jesus gives no direct reply. Instead, he tells the story of a
man who was beaten and robbed on the highway. Two
respectable Jews, a priest and a Levite, pass by and take no
notice, but a Samaritan gives every possible help to the injured
man. Jesus then asks the lawyer "which of these three, in
your opinion , was neighbor to the man who fell in with the
robbers? " The lawyer, as an orthodox respectable Jew, hates
and despises all Samaritans as outside the Law. He is too
embarrassed to reply " the Samaritan"; he can only mutter
"the one who treated him with compassion." Jesus' reply
—follow the example of a Samaritan is equally humiliating.*

✠ A reading from the holy gospel according to Luke

On one occasion a lawyer stood up to pose this problem to Jesus:
   "Teacher, what must I do to inherit everlasting life? "
Jesus answered him: "What is written in the law?
How do you read it? "
He replied:

   "You shall love the Lord your God
   with all your heart,
   with all your soul,
   with all your strength,
   and with all your mind;
   and your neighbor as yourself."

Jesus said, "You have answered correctly,
Do this and you shall live."
But because he wished to justify himself he said to Jesus,
   "And who is my neighbor? "
Jesus replied:
   "There was a man going down from Jerusalem to Jér-i-cho
   who fell prey to robbers.
They stripped him, beat him,
   and then went off leaving him half dead.
A priest happened to be going down the same road;
   he saw him but continued on.

Likewise there was a Levite who came the same way;
  he saw him and went on.
But a Sam-ár-i-tan who was journeying along
  came on him and was moved to pity at the sight.
He approached him and dressed his wounds,
  pouring in oil and wine.
He then hoisted him on his own beast
  and brought him to an inn, where he cared for him.
The next day he took out two silver pieces
  and gave them to the innkeeper with the request:
'Look after him, and if there is any further expense
  I will repay you on my way back.'

"Which of these three, in your opinion,
  was neighbor to the man who fell in with the robbers? "
The answer came, "The one who treated him with compassion."
Jesus said to him, "Then go and do the same."

  This is the gospel of the Lord.

SIXTEENTH SUNDAY OF THE YEAR

FIRST READING

Genesis 18, 1-10 Lord, do not bypass your servant.

Abraham had long given up all hope of a child by his wife Sarah when he received this visitation. Read as a mysterious story, and show how Abraham at once senses that his visitors are supernatural and therefore to be treated with the utmost respect.

A reading from the book of Gén-e-sis

The Lord appeared to A-bra-ham by the terebinth of Mám-re,
    as he sat in the entrance of his tent, while the day was growing hot.
Looking up, he saw three men standing nearby.
When he saw them,
    he ran from the entrance of the tent to greet them;
    and bowing to the ground, he said:
    "Sir, if I may ask you this favor,
    please do not go on past your servant.
Let some water be brought, that you may bathe your feet,
    and then rest yourselves under the tree.
Now that you have come this close to your servant,
    let me bring you a little food, that you may refresh yourselves;
    and afterward you may go on your way."
"Very well," they replied, "do as you have said."

Abraham hastened into the tent and told Sarah,
    "Quick, three seahs of fine flour!   Knead it and make rolls."
He ran to the herd, picked out a tender, choice steer,
    and gave it to a servant, who quickly prepared it.
Then he got some curds and milk,
    as well as the steer that had been prepared, and set these before them;
    and he waited on them under the tree while they ate.

"Where is your wife Sarah? " they asked him.
    "There in the tent," he replied.
    One of them said,
"I will surely return to you about this time next year,
    and Sarah will then have a son."

    This is the Word of the Lord.

RESPONSORIAL PSALM

Psalm 15, 2-3. 3-4. 5   After the reading the psalmist sings or says the responsorial verse and all repeat it. This response is also repeated after each verse of the psalm.

Common response:

The   Lord is   near to all who   call on him.

For other common responses see page 441.

Or:

℟. He who does justice will live in the presence of the Lord.

He who walks blamelessly and does justice;
   who thinks the truth in his heart
   and slanders not with his tongue.   ℟.

Who harms not his fellow man,
   nor takes up a reproach against his neighbor;
By whom the reprobate is despised,
   while he honors those who fear the Lord.   ℟.

Who lends not his money at usury
   and accepts no bribe against the innocent.
He who does these things
   shall never be disturbed.   ℟.

SECOND READING

Colossians 1, 24-28   The mystery hidden for centuries has now been revealed to his saints.

The reading should be in the form of a careful explanation of Paul's message. Christ suffered for his Church, which is his Body. Members of that Church must expect also to suffer. Paul's special mission is to show the Gentiles that God's promises are for them also. The mystery of Christ is that he lives in us and we in him.

A reading from the letter of Paul to the Col-ós-si-ans

Even now I find my joy in the suffering I endure for you.
In my own flesh I fill up what is lacking in the sufferings of Christ
    for the sake of his body, the church.
I became a minister of this church through the commission
    God gave me to preach among you his word in its fullness,
    that mystery hidden from ages and generations
    past but now revealed to his holy ones.
God has willed to make known to them the glory
    beyond price which this mystery brings to the Gentiles—
    the mystery of Christ in you, your hope of glory.
This is the Christ we proclaim while we admonish all men
    and teach them in the full measure of wisdom,
    hoping to make every man complete in Christ.

    This is the Word of the Lord.

GOSPEL

*The cantor sings the alleluia and the people repeat it; the cantor then
sings the verse and the people repeat the alleluia. Otherwise the alleluia
may be omitted.*

Al - le - lu - ia.

If an-y-one loves me, he will hold to my words, and my
Fa-ther will love him and — we — will come — to him.

For other alleluia verses see pages 437, 438 and 439.

Luke 10, 38-42 Jesus speaks with Martha and Mary.

*A very human little story of Jesus with Martha and Mary her
sister, who are entertaining God unawares.*

✠   A reading from the holy gospel according to Luke

Jesus entered a village where a woman named Martha
    welcomed him to her home.
She had a sister named Mary,
    who seated herself at the Lord's feet and listened to his words.
Martha, who was busy with all the details of hospitality,
    came to him and said, "Lord, are you not concerned
    that my sister has left me to do the household tasks all alone?
Tell her to help me."

The Lord in reply said to her:
    "Martha , Martha, you are anxious and upset about many things;
    one thing only is required.
Mary has chosen the better portion and she shall not be deprived of it."

    This is the gospel of the Lord.

SEVENTEENTH SUNDAY OF THE YEAR

FIRST READING

Genesis 18, 20-32   Lord, do not be angry if I speak.

Continuation from last Sunday. Three men had appeared before Abraham: the Lord and two others. The Lord now declares that he will destroy the people of Sodom and Gomorrah for their sins. Abraham pleads for them, for the sake of the few who are worthy of being saved. Bring out Abraham's fear in thus appealing to God direct, and the almost ritual repetition of request and answer, as Abraham persists in his plea. Also the sinister conclusion that underlies the last sentence for there were not even ten innocent persons in the two cities.

A reading from the book of Gén-e-sis

The Lord said: "The outcry against Sód-om and Go-mór-rah is so great,
   and their sin so grave, that I must go down and see
   whether or not their actions fully correspond
   to the cry against them that comes to me.
I mean to find out."

While the two men   walked on farther toward Sód-om,
   the Lord remained standing before Abraham.
Then Abraham drew nearer to him and said:
   "Will you sweep away the innocent with the guilty?
Suppose there were fifty innocent people in the city;
   would you wipe out the place,
   rather than spare it for the sake of the fifty innocent people within it?
Far be it from you to do such a thing,
   to make the innocent die with the guilty,
   so that the innocent and the guilty would be treated alike!
Should not the judge of all the world act with justice? "
The Lord replied, "If I find fifty innocent people in the city of Sód-om,
   I will spare the whole place for their sake."
Abraham spoke up again:
   "See how I am presuming to speak to my Lord,
   though I am but dust and ashes!
What if there are five less than fifty innocent people?
Will you destroy the whole city because of those five? "
"I will not destroy it," he answered,
   "if I find forty-five there."

But Abraham persisted, saying,
  "What if only forty are found there? "
He replied, "I will forbear doing it for the sake of the forty."
Then he said, "Let not my Lord grow impatient if I go on.
What if only thirty are found there? "
He replied, "I will forbear doing it if I can find but thirty there."
Still he went on,
  "Since I have thus dared to speak to my Lord,
  what if there are no more than twenty? "
"I will not destroy it," he answered, "for the sake of the twenty."
But he still persisted:
"Please, let not my Lord grow angry if I speak up this last time.
What if there are at least ten there? "
"For the sake of those ten," he replied, "I will not destroy it."

  This is the Word of the Lord.

RESPONSORIAL PSALM

*Psalm 138, 1-2. 2-3. 6-7. 7-8 After the reading the psalmist sings or says
the responsorial verse and all repeat it. This response is also repeated
after each verse of the psalm.*

Common response:

We   praise you, O Lord, for   all   your works are   won - der - ful.

For other common responses see page 441.

Or:

℟. Lord, on the day I called for help, you answered me.

I will give thanks to you, O Lord, with all my heart,
    for you have heard the words of my mouth;
    in the presence of the angels I will sing your praise;
    I will worship at your holy temple
    and give thanks to your name.   ℟.

Because of your kindness and your truth;
    for you have made great above all things
    your name and your promise.
When I called you answered me;
    you built up strength within me.   ℟.

The Lord is exalted, yet the lowly he sees,
   and the proud he knows from afar.
Though I walk amid distress, you preserve me;
   against the anger of my enemies you raise your hand. ℟.

Your right hand saves me.
The Lord will complete what he has done for me;
   Your kindness, O Lord, endures forever;
   forsake not the work of your hands. ℟.

SECOND READING

*Colossians 2, 12-14 He has made you alive with Christ for he has
forgiven all our sins.*

*A difficult reading. The thought is this: in Paul's time, in baptism
the convert was thrust under the water. Baptism thus symbolized
'death' and 'burial', and as he came up again, 'resurrection'. The
rite thus unites the convert with the death and resurrection of
Christ. Although the Colossians had not been made to accept the
Law of Moses (which included circumcision), yet by baptism, Paul
declares, they have received the forgiveness of their sins through
the cross of Christ.*

A reading from the letter of Paul to the Col-ós-si-ans

In baptism you were not only buried with him
   but also raised to life with him
   because you believed in the power of God
   who raised him from the dead.
Even when you were dead in sin and your flesh was uncircumcised,
   God gave you new life in company with Christ.
He pardoned all our sins.
He canceled the bond that stood against us with all its claims,
   snatching it up and nailing it to the cross.

   This is the Word of the Lord.

GOSPEL

*The cantor sings the alleluia and the people repeat it; the cantor then
sings the verse and the people repeat the alleluia. Otherwise the alleluia
may be omitted.*

Al - le - lu - ia.

I call you my friends, __ says the Lord, for I have made known to

you all that the Fa - ther has told _____ me.

For other alleluia verses see pages 437, 438 and 439.

Luke 11, 1-13 Ask, and it will be given to you.

*A vivid dialogue between Jesus and his disciples. Since the words
of the 'Lord's Prayer' differ somewhat from the usual version, read
each clause as a separate petition, and then go on to give life to
Jesus' words on prayer, emphasizing each homely illustration as if
your congregation had never heard this reading before.*

✠ A reading from the holy gospel according to Luke

One day Jesus was praying in a certain place.
When he had finished, one of his disciples asked him,
    "Lord, teach us to pray as John taught his disciples."
He said to them, "When you pray, say:
    "Father,
    hallowed be your name,
    your kingdom come.
Give us each day our daily bread.
Forgive us our sins
   .for we too forgive all who do us wrong;
    and subject us not to the trial."

Jesus said to them:

"If one of you knows someone who comes to him in the middle
 of the night
and says to him, 'Friend, lend me three loaves,
for a friend of mine has come in from a journey
and I have nothing to offer him ';
and he from inside should reply, 'Leave me alone.
The door is shut now and my children and I are in bed.
I can't get up to look after your needs'—
I tell you, even though he does not get up
and take care of the man because of friendship,
he will do so because of his persistence,
and give him as much as he needs.

"So I say to you, 'Ask and you shall receive;
seek and you shall find, knock and it shall be opened to you.'

"For whoever asks, receives; whoever seeks, finds;
whoever knocks, is admitted.
What father among you will give his son a snake if he asks for a fish,
or hand him a scorpion if he asks for an egg?
If you, with all your sins,
know how to give your children good things,
how much more will the heavenly Father
give the Holy Spirit to those who ask him."

This is the gospel of the Lord.

EIGHTEENTH SUNDAY OF THE YEAR

FIRST READING

Ecclesiastes 1, 2; 2, 21-23   What do all his labors profit a man?

*"Qoholeth' is a Hebrew word sometimes translated 'the Preacher.'
His theme is that everything is futile, but God knows best.   The
tone is slow melancholy, musing.*

A reading from the book of Ec-cle-si-ás-tes

Vanity of vanities, says Qo-hé-leth, vanity of vanities! All things
    are vanity!

Here is a man who has labored with wisdom and knowledge and skill,
    and to another, who has not labored over it,
    he must leave his property.
This also is vanity and a great misfortune.
For what profit comes to a man from all the toil and anxiety of heart
    with which he has labored under the sun?
All his days sorrow and grief are his occupation;
    even at night his mind is not at rest.
This also is vanity.

    This is the Word of the Lord.

RESPONSORIAL PSALM

*Psalm 95, 1-2. 6-7. 8-9   After the reading the psalmist sings or says the
responsorial verse and all repeat it.   This response is also repeated
after each verse of the psalm.*

Common response:

We   praise you, O Lord, for   all   your works are   won - der - ful.

For other common responses see page 441.

Or:

℟. If today you hear his voice, harden not your hearts.

Come, let us sing joyfully to the Lord;
    let us acclaim the Rock of our salvation.
Let us greet him with thanksgiving;
    let us joyfully sing psalms to him.   ℟.

Come, let us bow down in worship;
  let us kneel before the Lord who made us.
For he is our God,
  and we are the people he shepherds, the flock he guides.   ℟.

Oh, that today you would hear his voice;
  "Harden not your hearts as at Mer-í-bah,
  as in the day of Más-sah in the desert,
Where your fathers tempted me;
  they tested me though they had seen my works."   ℟.

SECOND READING

Colossians 3, 1-5. 9-11   Seek the things that are above where Christ is.

Clarify the argument: now that you have been baptized, you belong to heaven. You must put to death—that is, leave behind with your sinful old life— all your old sins, and become new men. Among Christians there is no distinction between people of different race and class.

A reading from the letter of Paul to the Col-ós-si-ans

Since you have been raised up in company with Christ,
  set your heart on what pertains to higher realms
  where Christ is seated at God's right hand.
Be intent on things above rather than on things of earth.
After all, you have died!
Your life is hidden now with Christ in God.
When Christ our life appears,
  then you shall appear with him in glory.

Put to death whatever in your nature is rooted in earth:
  fornication, uncleanness, passion, evil desires,
  and that lust which is idolatry.
Stop lying to one another.
What you have done is put aside your old self with its past deeds
  and put on a new man,
  one who grows in knowledge as he is formed anew
  in the image of his Creator.
There is no Greek or Jew here, circumcised or uncircumcised,
  foreigner, Scýth-i-an, slave, or freeman.
Rather, Christ is everything in all of you.

  This is the Word of the Lord.

GOSPEL

*The cantor sings the alleluia and the people repeat it; the cantor then
sings the verse and the people repeat the alleluia. Otherwise the alleluia
may be omitted.*

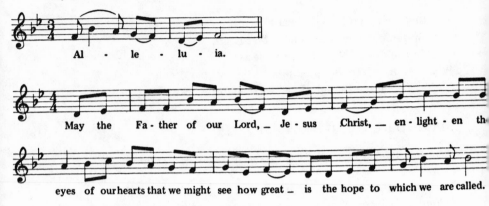

Al - le - lu - ia.

May the Fa - ther of our Lord, _ Je - sus Christ, _ en - light - en th

eyes of our hearts that we might see how great _ is the hope to which we are called.

For other alleluia verses see pages 437, 438 and 439.

Luke 12, 13-21 Why are you preparing these things?

*Jesus' words on the futility of great possessions. Read with
vigor as a message for our times.*

✠ A reading from the holy gospel according to Luke

Someone in the crowd said to Jesus,
"Teacher, tell my brother to give me my share of our inheritance."
He replied, "Friend,
who has set me up as your judge or arbiter? "
Then he said to the crowd,
"Avoid greed in all its forms.
A man may be wealthy,
but his possessions do not guarantee him life."

He told them a parable in these words:
"There was a rich man who had a good harvest.
'What shall I do? ' he asked himself.
'I have no place to store my harvest.
I know! ' he said.
'I will pull down my grain bins and build larger ones.
All my grain and my goods will go there.

Then I will say to myself:
  You have blessings in reserve for years to come. Relax!
Eat heartily, drink well. Enjoy yourself.'
But God said to him, 'You fool!
This very night your life shall be required of you.
To whom will all this piled-up wealth of yours go? '
That is the way it works with the man
  who grows rich for himself instead of growing rich in the sight of God."

  This is the gospel of the Lord.

NINETEENTH SUNDAY OF THE YEAR

FIRST READING

*Wisdom 18, 6-9 Just as you struck our enemies, you made us glorious
by calling us to you.*

*A difficult passage because it assumes in the hearers a knowledge
of the events told in Exodus chapters 11 and 12. An introductory
explanation is needed. The author has been showing at great length
how God looked after his people before and after the flight from
Egypt. Here he reminds his hearers that the Israelites were warned to
be ready to leave Egypt at once on the night that the angel passed
through to slay the first born of the Egyptians.*

A reading from the book of Wisdom

That night was known beforehand to our fathers,
   that, with sure knowledge of the oaths in
    which they put their faith, they might have courage.
Your people awaited.
   the salvation of the just and the destruction of their foes.
For when you punished our adversaries,
   in this you glorified us whom you had summoned.
For in secret the holy children of the good were offering sacrifice
   and putting into effect with one accord the divine institution.

   This is the Word of the Lord.

RESPONSORIAL PSALM

*Psalm 33, 1. 12. 18-19. 20-22 After the reading the psalmist sings or says
the responsorial verse and all repeat it. This response is also repeated
after each verse of the psalm.*

Common response:

We   praise you, O Lord, for   all   your works are   won - der - ful.

For other common responses see page 441.

Or:

℟. Happy the people the Lord has chosen to be his own.

Exult, you just, in the Lord;
  praise from the upright is fitting.
Happy the nation whose God is the Lord,
  the people he has chosen for his own inheritance.   ℟.

See, the eyes of the Lord are upon those who fear him,
  upon those who hope for his kindness,
To deliver them from death
  and preserve them in spite of famine.   ℟.

Our soul waits for the Lord,
  who is our help and our shield.
May your kindness, O Lord, be upon us
  who have put our hope in you.   ℟.

SECOND READING

*Long Form: Hebrews 11, 1-2. 8-19   We will look for the city designed
and built by God.*

*The reading consists of a definition of faith, followed by notable
examples of those who showed entire faith in God's promises.
Now translate the first sentence: "what is faith? It is that which
gives substance to our hope, which convinces us of things we cannot
see." Preserve the tone and the crescendo. Start with the unemotional
definition, increase in intensity in the list of the saints of old who
showed heroic faith, and rise to the climax at "wherefore God is
not ashamed to be called their God."*

A reading from the letter to the Hebrews

Faith is confident assurance concerning what we hope for,
  and conviction about things we do not see.
Because of faith the men of old were approved by God.
By faith Abraham obeyed when he was called,
  and went forth to the place he was to receive as a heritage;
  he went forth, moreover, not knowing where he was going.
By faith he sojourned in the promised land as in a foreign country,
  dwelling in tents with Isaac and Jacob,
  heirs of the same promise;
    for he was looking forward to the city with foundations,
    whose designer and maker is God.
By faith Sarah received power to conceive
  though she was past the age,
    for she thought that the One who had made the promise
    was worthy of trust.

As a result of this faith, there came forth from one man,
    who was himself as good as dead,
        descendants as numerous as the stars in the sky
        and the sands of the seashore.

All of these died in faith.
They did not obtain what had been promised
    but saw and saluted it from afar.
By acknowledging themselves to be strangers and foreigners on the earth,
    they showed that they were seeking a homeland.
If they had been thinking back
    to the place from which they had come,
    they would have had the opportunity of returning there.
But they were searching for a better, a heavenly home.
Wherefore God is not ashamed to be called their God,
    for he has prepared a city for them.
By faith Abraham, when put to the test,
    offered up Í-saac;
    he who had received the promises
    was ready to sacrifice his only son, of whom it was said,
    "Through Í-saac shall your descendants be called."
He reasoned that God was able to raise from the dead,
    and so he received Í-saac back as a symbol.

    This is the Word of the Lord.

*Short Form: Hebrews 11, 1-2. 8-12   We will look for the city designed
and built by God.*

Faith is confident assurance concerning what we hope for,
    and conviction about things we do not see.
Because of faith the men of old were approved by God.
By faith Abraham obeyed when he was called,
    and went forth to the place he was to receive as a heritage;
    he went forth, moreover, not knowing where he was going.
By faith he sojourned in the promised land as in a foreign country,
    dwelling in tents with Í-saac and Jacob,
    heirs of the same promise;
    for he was looking forward to the city with foundations,
    whose designer and maker is God.
By faith Sarah received power to conceive
    though she was past the age,
    for she thought that the One who had made the promise
    was worthy of trust.

As a result of this faith, there came forth from one man,
   who was himself as good as dead,
   descendants as numerous as the stars in the sky
   and the sands of the seashore.

This is the Word of the Lord.

GOSPEL

*The cantor sings the alleluia and the people repeat it; the cantor then
sings the verse and the people repeat the alleluia. Otherwise the alleluia
may be omitted.*

Al - le - lu - ia.

O - pen our hearts, _ O _ Lord, _ to lis-ten to the words of your Son.

For other alleluia verses see pages 437, 438 and 439.

Long Form: Luke 12, 32-48 See that you are prepared.

*Jesus warns his disciples that we are God's servants, who must always
be ready at any time to obey his commands. Read with vigor.*

☩   A reading from the holy gospel according to Luke

Jesus said to his disciples: "Do not live in fear, little flock.
It has pleased your Father to give you the kingdom.
Sell what you have and give alms.
Get purses for yourselves that do not wear out,
   a never-failing treasure with the Lord
   which no thief comes near nor any moth destroys.
Wherever your treasure lies, there your heart will be.

"Let your belts be fastened around your waists
   and your lamps be burning ready.
Be like men awaiting their master's return from a wedding,
   so that when he arrives and knocks,
   you will open for him without delay.
It will go well with those servants
   whom the master finds wide-awake on his return.

I tell you, he will put on an apron, seat them at table,
    and proceed to wait on them.
Should he happen to come at midnight or before sunrise
    and find them prepared, it will go well with them.
You know as well as I
    that if the head of the house knew when the thief was coming
    he would not let him break into his house.
Be on guard, therefore.
The Son of Man will come when you least expect him."

Peter said, "Do you intend this parable for us, Lord,
    or do you mean it for the whole world?"
The Lord said, "Who in your opinion is that faithful, farsighted steward
    whom the master will set over his servants
    to dispense their ration of grain in season?
That servant is fortunate whom his master finds busy when he returns.
Assuredly, his master will put him in charge of all his property.
But if the servant says to himself,
'My master is taking his time about coming,'
    and begins to abuse the housemen and servant girls,
    to eat and drink and get drunk,
    that servant's master will come back on a day
    when he does not expect him,
    at a time he does not know.
He will punish him severely
    and rank him among those undeserving of trust.
The slave who knew his master's wishes
    but did not prepare to fulfill them
    will get a severe beating,
    whereas the one who did not know them
    and who nonetheless deserved to be flogged
    will get off with fewer stripes.
When much has been given a man,
    much will be required of him.
More will be asked of a man to whom more has been entrusted.

    This is the gospel of the Lord.

Short Form: Luke 12, 35-40 See that you are prepared.

✠ A reading from the holy gospel according to Luke

Jesus said to his disciples: "Let your belts be fastened around your waists
  and your lamps be burning ready.
Be like men awaiting their master's return from a wedding,
    so that when he arrives and knocks, you will open for him without
      delay.
It will go well with those servants whom the master finds wide-awake
    on his return.
I tell you, he will put on an apron, seat them at table,
    and proceed to wait on them.
Should he happen to come at midnight or before sunrise
    and find them prepared, it will go well with them.
You know as well as I
    that if the head of the house knew when the thief was coming
    he would not let him break into his house.
Be on guard, therefore.
The son of Man will come when you least expect him."

  This is the gospel of the Lord.

TWENTIETH SUNDAY OF THE YEAR

FIRST READING

Jeremiah 38, 4-6. 8-10   You bore me to be a man of strife for the whole world.

In the last days of Jerusalem, Jeremiah the prophet had advised the people to leave the city and make their peace with the Babylonian army. Thereupon, as the reading tells us, the princes tried to have him killed. Afterward Jeremiah urged the King Zedekiah to surrender to the enemy, but the princes would not allow this. As a result, Jerusalem was captured and destroyed, and Zedekiah was blinded and carried away in chains to Babylon. Read as an incident in history, which shows that God's servants must always expect to suffer for doing his will.

A reading from the book of the prophet Je-re-mí-ah

The princes said to the king:
    "Je-re-mí-ah ought to be put to death;
    he demoralizes the soldiers who are left in this city,
    and all the people, by speaking such things to them;
    he is not interested in the welfare of our people,
    but in their ruin."
King Ze-de-kí-ah answered:
    "He is in your power"; for the king could do nothing with them.
And so they took Je-re-mí-ah
    and threw him into the cistern of Prince Mal-chí-ah,
    which was in the quarters of the guard,
        letting him down with ropes.
There was no water in the cistern, only mud,
    and Jeremiah sank into the mud.

Ébed-mé-lech went to the Gate of Benjamin from the palace
    and said to the king:
"My lord king,
    these men have been at fault
    in all they have done to the prophet Je-re-mí-ah,
    casting him into the cistern.
He will die of famine on the spot,
    for there is no more food in the city."
Then the king ordered Ébed-mé-lech the Cúsh-ite
    to take three men along with him,
    and draw the prophet Je-re-mí-ah out of the cistern before he
        should die.

    This is the Word of the Lord.

RESPONSORIAL PSALM

*Psalm 40, 2. 3. 4. 18   After the reading the psalmist sings or says the
responsorial verse and all repeat it. This response is also repeated
after each verse of the psalm.*

Common response:

The   Lord   is   kind and   mer - ci - ful.

For other common responses see page 441.

Or:

℞. Lord, come to my aid!

I have waited, waited for the Lord,
   and he stooped toward me.   ℞.

The Lord heard my cry.
He drew me out of the pit of destruction,
   out of the mud of the swamp;
    He set my feet upon a crag;
     he made firm my steps.   ℞.

And he put a new song into my mouth,
   a hymn to our God.
Many shall look on in awe
   and trust in the Lord.   ℞.

Though I am afflicted and poor,
   yet the Lord thinks of me.
You are my help and my deliverer;
   O my God, hold not back!   ℞.

SECOND READING

Hebrews 12, 1-4   Let us bear patiently the struggle placed upon us.

An inspiring appeal that Christians shall endure their sufferings, since Jesus first suffered for us and is now in glory.

A reading from the letter to the Hebrews

Since we for our part are surrounded by a cloud of witnesses
    let us lay aside every encumbrance of sin which clings to us
    and persevere in running the race which lies ahead;
    let us keep our eyes fixed on Jesus,
    who inspires and perfects our faith.
For the sake of the joy which lay before him
    he endured the cross, heedless of its shame.
He has taken his seat at the right of the throne of God.
Remember how he endured the opposition of sinners;
    hence do not grow despondent or abandon the struggle.

    This is the Word of the Lord.

GOSPEL

The cantor sings the alleluia and the people repeat it; the cantor then sings the verse and the people repeat the alleluia. Otherwise the alleluia may be omitted.

Al - le - lu - ia.

Speak, O Lord, your ser - vant is lis - ten - ing; you ___ have the words of ev-er - last - ing life.

For other alleluia verses see pages 437, 438 and 439.

Luke 12, 49-53 I have come not to give peace, but discord.

Jesus warns his disciples that his message will not bring peace but a fire—both burning zeal in those who follow him and destruction from their enemies. A strong warning that Christianity is not an easy, comfortable faith. Read with vigor.

✟   A reading from the holy gospel according to Luke

Jesus said to his disciples:

"I have come to light a fire on the earth.
How I wish the blaze were ignited!
I have a baptism to receive.
What anguish I feel till it is over!
Do you think I have come to establish peace on the earth?
I assure you, the contrary is true; I have come for division.
From now on, a household of five will be divided
 three against two and two against three;
 father will be split against son and son against father,
 mother against daughter and daughter against mother,
 mother -in-law against daughter-in-law,
 daughter-in-law against mother-in-law."

This is the gospel of the Lord.

TWENTY-FIRST SUNDAY OF THE YEAR

FIRST READING

Isaiah 66, 18-21   They will gather all of your brothers from all nations.

*Read as an exalted vision of the end of the world when all nations,
and the Jews scattered throughout the world, will come together
to Jerusalem to worship the Lord.*

A reading from the book of the prophet I-saí-ah

I come to gather nations of every language;
    they shall come and see my glory.
I will set a sign among them;
    from them I will send fugitives to the nations:
    to Tár-shish, Put and Lud, Mó-soch, Tú-bal and Já-van,
    to the distant coastlands that have never heard of my fame,
    or seen my glory;
    and they shall proclaim my glory among the nations.
They shall bring all your brethren from all the nations
    as an offering to the Lord,
    on horses and in chariots, in carts, upon mules and dróm-e-da-ries,
    to Jerusalem, my holy mountain, says the Lord,
    just as the Ís-ra-el-ites bring their offering
    to the house of the Lord in clean vessels.
Some of these I will take as priests and Lé-vites, says the Lord.

This is the Word of the Lord.

RESPONSORIAL PSALM

*Psalm 117, 1. 2   After the reading the psalmist sings or says the responsorial
verse and all repeat it. This response is also repeated after each verse of
the psalm.*

Common Response:

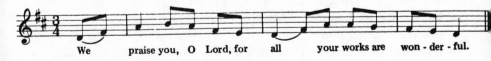

We   praise you, O Lord, for   all   your works are   won - der - ful.

For other common responses see page 441.

Or:

℞. Go out to all the world and tell the Good News.

Praise the Lord, all you nations;
　glorify him, all you peoples!   ℟.

For steadfast is his kindness toward us,
　and fidelity of the Lord endures forever.   ℟.

SECOND READING

Hebrews 12, 5-7. 11-13   The Lord disciplines those he loves.

*Your sufferings are part of God's discipline; they are a sign that
he loves you and treats you as his own children. Since this idea of
discipline is so contrary to most modern theories, state it very clearly.*

A reading from the letter to the Hebrews

You have forgotten the encouraging words addressed to you as sons:
　"My sons, do not disdain the discipline of the Lord
　　nor lose heart when he reproves you;
For, whom the Lord loves, he disciplines;
　he scourges every son he receives."

Endure your trials as the discipline of God,
　who deals with you as sons.
For what son is there whom his father does not discipline?
At the time it is administered,
　all discipline seems a cause for grief and not for joy,
　　but later it brings forth the fruit of peace and justice
　　to those who are trained in its school.

So strengthen your drooping hands and your weak knees.
Make straight the paths you walk on,
　that your halting limbs may not be dislocated but healed.

　This is the Word of the Lord.

GOSPEL

*The cantor sings the alleluia and the people repeat it; the cantor then
sings the verse and the people repeat the alleluia. Otherwise the alleluia
may be omitted.*

Al - le - lu - ia.

Your word, _ O Lord, _ is _ truth;make us ho - ly in _ the trut

For other alleluia verses see pages 437, 438 and 439.

Luke 13, 22-30 Men from the east and from the west will come to take their place in the kingdom of God.

Bring out the note of stern warning in these words of Jesus.

✠   A reading from the holy gospel according to Luke

Jesus went through cities and towns teaching
  —all the while making his way toward Jerusalem.
Someone asked him,
  "Lord, are they few in number who are to be saved? "
He replied: "Try to come in through the narrow door.
Many, I tell you, will try to enter and be unable.
When once the master of the house has risen to lock the door
  and you stand outside knocking and saying,
  'Sir, open for us,' he will say in reply,
  'I do not know where you come from.'
Then you will begin to say,
  'We ate and drank in your company.
You taught in our streets.'
But he will answer, 'I tell you, I do not know where you come from.
Away from me, you evildoers! '

"There will be wailing and grinding of teeth
  when you see Abraham, Isaac, Jacob,
  and all the prophets safe in the kingdom of God,
    and you yourselves rejected.
People will come from the east and the west,
  from the north and the south,
  and will take their place at the feast in the kingdom of God.
Some who are last will be first and some who are first will be last."

    This is the gospel of the Lord.

TWENTY-SECOND SUNDAY OF THE YEAR

FIRST READING

Sirach 3, 17-18. 20. 28-29   Humble yourself and you will find favor with the Lord.

As with other passages from this book, read each of these five proverbial sayings separately, making a full pause after each so that everyone can take it in.

A reading from the book of Sí-rach

My son, conduct your affairs with humility,
   and you will be loved more than a giver of gifts.
Humble yourself the more, the greater you are,
   and you will find favor with God.
What is too sublime for you, seek not,
   into things beyond your strength search not.
The mind of a sage appreciates proverbs,
   and an attentive ear is the wise man's joy.
Water quenches a flaming fire,
   and alms atone for sins.

   This is the Word of the Lord.

RESPONSORIAL PSALM

Psalm 68, 4-5. 6-7. 10-11   After the reading the psalmist sings or says the responsorial verse and all repeat it. This response is also repeated after each verse of the psalm.

Common response:

We   praise you, O Lord, for   all   your works are   won - der - ful.

For other common responses see page 441.

Or:

℞. God, in your goodness, you have made a home for the poor.

The just rejoice and exult before God;
    they are glad and rejoice.
Sing to God, chant praise to his name;
    whose name is the Lord.   ℞.

The father of orphans and the defender of widows
    is God in his holy dwelling.
God gives a home to the forsaken;
    he leads forth prisoners to prosperity.   ℞.

A bountiful rain you showered down, O God,
    upon your inheritance;
    you restored the land when it languished;
Your flock settled in it;
    in your goodness, O God, you provided it for the needy.   ℞.

SECOND READING

*Hebrews 12, 18-19. 22-24 You have come to Mount Zion and to the
city of the living God.*

*Show the contrast between the old covenant and the new. The
people below were in terror when Moses went up Mount Sinai to
commune with the Lord and to receive the old covenant. Now
because of the new covenant made through Jesus we go up to
Mount Zion with joy to be received by God. The key words are
"You have not drawn near an untouchable mountain. . . you
have drawn near to Mount Zion." As preparation for this reading,
study Exodus 19: 1-25.*

A reading from the letter to the Hebrews

You have not drawn near
   to an untouchable mountain and a blazing fire,
   and gloomy darkness and storm and trumpet blast,
   and a voice speaking words such that those who heard
   begged that they be not addressed to them.
No, you have drawn near to Mount Zí-on
   and the city of the living God, the heavenly Jerusalem,
   to myriads of angels in festal gathering,
   to the assembly of the first-born enrolled in heaven,
   to God the judge of all,
   to the spirits of just men made perfect,
   to Jesus, the mediator of a new covenant.

This is the Word of the Lord.

GOSPEL

*The cantor sings the alleluia and the people repeat it; the cantor then
sings the verse and the people repeat the alleluia. Otherwise the alleluia
may be omitted.*

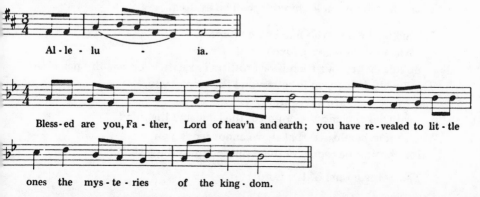

Al - le - lu - ia.

Bless-ed are you, Fa - ther, Lord of heav'n and earth; you have re - vealed to lit - tle

ones the mys - te - ries of the king - dom.

For other alleluia verses see pages 437, 438 and 439.

*Luke 14, 1. 7-14   The man who exalts himself shall be humbled and
he who humbles himself shall be exalted.*

*Convey the atmosphere of this scene.   Jesus had been invited to a
meal by one of the leading Pharisees—a formal occasion when the
guests are very conscious of their own importance, Jesus, as always,
has been observing closely; and he has noticed the jealous rivalry
for the chief places.   In the last section bring out the irony of Jesus'
words to his host—a man of great social standing who must have
wondered uneasily just how far Jesus meant his words to be taken
literally.*

✠ A reading from the holy gospel according to Luke

When Jesus came on a sabbath
    to eat a meal in the house of one of the leading Phár-i-sees,
    they observed him closely.

He went on to address a parable to the guests,
    noticing how they were trying to get the places of honor at the table:
    "When you are invited by someone to a wedding party,
    do not sit in the place of honor
    in case some greater dignitary has been invited.
Then the host might come and say to you,
    'Make room for this man,'
    and you would have to proceed shamefacedly to the lowest place.
What you should do when you have been invited
    is go and sit in the lowest place,
    so that when your host approaches you he will say,
    'My friend, come up higher.'
This will win you the esteem of your fellow guests.
For everyone who exalts himself shall be humbled
    and he who humbles himself shall be exalted."

He said to the one who had invited him:
    "Whenever you give a lunch or dinner,
    do not invite your friends or brothers or relatives or wealthy neighbors.
They might invite you in return and thus repay you.
No, when you have a reception,
    invite beggars and the crippled, the lame and the blind.
You should be pleased that they cannot repay you,
    for you will be repaid in the resurrection of the just."

    This is the gospel of the Lord.

TWENTY-THIRD SUNDAY OF THE YEAR

FIRST READING

Wisdom 9, 13-18   Who can comprehend the will of God?

An extract from Solomon's moving prayer that God will give him wisdom to be his guide. Wisdom is the image of God's goodness, enlightening the heart. An exalted expression of prayer, praise and blessing. Prepare by studying the whole chapter.

A reading from the book of Wisdom

For what man knows God's counsel,
　　or who can conceive what the Lord intends?
For the deliberations of mortals are timid,
　　and unsure are our plans.
For the corruptible body burdens the soul
　　and the earthen shelter weighs down the mind that has many concerns.
And scarce do we guess the things on earth,
　　and what is within our grasp we find with difficulty;
　　but when things are in heaven, who can search them out?
Or who ever knew your counsel, except you had given Wisdom
　　and sent your holy spirit from on high?
And thus were the paths of those on earth made straight.

　　This is the Word of the Lord.

RESPONSORIAL PSALM

Psalm 90, 3-4. 5-6. 12-13. 14-17 After the reading the psalmist sings or says the responsorial verse and all repeat it. This response is also repeated after each verse of the psalm.

Common response

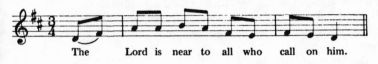

The   Lord is near to all who   call on him.

For other common responses see page 441.

Or:

℟. In every age, O Lord, you have been our refuge.

You turn man back to dust,
   saying, "Return, O children of men."
For a thousand years in your sight
   are as yesterday, now that it is past,
   or as a watch of the night.   ℟.

You make an end of them in their sleep;
   the next morning they are like the changing grass,
Which at dawn springs up anew,
   but by evening wilts and fades.   ℟.

Teach us to number our days aright,
   that we may gain wisdom of heart.
Return, O Lord! How long?
Have pity on your servants!   ℟.

Fill us at daybreak with your kindness,
   that we may shout for joy and gladness all our days.
And may the gracious care of the Lord our God be ours;
   prosper the work of our hands for us!
Prosper the work of our hands!   ℟.

SECOND READING

Philemon 9-10. 12-17   Receive him, not as a slave anymore, but as a very dear brother.

Paul's letter to Philemon is very short and personal. Philemon had a slave called Onesimus who ran away. Later Onesimus encountered Paul and was converted. Now Paul sends him back to his master, not as a slave but as a brother. Show the moving personal affection in this letter.

A reading from the letter of Paul to Phíl-e-mon

I, Paul, ambassador of Christ and now a prisoner for him,
  appeal to you for my child,
    whom I have begotten during my imprisonment.
It is he I am sending to you—
    and that means I am sending my heart!

I had wanted to keep him with me,
    that he might serve me in your place
    while I am in prison for the gospel;
      but I did not want to do anything without your consent,
      that kindness might not be forced on you but freely bestowed.
Perhaps he was separated from you for a while for this reason:
    that you might possess him forever,
    no longer as a slave but as more than a slave,
    a beloved brother, especially dear to me;
    and how much more than a brother to you,
      since now you will know him both as a man and in the Lord.

If then you regard me as a partner,
    welcome him as you would me.

   This is the Word of the Lord.

GOSPEL

The cantor sings the alleluia and the people repeat it; the cantor then sings the verse and the people repeat the alleluia. Otherwise the alleluia may be omitted.

Al - le - lu - ia.

Bless-ed is the king who   comes_ in the name of the Lord: peace on _

earth   and   glo - ry   in   heav - en.

For other alleluia verses see pages 437, 438 and 439.

Luke 14, 25-33   The man who does not renounce his possessions cannot be my disciple.

Jesus again warns those who would be his followers to count the cost before they commit themselves. They must be ready to give up everything. Emphasize the threefold repetition of the thought "you cannot be my disciples unless. . ."

✠ A reading from the holy gospel according to Luke

On one occasion when a great crowd was with Jesus,
> he turned to them and said,
> "If anyone comes to me without turning his back on his father
>   and mother,
> his wife and his children, his brothers and sisters,
> indeed his very self, he cannot be my follower.
Anyone who does not take up his cross and follow me cannot be
>   my disciple.
If one of you decides to build a tower,
> will he not first sit down and calculate the outlay
> to see if he has enough money to complete the project?
He will do that for fear of laying the foundation
> and then not being able to complete the work;
> at which all who saw it would then jeer at him, saying,
> 'That man began to build what he could not finish.'

"Or if a king is about to march on another king to do battle
>   with him,
> will he not sit down first and consider whether,
> with ten thousand men, he can withstand an enemy
> coming against him with twenty thousand?
If he cannot, he will send a delegation
> while the enemy is still at a distance,
> asking for terms of peace.
In the same way, none of you can be my disciple
> if he does not renounce all his possessions."

> This is the gospel of the Lord.

TWENTY-FOURTH SUNDAY OF THE YEAR

All three readings are concerned with God's mercy and forgiveness.

FIRST READING

Exodus 32, 7-11. 13-14 The Lord relented and did not send the evil he had threatened.

Moses had gone up Mount Sinai to commune with the Lord, when he is told that the people have made a golden calf and are sacrificing to it as their god. Tell the story with vigor stressing both the anger of the Lord and the pleading of Moses.

A reading from the book of Éx-o-dus

The Lord said to Moses,
   "Go down at once to your people,
   whom you brought out of the land of Egypt,
   for they have become depraved.
They have soon turned aside from the way I pointed out to them,
   making for themselves a molten calf and worshiping it,
   sacrificing to it and crying out,
   'This is your God, O Israel,
   who brought you out of the land of Egypt! '
I see how stiff-necked this people is,"
   continued the Lord to Moses.
"Let me alone, then,
   that my wrath may blaze up against them to consume them.
Then I will make of you a great nation."

But Moses implored the Lord, his God, saying,
   "Why, O Lord, should your wrath blaze up
   against your own people, whom you brought out of the land of Egypt
   with such great power and with so strong a hand?
Remember your servants Abraham, Í-saac and Israel,
   and how you swore to them by your own self, saying,
   'I will make your descendants as numerous as the stars
     in the sky;
   and all this land that I promised,
   I will give your descendants as their perpetual heritage.' "
So the Lord relented in the punishment
   he had threatened to inflict on his people.

   This is the Word of the Lord.

RESPONSORIAL PSALM

Psalm 51, 3-4. 12-13. 17. 19   After the reading the psalmist sings or says the responsorial verse and all repeat it. This response is also repeated after each verse of the psalm.

Common response:

The   Lord   is kind and   mer - ci - ful.

For other common responses see page 441.

Or:

℟. I will rise and go to my father.

Have mercy on me, O God, in your goodness;
    in the greatness of your compassion wipe out my offense.
Thoroughly wash me from my guilt
    and of my sin cleanse me.   ℟.

A clean heart create for me, O God,
    and a steadfast spirit renew within me.
Cast me not out from your presence,
    and your holy spirit take not from me.   ℟.

O Lord, open my lips,
    and my mouth shall proclaim your praise.
My sacrifice, O God, is a contrite spirit;
    a heart contrite and humble, O God, you will not spurn.   ℟.

SECOND READING

1 Timothy 1, 12-17   Christ came to save sinners.

*Paul sent Timothy to Ephesus to counter certain false doctrines
which were being put about by some who were converts from
the Jewish faith. In this opening section, Paul stresses the special
mercy by which he himself had been saved, and become thereby
an example of God's infinite patience and mercy. Read with feeling.*

A reading from the first letter of Paul to Timothy

I thank Christ Jesus our Lord, who has strengthened me,
    that he has made me his servant and judged me faithful.

I was once a blasphemer,
  a persecutor, a man filled with arrogance;
  but because I did not know what I was doing in my unbelief,
  I have been treated mercifully,
  and the grace of our Lord has been granted me
  in overflowing measure,
  along with the faith and love which are in Christ Jesus.
You can depend on this as worthy of full acceptance:
  that Christ Jesus came into the world to save sinners.
Of these I myself am the worst.
But on that very account I was dealt with mercifully,
  so that in me, as an extreme case,
  Jesus Christ might display all his patience,
  and that I might become an example to those
  who would later have faith in him and gain everlasting life.
To the King of ages, the inmortal, the invisible,
  the only God, be honor and glory forever and ever! Amen.

  This is the Word of the Lord.

GOSPEL

The cantor sings the alleluia and the people repeat it; the cantor then
sings the verse and the people repeat the alleluia. Otherwise the alleluia
may be omitted. Reference:

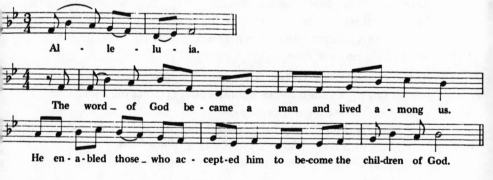

Al - le - lu - ia.

The word of God be-came a man and lived a-mong us.

He en-a-bled those who ac-cept-ed him to be-come the chil-dren of God.

For other alleluia verses see pages 437, 438 and 439.

Long Form: Luke 15, 1-32   There will be joy in heaven over one sinner
who does penance.

The Pharisees and scribes, being most orthodox in their conduct,
condemn Jesus because he is so friendly with sinners. He replies
with two short parables that underline the joy of bringing one
sinner to repentance. Then Luke records a third usually called
The Prodigal Son, which is more a short story than a parable. Read
it with zest as if the story was quite unfamiliar to your hearers. Bring
out the characters of the two brothers, and give slight extra emphsis
to the word 'one' in the final sentence.

✠ A reading from the holy gospel according to Luke

The tax collectors and sinners were all gathering around to hear Jesus,
　　at which the Pharisees and the scribes murmured,
　　"This man welcomes sinners and eats with them."
Then he addressed this parable to them:
　　"Who among you, if he has a hundred sheep
　　and loses one of them, does not leave the ninety-nine in the wasteland
　　and follow the lost one until he finds it?
And when he finds it, he puts it on his shoulders in jubilation.
Once arrived home, he invites friends and neighbors in
　　and says to them, 'Rejoice with me
　　because I have found my lost sheep.'
I tell you, there will likewise be more joy in heaven
　　over one repentant sinner than over ninety-nine righteous people
　　who have no need to repent.

"What woman, if she has ten silver pieces and loses one,
　　does not light a lamp and sweep the house in a diligent search
　　until she has retrieved what she lost?
And when she finds it, she calls in her friends and neighbors to say,
　　'Rejoice with me!   I have found the silver piece I lost. '
I tell you, there will be the same kind of joy before the angels
　　　of God
　　over one repentant sinner."

Jesus said to them: "A man had two sons.
The younger of them said to his father,
　　'Father, give me the share of the estate that is coming to me.'
So the father divided up the property.
Some days later this younger son collected all his belongings
　　and went off to a distant land,
　　where he squandered his money on dissolute living.

After he had spent everything,
    a great famine broke out in that country and he was in dire need.
So he attached himself to one of the propertied class of the place,
    who sent him to his farm to take care of the pigs.
He longed to fill his belly with the husks
    that were fodder for the pigs,
    but no one made a move to give him anything.
Coming to his senses at last, he said:
    'How many hired hands at my father's place have more than
        enough to eat,
    while here I am starving!
I will break away and return to my father, and say to him,
    "Father, I have sinned against God and against you;
    I no longer deserve to be called your son.
Treat me like one of your hired hands." '
With that he set off for his father's house.
While he was still a long way off,
    his father caught sight of him and was deeply moved.
He ran out to meet him,
    threw his arms around his neck, and kissed him.
The son said to him, 'Father, I have sinned against God and against
    you;
    I no longer deserve to be called your son.'
The father said to his servants:
    'Quick! bring out the finest robe and put it on him;
    put a ring on his finger and shoes on his feet.
Take the fatted calf and kill it.
Let us eat and celebrate
    because this son of mine was dead and has come back to life.
He was lost and is found.'
Then the celebration began.

"Meanwhile the elder son was out on the land.
As he neared the house on his way home,
    he heard the sound of music and dancing.
He called one of the servants
    and asked him the reason for the dancing and the music.
The servant answered, 'Your brother is home,
    and your father has killed the fatted calf
    because he has him back in good health.'
The son grew angry at this and would not go in;
    but his father came out and began to plead with him.

"He said in reply to his father:
    'For years now I have slaved for you.
I never disobeyed one of your orders,
    yet you never gave me so much as a kid goat to
    to celebrate with my friends.
Then, when this son of yours returns
    after having gone through your property with loose women,
    you kill the fatted calf for him.'

" 'My son,' replied the father, 'you are with me always,
    and everything I have is yours.
But we had to celebrate and rejoice!
This brother of yours was dead, and has come back to life.
He was lost, and is found.' "

    This is the gospel of the Lord.

*Short Form: Luke 15, 1-10 There will be joy in heaven over one sinner
who does penance.*

The tax collectors and sinners were all gathering around to hear Jesus,
    at which the Phár-i-sees and the scribes murmured,
    "This man welcomes sinners and eats with them."
Then he addressed this parable to them:
    "Who among you, if he has a hundred sheep
    and loses one of them, does not leave the ninety-nine in the wasteland
    and follow the lost one until he finds it?
And when he finds it, he puts it on his shoulders in jubilation.
Once arrived home, he invites friends and neighbors in
    and says to them, 'Rejoice with me
    because I have found my lost sheep.'
I tell you, there will likewise be more joy in heaven
    over one repentant sinner than over ninety-nine righteous people
    who have no need to repent.

"What woman, if she has ten silver pieces and loses one,
    does not light a lamp and sweep the house in a diligent search
    until she has retrieved what she lost?
And when she finds it, she calls in her friends and neighbors to say,
    'Rejoice with me! I have found the silver piece I lost.'
I tell you, there will be the same kind of joy before the angels of God
    over one repentant sinner."

    This is the gospel of the Lord.

TWENTY-FIFTH SUNDAY OF THE YEAR

FIRST READING

Amos 8, 4-7 The Lord God spoke against those who buy the poor for money.

Amos denounces those who swindle the poor. Then he imagines the business men in committee, discussing how they can extract greater profits by falsifying the weights, "even the refuse of the wheat will we sell!" In the last sentence this eager scheming is followed by the crashing denunciation.

A reading from the book of the prophet Á-mos

Hear this, you who trample upon the needy
    and destroy the poor of the land!
"When will the new moon be over," you ask,
   "that we may sell our grain,
   and the sabbath, that we may display the wheat?
We will diminish the éph-ah,
   add to the shekel,
   and fix our scales for cheating!
We will buy the lowly man for silver,
   and the poor man for a pair of sandals;
   even the refuse of wheat we will sell! "
The Lord has sworn by the pride of Jacob:
   Never will I forget a thing they have done!

   This is the Word of the Lord.

RESPONSORIAL PSALM

*Psalm 113, 1-2. 4-6. 7-8   After the reading the psalmist sings or says the
responsorial verse and all repeat it. This response is also repeated after
each verse of the psalm.*

Common response:

We   praise you, O Lord, for   all   your works are   won - der - ful.

For other common responses see page 441.

Or:

℟. Praise the Lord who lifts up the poor.

Praise, you servants of the Lord,
   praise the name of the Lord.
Blessed be the name of the Lord
   both now and forever.   ℟.

High above all nations is the Lord;
   above the heavens is his glory.
Who is like the Lord, our God, who is enthroned on high
   and looks upon the heavens and the earth below?   ℟.

He raises up the lowly from the dust;
   from the dunghill he lifts up the poor
To seat them with princes,
   with the princes of his own people.   ℟.

SECOND READING

*1 Timothy 2, 1-8   Let prayers be offered to God for everyone, for he
wishes that all men be saved.*

*Continuation from last Sunday of Paul's advice to Timothy. Pray
for all men, especially for those in authority—kings, the Roman Emperor
and his officials. This was important because the Romans regarded
Christans and Jews as one party; and the Jews were suspect as
likely to cause trouble. Besides, Paul adds, God loves everyone.
There is one God and Jesus Christ, mediator between God and
man. An earnest plea for quiet charity especially for those in
responsible positions.*

A reading from the letter of Paul to Tim-o-thy

First of all, I urge that petitions, prayers, intercessions,
  and thanksgivings be offered for all men,
  especially for kings and those in authority,
  that we may be able to lead
  undisturbed and tranquil lives in perfect piety and dignity.
Prayer of this kind is good, and God our savior is pleased with it,
  for he wants all men to be saved and come to know the truth.
And the truth is this:
  "God is one.
One also is the mediator between God and men,
  the man Christ Jesus,
  who gave himself as a ransom for all."
This truth was attested at the fitting time.
I have been made its herald and apostle

  (believe me, I am not lying but speak the truth),
  the teacher of the nations in the true faith.

It is my wish, then, that in every place
  the men shall offer prayers with blameless hands held aloft,
  and be free from anger and dissension.

  This is the Word of the Lord.

GOSPEL

*The cantor sings the alleluia and the people repeat it; the cantor then
sings the verse and the people repeat the alleluia. Otherwise the alleluia
may be omitted.*

Al - le - lu - ia.

O - pen our hearts, _ O __ Lord, _ to lis-ten to the words of your Son.

For other alleluia verses see pages 437, 438 and 439.

Long Form: Luke 16, 1-13   You cannot be slaves both of God and of money.

This is a difficult parable because on the surface it seems that Jesus,
who usually condemns riches as evil, is here apparently advising his
disciples on the worldly use of money. The reading is in three
sections. The first is the story of the dishonest manager who
schemes to prey on his master's debtors. His method is to persuade
them to falsify their accounts so that thereafter he may live on
blackmail. The owner, who is also somewhat of a sharp dealer,
admires such roguery. In the second section Jesus comments on
the prudent use of money to buy friends. The words are not
addressed to the disciples: rather they are ironical advise to the
worldly on how to get on. In the last section Jesus changes the
tone as Jesus turns to his own and warns them solemnly that
we cannot give ourselves to God and money.

✠ A reading from the holy gospel according to Luke

Jesus said to his disciples: "A rich man had a manager
   who was reported to him for dissipating his property.
He summoned him and said, 'What is this I hear about you?
Give me an account of your service, for it is about to come to an end.'
The manager thought to himself, 'What shall I do next?
My employer is sure to dismiss me.
I cannot dig ditches. I am ashamed to go begging.
I have it!   Here is a way to make sure
   that people will take me into their homes when I am let go.'

"So he called in each of his master's debtors, and said to the first,
   'How much do you owe my master? '
The man replied, 'A hundred jars of oil.'
The manager said, 'Take your invoice,
   sit down quickly, and make it fifty.'
Then he said to a second, 'How much do you owe? '
The answer came, 'A hundred measures of wheat,'
   and the manager said, 'Take your invoice and make it eighty.'

"The owner then gave his devious employee credit for being enterprising!
Why?   Because the worldly take more initiative than the other worldly
   when it comes to dealing with their own kind.

"What I say to you is this:
   Make friends for yourselves through your use of this world's
      goods,
   so that when they fail you, a lasting reception will be yours.
If you can trust a man in little things,
   you can also trust him in greater;
   while anyone unjust in a slight matter is also unjust in greater.
If you cannot be trusted with elusive wealth,
   who will trust you with lasting?
And if you have not been trustworthy with someone else's money,
   who will give you what is your own?

"No servant can serve two masters.
Either he will hate the one and love the other
   or be attentive to the one and despise the other.
You cannot give yourself to God and money."

   This is the gospel of the Lord.

Short Form: Luke 16, 10-13 You cannot be slaves both of God and of
money.

Jesus said to his disciples:
   "If you can trust a man in little things,
   you can also trust him in greater;
   while anyone unjust in a slight matter is also unjust in greater.
If you cannot be trusted with elusive wealth,
   who will trust you with lasting?
And if you have not been trustworthy with someone else's money,
   who will give you what is your own?

"No servant can serve two masters.
Either he will hate the one and love the other
   or be attentive to the one and despise the other.
You cannot give yourself to God and money."

   This is the gospel of the Lord.

TWENTY-SIXTH SUNDAY OF THE YEAR

FIRST READING

Amos 6, 1. 4-7   You who give yourself to licentiousness and revelry will be exiled.

Amos prophesied in the Kingdom of Israel shortly before its destruction. In this passage he denounces the selfish luxury of the rich and ends with a solemn warning of ruin shortly to come.

A reading from the book of the prophet Á-mos

Woe to the complacent in Zí-on!
Lying upon beds of ivory,
    stretched comfortably on their couches,
They eat lambs taken from the flock,
    and calves from the stall!
Improvising to the music of the harp,
    like David, they devise their own accompaniment.
They drink wine from bowls
    and anoint themselves with the best oils;
    yet they are not made ill by the collapse of Joseph!
Therefore, now they shall be the first to go into exile,
    and their wanton revelry shall be done away with.

This is the Word of the Lord.

RESPONSORIAL PSALM

Psalm 146, 7. 8-9. 9-10   After the reading the psalmist sings or says the responsorial verse and all repeat it. This response is also repeated after each verse of the psalm.

Common response:

We   praise you, O Lord, for   all   your works are   won - der - ful.

For other common responses see page 441.

Or:

℟. Praise the Lord, my soul!

Happy he who keeps faith forever,
    secures justice for the oppressed,

gives food to the hungry.
The Lord sets captives free.   ℟.

The Lord gives sight to the blind.
The Lord raises up those that were bowed down;
  The Lord loves the just.
The Lord protects strangers.   ℟.

The fatherless and the widow he sustains,
  but the way of the wicked he thwarts.
The Lord shall reign forever;
  your God, O Zion, through all generations. Alleluia.   ℟.

SECOND READING

1 Timothy 6, 11-16   Obey the commandments until the coming of the Lord.

*From the concluding passage of the letter, Paul exhorts Timothy
to continue to be an example of a good Christian. Read as if this
was a public charge to a leader assuming a great responsibility,
and bring out the key words distinctly 'integrity. . .' 'everlasting
life'. .I charge you'. End on a high note with the concluding words
of praise and honor to God: "He is the blessed. . .everlasting rule!
Amen."*

A reading from the first letter of Paul to Timothy

Man of God that you are, seek after integrity,
  piety, faith, love, steadfastness, and a gentle spirit.
Fight the good fight of faith.
Take firm hold on the everlasting life to which you were called
  when, in the presence of many witnesses,
  you made your noble profession of faith.
Before God, who gives life to all,
  and before Christ Jesus, who in bearing witness
  made his noble profession before Pontius Pilate,
  I charge you to keep God's command
  without blame or reproach until our Lord Jesus Christ shall appear.
This appearance God will bring to pass at his chosen time.
He is the blessed and only ruler,
  the King of kings and Lord of lords who alone has immortality
  and who dwells in inapproachable light,
  whom no human being has ever seen or can see.
To him be honor and everlasting rule! Amen.

  This is the Word of the Lord.

GOSPEL

The cantor sings the alleluia and the people repeat it; the cantor then sings the verse and the people repeat the alleluia. Otherwise the alleluia may be omitted.

Al - le - lu - ia.

If an-y-one loves me, he will hold to my words, and my

Fa - ther will love him and — we — will come — to him.

For other alleluia verses see pages 437, 438 and 439.

Luke 16, 19-31 During your life good things came your way just as bad things came the way of Lazarus. Now he is being comforted while you are in agony.

The parable of the rich man and the beggar (Dives and Lazarus) illustrates a theme frequent in Jesus' teaching—the danger of riches. After death the position of rich man and beggar is reversed. The rich man is now in torment, the beggar is the honored guest of Abraham the founder of the Jewish people. The phrase "resting in his bosom" sometimes causes difficulty. In formal banquets, the guests lay on couches, with the head propped on the left hand and arm. The most honored guest lay on the right side of his host, with his head leaning back on the host's breast. In the concluding passage Jesus is referring to the Pharisees who claimed that since they were the true followers of Abraham they were heirs to the blessings which God had promised. Jesus' words mean "You have had plenty of warning from Moses and the prophets, but you take no heed. Nor will you if I rise again from the dead." Read as an interesting story, but with a bitter ending.

✠ A reading from the holy gospel according to Luke

Jesus said to the Phár-i-sees:
  "Once there was a rich man who dressed in purple and linen
  and feasted splendidly every day.
At his gate lay a beggar named Láz-a-rus who was covered with sores.
Láz-a-rus longed to eat the scraps that fell from the rich man's table.
The dogs even came and licked his sores.
Eventually the beggar died.
He was carried by angels to the bosom of Abraham.
The rich man likewise died and was buried.
From the abode of the dead where he was in torment,
  he raised his eyes and saw Abraham afar off,
  and Láz-a-rus resting in his bosom.

"He called out, 'Father Abraham, have pity on me.
Send Láz-a-rus to dip the tip of his finger in water
  to refresh my tongue, for I am tortured in these flames.'
'My child,' replied Abraham,
  'remember that you were well off in your lifetime,
  while Láz-a-rus was in misery.
Now he has found consolation here,
  but you have found torment.
And that is not all.
Between you and us there is fixed a great abyss,
  so that those who might wish to cross from here to you cannot do so,
  nor can anyone cross from your side to us.'

" 'Father, I ask you, then,' the rich man said,
  'send him to my father's house where I have five brothers.
Let him be a warning to them
  so that they may not end in this place of torment.'
Abraham answered, 'They have Moses and the prophets.
Let them hear them.'
No, Father Abraham,' replied the rich man.
'But if someone would only go to them from the dead,
  then they would repent.'
Abraham said to him,
  'If they do not listen to Moses and the prophets,
  they will not be convinced even if one should rise from the dead.' "

  This is the gospel of the Lord.

TWENTY-SEVENTH SUNDAY OF THE YEAR

FIRST READING

Habakkuk 1, 2-3; 2, 2-4   The just man will live by his faithfulness.

Habbakuk prophesied just before the fall of Jerusalem; he was disgusted at the general depravity. In the first section (from chapter 1) he complains to the Lord for allowing such things to continue; in the second (from chapter 2) the Lord answers. The first eight lines are a cry of angry despair. At line 9 comes the answer. Read with force. As preparation read the two chapters in Habbakuk.

A reading from the book of the prophet Háb-ak-kuk

How long, O Lord? I cry for help
  but you do not listen!
I cry out to you, "Violence! "
  but you do not intervene.
Why do you let me see ruin;
  why must I look at misery?
Destruction and violence are before me;
  there is strife, and clamorous discord.
Then the Lord answered me and said:
  Write down the vision
  Clearly upon the tablets,
  so that one can read it readily.
For the vision still has its time,
  presses on to fulfillment, and will not disappoint;
  If it delays, wait for it,
  it will surely come, it will not be late.
The rash man has no integrity;
  but the just man, because of his faith, shall live.

  This is the Word of the Lord.

RESPONSORIAL PSALM

Psalm 95, 1-2. 6-7. 8-9   After the reading the psalmist sings or says the responsorial verse and all repeat it. This response is also repeated after each verse of the psalm.

Common response:

We   praise you, O Lord, for all   your works are won - der - ful.

For other common responses see page 441.

Or:

R̈. If today you hear his voice, harden not your hearts.

Come, let us sing joyfully to the Lord;
 let us acclaim the Rock of our salvation.
Let us greet him with thanksgiving;
 let us joyfully sing psalms to him.   R̈.

Come, let us bow down in worship;
 let us kneel before the Lord who made us.
For he is our God,
 and we are the people he shepherds, the flock he guides.   R̈.

Oh, that today you would hear his voice:
 "Harden not your hearts as at Mer-í-bah,
 as in the day of Más-sah in the desert,
Where your fathers tempted me;
 they tested me though they had seen my works.   R̈.

SECOND READING

2 Timothy 1, 6-8. 13-14   Never be ashamed of witnessing the Lord.

*The second letter to Timothy was written by Paul when a
prisoner in Rome, awaiting trial and expecting execution.
Convey the powerful feeling of urgency in Paul's words.*

A reading from the second letter of Paul to Timothy

I remind you to stir into flame
 the gift of God bestowed when my hands were laid on you.
The Spirit God has given us is no cowardly spirit,
 but rather one that makes us strong, loving and wise.
Therefore, never be ashamed of your testimony to our Lord,
 nor of me, a prisoner for his sake;
 but with the strength which comes from God
 bear your share of the hardship which the gospel entails.

Take as a model of sound teaching what you have heard me say,
 in faith and love in Christ Jesus.
Guard the rich deposit of faith
 with the help of the Holy Spirit who dwells within us.

This is the Word of the Lord.

GOSPEL

*The cantor sings the alleluia and the people repeat it; the cantor then
sings the verse and the people repeat the alleluia. Otherwise the alleluia
may be omitted.*

Al - le - lu - ia.

I call you my friends, — says the Lord, for I have made known to

you all that the Fa - ther has told _____ me.

For other alleluia verses see pages 437, 438 and 439.

Luke 17, 5-10 If you had faith!

*Two separate sayings of Jesus. The first is a strong and
surprising statement on the power of prayer. The second reminds
man that since he is God's servant he is so bound to do everything
that God commands. Stress the last sentence.*

✠ A reading from the holy gospel according to Luke

The apostles said to the Lord,
    "Increase our faith," and he answered:
    "If you had faith the size of a mustard seed,
    you could say to this sycamore, 'Be uprooted
    and transplanted into the sea,'
    and it would obey you.

"If one of you had a servant plowing or herding sheep
    and he came in from the fields,
    would you say to him, 'Come and sit down at table'?
Would you not rather say, 'Prepare my supper.
Put on your apron and wait on me while I eat and drink.
You can eat and drink afterward'?
Would he be grateful to the servant
    who was only carrying out his orders?
It is quite the same with you who hear me.
When you have done all you have been commanded to do,
    say, 'We are useless servants.
We have done no more than our duty.' "

    This is the gospel of the Lord.

TWENTY-EIGHTH SUNDAY OF THE YEAR

FIRST READING

2 Kings 5, 14-17 He returned to Naaman and acknowledged the Lord to this man of God.

Prepare by reading the whole story of Naaman the Syrian General —one of the best stories in the books of Kings (2 Kings chap. 5). Here only four verses from the end of the story are read; they show the gratitude of a man cured of leprosy for God's mercy; they have therefore some connection with today's gospel. Naaman's desire to carry away some of the earth of Palestine is that he may, as it were, hereafter worship the Lord on his own soil.

A reading from the second book of Kings

Ná-a-man went down and plunged into the Jordan seven times
    at the word of El-í-sha, the man of God.
His flesh became again like the flesh of a little child,
    and he was clean [of his leprosy].

He returned with his whole retinue to the man of God.
On his arrival he stood before him and said,
    "Now I know that there is no God in all the earth,
        except in Israel.
Please accept a gift from your servant."

"As the Lord lives whom I serve, I will not take it," El-í-sha replied;
    and despite Ná-a-man's urging, he still refused.
Ná-a-man said: "If you will not accept,
    please let me, your servant, have two mule-loads of earth,
    for I will no longer offer holocaust or sacrifice
    to any other god except to the Lord."

This is the Word of the Lord.

RESPONSORIAL PSALM

Psalm 98, 1. 2-3. 3-4 After the reading the psalmist sings or says the
responsorial verse and all repeat it. This response is also repeated
after each verse of the psalm.

Common response:

Sing   to   the Lord a   new   song.

For other common responses see page 441.

Or: .

℟. The Lord has revealed to the nations his saving power.

Sing to the Lord a new song,
    for he has done wondrous deeds;
      His right hand has won victory for him, his holy arm.   ℟.

The Lord has made his salvation known:
    in the sight of the nations he has revealed his justice.
He has remembered his kindness and his faithfulness
    toward the house of Israel.   ℟.

All the ends of the earth have seen
    the salvation by our God.
Sing joyfully to the Lord, all you lands:
    break into song; sing praise.   ℟.

SECOND READING

2 Timothy 2, 8-13 If we hold firm, we shall reign with Christ.

Continuation of Paul's exhortation to Timothy. In the first words
he sums up the meaning of the gospel: Jesus was descended
from David and so was the Messiah; he rose from the dead. As
a result we are saved. The four lines "If we have died. . . with him"
are a quotation from an early Christian hymn. Bring out the feeling
of tranquil faith in Paul's words.

A reading from the letter of Paul to Timothy

Remember that Jesus Christ, a descendant of David,
   was raised from the dead.
This is the gospel I preach;
   in preaching it I suffer as a criminal,
   even to the point of being thrown into chains—
   but there is no chaining the word of God!
Therefore I bear with all of this
   for the sake of those whom God has chosen,
   in order that they may obtain the salvation
   to be found in Christ Jesus and with it eternal glory.

You can depend on this:
   If we have died with him
   we shall also live with him;
   If we hold out to the end
   we shall also reign with him.
But if we deny him he will deny us.
If we are unfaithful he will still remain faithful;
   for he cannot deny himself.

   This is the Word of the Lord.

GOSPEL

*The cantor sings the alleluia and the people repeat it; the cantor then
sings the verse and the people repeat the alleluia. Otherwise the alleluia
may be omitted.*

Al - le - lu - ia.

May the Fa - ther of our Lord, — Je - sus Christ, — en - light - en the

eyes of our hearts that we might see how great — is the hope to which we are called.

For other alleluia verses see pages 437, 438 and 439.

Luke 17, 11-19 It seems that no one has returned to give thanks to God except this stranger.

Continuation of last Sunday's gospel. Convey the sadness of Jesus that only one of those healed came back to show thanks, and his joy in the Samaritan; and stress the last words, which so often recur in the gospels —"your faith has saved you."

✝   A reading from the holy gospel according to Luke

On his journey to Jerusalem Jesus passed along the borders of Sa-má-ri-a
    and Gál-i-lee.
As he was entering a village, ten lepers met him.
Keeping their distance, they raised their voices and said,
    "Jesus, Master, have pity on us! "
When he saw them, he responded,
    "Go and show yourselves to the priests."
On their way there they were cured.
One of them, realizing that he had been cured,
    came back praising God in a loud voice.
He threw himself on his face at the feet of Jesus
    and spoke his praises.
This man was a Sa-má-ri-tan.

Jesus took the occasion to say,
    "Were not all ten made whole?
Where are the other nine?
Was there no one to return and give thanks to God except this foreigner? "
He said to the man, "Stand up and go your way;
    your faith has been your salvation."

    This is the gospel of the Lord.

TWENTY-NINTH SUNDAY OF THE YEAR

FIRST READING

Exodus 17, 8-13   As long as Moses kept his arms raised, Israel had the advantage.

An episode during the desert wanderings of the people of Israel. Tell as a traditional tale of Moses, of God's dealings with his people, and the power of prayer.

A reading from the book of Éx-o-dus

Ám-a-lek came and waged war against Israel.
Moses, therefore, said to Jósh-u-a,
   "Pick out certain men, and tomorrow go out and engage
     Ám-a-lek in battle.
I will be standing on top of the hill
   with the staff of God in my hand."
So Jósh-u-a did as Moses told him:
   he engaged Ám-a-lek in battle
     after Moses had climbed to the top of the hill with Á-ar-on and Húr.
As long as Moses kept his hands raised up,
   Israel had the better of the fight,
   but when he let his hands rest,
   Ám-a-lek had the better of the fight.
Moses' hands, however, grew tired;
   so they put a rock in place for him to sit on.
Meanwhile Á-ar-on and Húr supported his hands,
   one on one side and one on the other,
   so that his hands remained steady till sunset.
And Jósh-u-a mowed down Ám-a-lek and his people
   with the edge of the sword.

   This is the Word of the Lord.

RESPONSORIAL PSALM

Psalm 121, 1-2. 3-4. 5-6. 7-8   After the reading the psalmist sings or says the responsorial verse and all repeat it. This response is also repeated after each verse of the psalm.

Common response:

The   Lord   is kind and   mer - ci - ful.

For other common responses see page 441.

Or:

℟. Our help is from the Lord who made heaven and earth.

I lift up my eyes toward the mountains;
  whence shall help come to me?
My help is from the Lord,
  who made heaven and earth.   ℟.

May he not suffer your foot to slip;
  may he slumber not who guards you:
Indeed he neither slumbers nor sleeps,
  the guardian of Israel.   ℟.

The Lord is your guardian; the Lord is your shade;
  he is beside you at your right hand.
The sun shall not harm you by day,
  nor the moon by night.   ℟.

The Lord will guard you from all evil;
  he will guard your life.
The Lord will guard your coming and your going,
  both now and forever.   ℟.

SECOND READING

*2 Timothy 3, 14-4, 2   This is how the man of God becomes equipped
and ready for every good work.*

*Continuation of Paul's exhortation to Timothy. He strongly
urges Timothy to regard the scriptures as inspired by God, and
the source of all wisdom. The whole is a powerful appeal with
special stress on the last two sentences — "In the presence of
God. . ." — a most solemn charge that Timothy shall never falter
in his duty of preaching the gospel.*

A reading from the second letter of Paul to Timothy

You must remain faithful to what you have learned and believed,
   because you know who your teachers were.
Likewise, from your infancy you have known the sacred Scriptures,
   the source of the wisdom
      which through faith in Jesus Christ leads to salvation.
All Scripture is inspired of God and is useful for teaching—
   for reproof, correction, and training in holiness
   so that the man of God may be fully competent
   and equipped for every good work.
In the presence of God and of Christ Jesus,
   who is coming to judge the living and the dead,
   and by his appearing and his kingly power,
   I charge you to preach the word,
   to stay with this task whether convenient or inconvenient
   —correcting, reproving, appealing—
   constantly teaching and never losing patience.

This is the Word of the Lord.

GOSPEL

*The cantor sings the alleluia and the people repeat it; the cantor then
sings the verse and the people repeat the alleluia. Otherwise the alleluia
may be omitted.*

Al - le - lu - ia.

Your words, O Lord, __ are __ spir - it and life, __

you have the words of ev - er - last - ing life.

For other alleluia verses see pages 437, 438 and 439.

Luke 18, 1-8   God will see those who cry to him vindicated.

*Jesus insists that we must not cease from prayer to God for help,
illustrated by the story of the corrupt judge. Underline the meaning
by giving increased weight to the last section; "Will not God. . .swift
justice." But the reading ends on a note of sadness, with the key word
word "any faith."*

✟ A reading from the holy gospel according to Luke

Jesus told his disciples a parable
   on the necessity of praying always and not losing heart:
   "Once there was a judge in a certain city who respected neither
     God nor man.
A widow in that city kept coming to him saying,
   'Give me my rights against my opponent.'
For a time he refused, but finally he thought,
   'I care little for God or man,
   but this widow is wearing me out.
I am going to settle in her favor
   or she will end by doing me violence.' "
The Lord said, "Listen to what the corrupt judge has to say.
Will not God then do justice to his chosen
   who call out to him day and night?
Will he delay long over them, do you suppose?
I tell you, he will give them swift justice.
But when the Son of Man comes,
   will he find any faith on the earth? "

   This is the gospel of the Lord.

THIRTIETH SUNDAY OF THE YEAR

FIRST READING

Sirach 35, 12-14. 16-18   The prayer of the humble man will penetrate the heavens.

From a chapter on the justice of God who (unlike some human judges) listens to the humble. Read each couplet as a separate saying, with a pause after each.

A reading from the book of Sí-rach

The Lord is a God of justice,
  who knows no favorites.
Though not unduly partial toward the weak,
  yet he hears the cry of the oppressed.
He is not deaf to the wail of the orphan,
  nor to the widow when she pours out her complaint.

He who serves God willingly is heard;
  his petition reaches the heavens.
The prayer of the lowly pierces the clouds;
  it does not rest till it reaches its goal,
Nor will it withdraw till the Most High responds,
  judges justly and affirms the right.

  This is the Word of the Lord.

RESPONSORIAL PSALM

Psalm 34, 2-3. 17-18. 19. 23   After the reading the psalmist sings or says the responsorial verse and all repeat it. This response is also repeated after each verse of the psalm.

Common response:

Praise the   Lord   for he is   good.

For other common responses see page 441.

Or:

℟. The Lord hears the cry of the poor.

I will bless the Lord at all times;
   his praise shall be ever in my mouth.
Let my soul glory in the Lord;
   the lowly will hear me and be glad.   ℟.

The Lord confronts the evildoers,
   to destroy remembrance of them from the earth.
When the just cry out, the Lord hears them,
   and from all their distress he rescues them.   ℟.

The Lord is close to the brokenhearted;
   and those who are crushed in spirit he saves.
The Lord redeems the lives of his servants;
   no one incurs guilt who takes refuge in him.   ℟.

SECOND READING

2 Timothy 4, 6-8. 16-18   All that remains is the crown of righteousness reserved for me.

Continuation from last Sunday. Paul senses that he is near the end of his labors, and he looks back happily on a mission faithfully completed. Express the dignity of this farewell, and continue in a more personal tone as Paul relates what happened at his trial. End on the same high note as the beginning.

A reading from the second letter of Paul to Timothy

I am already being poured out like a libation.
The time of my dissolution is near.
I have fought the good fight, I have finished the race,
 I have kept the faith.
From now on a merited crown awaits me;
 on that Day the Lord, just judge that he is, will award it to me—
 and not only to me but to all
 who have looked for his appearing with eager longing.

At the first hearing of my case in court, no one took my part.
In fact, everyone abandoned me.
May it not be held against them!
But the Lord stood by my side and gave me strength,
 so that through me the preaching task might be completed
 and all the nations might hear the gospel.
That is how I was saved from the lion's jaws.
The Lord will continue to rescue me
 from all attempts to do me harm
 and will bring me safe to his heavenly kingdom.
To him be glory forever and ever. Amen.

 This is the Word of the Lord.

GOSPEL

*The cantor sings the alleluia and the people repeat it; the cantor then
sings the verse and the people repeat the alleluia. Otherwise the alleluia
may be omitted.*

Al - le - lu - ia.

I am the light of the world, — says the Lord; the
man who fol-lows me will have the light — of life.

For other alleluia verses see pages 437, 438 and 439.

Luke 18, 9-14   The publican returned home justified; the pharisee did not.

The parable of the Pharisee and the tax collector (once called the Publican). As often Jesus condemns the Pharisees for their self righteousness in religion and their certainty that God loves them all as he parodies the man's complacent prayer. Compared with this Pharisee, the tax collector, whom all orthodox Jews despised as an utter sinner, finds mercy in the sight of God because he is humble and penitent. Contrast the tone of the Pharisee's prayer with the almost whispered words of the tax collector. End with strong stress on "the other did not." Emphasize the final judgment.

✠ A reading from the holy gospel according to Luke

Jesus spoke this parable
    addressed to those who believed in their own self-righteousness
    while holding everyone else in contempt:
    "Two men went up to the temple to pray;
    one was a Phár-i-see, the other a tax collector.
The Phár-i-see with head unbowed prayed in this fashion:
    'I give you thanks, O God, that I am not like the rest of men—
    grasping, crooked, adulterous—or even like this tax collector.
I fast twice a week. I pay tithes on all I possess.'
The other man, however, kept his distance,
    not even daring to raise his eyes to heaven.
All he did was beat his breast and say,
    'O God, be merciful to me, a sinner.'
Believe me, this man went home from the temple justified
    but the other did not.
For everyone who exalts himself shall be humbled
    while he who humbles himself shall be exalted."

    This is the gospel of the Lord.

THIRTY-FIRST SUNDAY OF THE YEAR

FIRST READING

Wisdom 11, 23-12, 2 *You have mercy on all things because you love everything that exists.*

A hymn of praise for God's infinite love for the creatures he has created. Convey the overwhelming emotion of this expression of humility, gratitude and wonder.

A reading from the book of Wisdom

You have mercy on all, because you can do all things;
   and you overlook the sins of men that they may repent.
For you love all things that are
   and loathe nothing that you have made;
   for what you hated, you would not have fashioned.
And how could a thing remain, unless you willed it;
   or be preserved, had it not been called forth by you?
But you spare all things, because they are yours,
   O Lord and lover of souls,
   for your imperishable spirit is in all things!
Therefore you rebuke offenders little by little,
   warn them and remind them of the sins they are committing,
   that they may abandon their wickedness
   and believe in you, O Lord!

   This is the Word of the Lord.

RESPONSORIAL PSALM

Psalm 145, 1-2. 8-9. 10-11. 13. 14 After the reading the psalmist sings or
says the responsorial verse and all repeat it. This response is also repeated
after each verse of the psalm.

Common response:

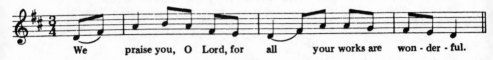

We praise you, O Lord, for all your works are won - der - ful.

For other common responses see page 441.

Or:

℟. I will praise your name for ever, my king and my God.

I will extol you, O my God and King,
    and I will bless your name forever and ever.
Every day will I bless you,
    and I will praise your name forever and ever. ℟.

The Lord is gracious and merciful,
    slow to anger and of great kindness.
The Lord is good to all
    and compassionate toward all his works. ℟.

Let all your works give you thanks, O Lord,
    and let your faithful ones bless you
Let them discourse of the glory of your kingdom
    and speak of your might. ℟.

The Lord is faithful in all his words
    and holy in all his works.
The Lord lifts up all who are falling
    and raises up all who are bowed down. ℟.

SECOND READING

2 Thessalonians 1, 11-2, 2   The name of our Lord Jesus Christ will be glorified in you and you in him.

Paul first visited Thessalonica on his second missionary journey His preaching of the gospel caused trouble with the Jewish community, who after his departure began to persecute the converts. From Corinth, Paul wrote two letters to the Thessalonians. The second was to direct them in the matter of Christ's second coming which was troubling some. Do not believe, says he, every false rumor, or 'reliable source'; we do not know the answer. Read as a calming reply to an anxious inquiry.

A reading from the second letter of Paul to the Thes-sa-ló-ni-ans

We pray for you always that our God may make you worthy of his call,
   and fulfill by his power every honest intention and work of faith.
In this way the name of our Lord Jesus
   may be glorified in you and you in him,
      in accord with the gracious gift of our God and of the Lord Jesus Christ.

On the question of the coming of our Lord Jesus Christ
   and our being gathered to him, we beg you, brothers
   not to be so easily agitated or terrified,
   whether by an oracular utterance or rumor
   or a letter alleged to be ours,
   into believing that the day of the Lord is here.

   This is the Word of the Lord.

GOSPEL

The cantor sings the alleluia and the people repeat it; the cantor then sings the verse and the people repeat the alleluia. Otherwise the alleluia may be omitted.

Al - le - lu - ia.

Be faith-ful un - til death, says the Lord, and — I — will —

give — you the crown — of life. —

For other alleluia verses see page 440.

An account of a homely event in Jesus' life. Show the eagerness of Zacchaeus; his excitement at Jesus' visit; the disgust of the orthodox and respectable; and the happy ending.

Luke 19, 1-10   *The Son of Man came to seek and to find that which was lost.*

✠ A reading from the holy gospel according to Luke

Jesus, upon entering Jér-i-cho, passed through the city.
There was a man there named Zach-áe-us,
    the chief tax collector and a wealthy man.
He was trying to see what Jesus was like,
    but being small of stature, was unable to do so because of the crowd.
He first ran on in front,
    then climbed a sycamore tree which was along Jesus' route,
    in order to see him.
When Jesus came to the spot he looked up and said,
    "Zach-áe-us, hurry down. I mean to stay at your house today."
He quickly descended, and welcomed him with delight.
When this was observed, everyone began to murmur,
    "He has gone to a sinner's house as a guest."
Zach-áe-us stood his ground and said to the Lord:
    "I give half my belongings, Lord, to the poor.
If I have defrauded anyone in the least, I pay him back fourfold."
Jesus said to him:
    "Today salvation has come to this house,
    for this is what it means to be a son of Á-bra-ham.
The Son of Man has come to search out and save what was lost."

    This is the gospel of the Lord.

THIRTY-SECOND SUNDAY OF THE YEAR

FIRST READING

2 Maccabees 7, 1-2. 9-14 The king of the world will receive us into life eternal at the resurrection.

The heroic behavior of a Jewish family during the brutal persecution in the time of Antiochus Epiphanes who tried to destroy the Jewish religion. Bring out not only the courage of the victims but also their strong belief in a life to come. As preparation, read the whole chapter.

A reading from the second book of Mác-ca-bees

It happened that seven brothers with their mother
    were arrested and tortured with whips and scourges by the king,
    to force them to eat pork in violation of God's law.
One of the brothers, speaking for the others, said:
    "What do you expect to achieve by questioning us?
We are ready to die rather than transgress the laws of our ancestors."

At the point of death the second brother said:
    "You accursed fiend, you are depriving us of this present life,
    but the King of the world will raise us up to live again forever.
It is for his laws that we are dying."

After him the third suffered their cruel sport.
He put out his tongue at once when told to do so,
    and bravely held out his hands, as he spoke these noble words:
    "It was from Heaven that I received these;
    for the sake of his laws I disdain them;
    from him I hope to receive them again."
Even the king and his attendants marveled at the young man's courage,
    because he regarded his sufferings as nothing.

After he had died,
    they tortured and maltreated the fourth brother in the same way.
When he was near death, he said,
    "It is my choice to die at the hands of men
    with the God-given hope of being restored to life by him;
    but for you, there will be no resurrection to life."

This is the Word of the Lord.

RESPONSORIAL PSALM

Psalm 17, 1. 5-6. 8. 15   After the reading the psalmist sings or says the
responsorial verse and all repeat it. This response is also repeated
after each verse of the psalm.

Common response:

The   Lord is   near to   all who   call   on him.

For other common responses see page 441.

Or:

℟. Lord, when your glory appears, my joy will be full.

Hear, O Lord, a just suit;
    attend to my outcry;
       hearken to my prayer from lips without deceit.   ℟.

My steps have been steadfast in your paths,
    my feet have not faltered.
I call upon you, for you will answer me, O God;
    incline your ear to me; hear my word.   ℟.

Keep me as the apple of your eye,
    hide me in the shadow of your wings.
But I in justice shall behold your face;
    on waking I shall be content in your presence.   ℟.

SECOND READING

2 Thessalonians 2, 16-3, 5   May the Lord strengthen you in everything
good that you do or say.

From the final section of the letter. Words of encouragement
and hope for converts who are suffering from doubts raised by
false teachers. Paul's message is that God will strengthen them.
He asks them to pray for him. A message of hope.

A reading from the second letter of Paul to the Thes-sa-ló-ni-ans

May our Lord Jesus Christ himself,
  may God our Father who loved us
  and in his mercy gave us eternal consolation and hope,
  console your hearts and strengthen them
  for every good work and word.

For the rest, brothers, pray for us
  that the word of the Lord may make progress
  and be hailed by many others, even as it has been by you.
Pray that we may be delivered from confused and evil men.
For not everyone has faith,
  but the Lord keeps faith;
  he it is who will strengthen you and guard you against the evil one.
In the Lord we are confident that you are doing
  and will continue to do whatever we enjoin.
May the Lord rule your hearts
  in the love of God and the constancy of Christ.

  This is the Word of the Lord.

GOSPEL

*The cantor sings the alleluia and the people repeat it; the cantor then
sings the verse and the people repeat the alleluia. Otherwise the alleluia
may be omitted.*

Al - le - lu - ia.

Be watch-ful, pray _ con-stant-ly that you _ may be wor - thy to

stand be - fore the Son _ of Man. _

For other alleluia verses see page 440.

Long Form: Luke 20, 27-38 He is not a God of the dead but of the living.

*The Sadducees accepted the scriptures but rejected the strict
interpretations and traditions of the Pharisees; they were not
opposed to foreigners and they did not believe in any resurrection.*

*They try to confuse Jesus by this theoretical problem of a
woman who had seven husbands. He refutes them out of one
of the most important passages in the Old Testament: the direct
call of Moses in the desert when God spoke to him from the
burning bush: "I am the God of your father, the God of Abraham,
the God of Isaac, the God of Jacob." Show the decisive authority
of Jesus' answer.*

✝ A reading from the holy gospel according to Luke

Some Sád-du-cees came forward
   (the ones who claim there is no resurrection)
   to pose this problem to Jesus:
   "Master, Moses prescribed that if a man's brother dies
   leaving a wife and no child,
   the brother should marry the widow and raise posterity to his brother.
Now there were seven brothers.
The first one married and died childless.
Next, the second brother married the widow,
   then the third, and so on.
All seven died without leaving her any children.
Finally the widow herself died.
At the resurrection, whose wife will she be?
Remember, seven married her.

Jesus said to them:
   "The children of this age marry and are given in marriage,
   but those judged worthy of a place in the age to come
   and of resurrection from the dead do not.
They become like angels and are no longer liable to death.
Sons of the resurrection, they are sons of God.
Moses in the passage about the bush
   showed that the dead rise again when he called the Lord the God
     of Abraham,
   and the God of Í-saac, and the God of Jacob.
God is not the God of the dead but of the living.
All are alive for him."

   This is the gospel of the Lord.

Short Form: Luke 20, 27. 34-38   He is not a God of the dead but of the living.

Some Sád-du-cees came forward (the ones who claim there is
   no resurrection).

Jesus said to them: "The children of this age marry and are
   given in marriage,
  but those judged worthy of a place in the age to come
  and of resurrection from the dead do not.
They become like angels and are no longer liable to death.
Sons of the resurrection, they are sons of God.
Moses in the passage about the bush
  showed that the dead rise again when he called the Lord
    God of Abraham,
  and the God of Í-saac, and the God of Jacob.
God is not the God of the dead but of the living.
All are alive for him."

   This is the gospel of the Lord.

THIRTY-THIRD SUNDAY OF THE YEAR

FIRST READING

Malachi 3, 19-20   The sun of righteousness will shine on you.

The short prophecy of Malachi was composed after the exiles had returned from Babylon and religious life in Jerusalem was in chaos. Malachi begins in denunciation but ends with the prophecy that God will send a messenger to prepare the way. Show that these verses were a prophecy of the Messiah whose feast we are soon to celebrate on Christmas Day.

A reading from the book of the prophet Mál-a-chi

Lo, the day is coming, blazing like an oven,
>   when all the proud and all evildoers will be stubble,
And the day that is coming will set them on fire,
>   leaving them neither root nor branch,
>   says the Lord of hosts.
But for you who fear my name, there will arise
>   the sun of justice with its healing rays.

>   This is the Word of the Lord.

RESPONSORIAL PSALM

Psalm 98, 5-6. 7-8. 9   After the reading the psalmist sings or says the responsorial verse and all repeat it. This response is also repeated after each verse of the psalm.

Common response:

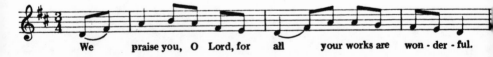

We   praise you, O Lord, for   all   your works are   won - der - ful.

For other common responses see page 441.

Or:

℟. The Lord comes to rule the earth with justice.

Sing praise to the Lord with the harp,
>   with the harp and melodious song.
With trumpets and the sound of the horn
>   sing joyfully before the King, the Lord.   ℟.

Let the sea and what fills it resound,
  the world and those who dwell in it;
Let the rivers clap their hands,
  the mountains shout with them for joy.   ℟.

Before the Lord, for he comes,
  for he comes to rule the earth,
He will rule the world with justice
  and the peoples with equity.   ℟.

SECOND READING

2 Thessalonians 3, 7-12   If anyone refuses to work then do not let him eat.

From the concluding words of Paul's letter. Some of the Thessalonians, professing to believe that the second coming of Christ was due at any moment, stopped working and were relying on their neighbors for support. Paul denounced this abuse. On his journeys he always supported himself by working at his trade. A straight command that every Christian must work for his own living.

A reading from the second letter of Paul to the Thes-sa-ló-ni-ans

You know how you ought to imitate us.
We did not live lives of disorder when we were among you,
  nor depend on anyone for food.
Rather, we worked day and night,
  laboring to the point of exhaustion so as not to impose on any of you.
Not that we had no claim on you,
  but that we might present ourselves as an example for you to imitate.
Indeed, when we were with you we used to lay down the rule
  that anyone who would not work should not eat.

We hear that some of you are unruly,
  not keeping busy but acting like busybodies.
We enjoin all such,
  and we urge them strongly in the Lord Jesus Christ
  to earn the food they eat by working quietly.

  This is the Word of the Lord.

GOSPEL

*The cantor sings the alleluia and the people repeat it; the cantor then
sings the verse and the people repeat the alleluia. Otherwise the alleluia
may be omitted.*

Al - le - lu - ia.

Be watch - ful and read - y: you know not when the Son of Man is com - ing.

For other alleluia verses see page 440.

Luke 21, 5-19   Your endurance will win you your life.

*This solemn warning was made by Jesus during the last days before
the passion. Christians will always live in a troubled world and
must be ready to suffer persecution. Climax on the last sentence:
"by patient endurance, you will save your lives.."*

✠ A reading from the holy gospel according to Luke

Some were speaking of how the temple was adorned
   with precious stones and votive offerings.
Jesus said,
   "These things you are contemplating—
   the day will come when not one stone will be left on another,
   but it will all be torn down."
They asked him, "When will this occur, Teacher?
And what will be the sign it is going to happen? "
He said, "Take care not to be misled.

Many will come in my name, saying, 'I am he'
  and 'The time is at hand.'
Do not follow them.
Neither must you be perturbed
  when you hear of wars and insurrections.
These things are bound to happen first,
  but the end does not follow immediately."

He said to them further:
  "Nation will rise against nation and kingdom against kingdom.
There will be great earthquakes, plagues and famines in various places—
  and in the sky fearful omens and great signs.
But before any of this, they will manhandle and persecute you,
  summoning you to synagogues and prisons,
  bringing you to trial before kings and governors,
  all because of my name.
You will be brought to give witness on account of it.
I bid you resolve not to worry about your defense beforehand,
  for I will give you words and a wisdom
  which none of your adversaries can take exception to or contradict.
You will be delivered up even by your parents,
  brothers, relatives and friends,
  and some of you will be put to death.
All will hate you because of me,
  yet not a hair of your head will be harmed.
By patient endurance you will save your lives.

  This is the gospel of the Lord.

TRINITY SUNDAY

FIRST READING

Proverbs 8, 22-31 Wisdom was born before the earth was made.

*The praise of Wisdom is a kind of foreshadowing of the doctrine of
the Blessed Trinity. Wisdom is personified as the creative spirit of
God speaking in her own person, and later to be manifested in the
person of Jesus Christ. Read with controlled exaltation, culminating
in the last sentence which starts with stress on "Then was I...found delight."*

A reading from the book of Proverbs

Thus says the Wisdom of God:
    "The Lord begot me, the first-born of his ways,
    the forerunner of his prodigies of long ago;
    From of old I was poured forth,
    at the first, before the earth.
When there were no depths I was brought forth,
    when there were no fountains or springs of water;
    Before the mountains were settled into place,
    before the hills, I was brought forth;
While as yet the earth and the fields were not made,
    nor the first clods of the world.

"When he established the heavens I was there,
    when he marked out the vault over the face of the deep;
When he made firm the skies above,
    when he fixed fast the foundations of the earth;
When he set for the sea its limit,
    so that the waters should not transgress his command;
Then was I beside him as his craftsman,
    and I was his delight day by day,
Playing before him all the while,
    playing on the surface of his earth;
    and I found delight in the sons of men."

    This is the Word of the Lord.

RESPONSORIAL PSALM

Psalm 8, 4-5. 6-7. 8-9 After the reading the psalmist sings or says the responsorial verse and all repeat it. This response is also repeated after each verse of the psalm.

Common response:

We praise you, O Lord, for all your works are won - der - ful.

For other common responses see page 441.

Or:

℟. O Lord, our God,
how wonderful your name in all the earth!

When I behold your heavens, the work of your fingers,
the moon and the stars which you set in place—
What is man that you should be mindful of him,
or the son of man that you should care for him? ℟.

You have made him little less than the angels,
and crowned him with glory and honor.
You have given him rule over the works of your hands,
putting all things under his feet: ℟.

All sheep and oxen,
yes, and the beasts of the field,
The birds of the air, the fishes of the sea,
and whatever swims the paths of the seas. ℟.

SECOND READING

Romans 5, 1-5   To God through Christ in the love which is poured out through the Spirit

Paul reminds us that we are saved through faith in Jesus Christ. From faith comes hope that we shall see the glory of God. This hope will not be disappointed because the Holy Spirit, sent by God, shows his love for us. The tone is assured conviction, to bring out the argument, with slight emphasis on 'faith,' 'hope,' and 'love.'

A reading from the letter of Paul to the Romans

Now that we have been justified by faith,
  we are at peace with God through our Lord Jesus Christ.
Through him we have gained access by faith
  to the grace in which we now stand,
  and we boast of our hope for the glory of God.
But not only that—we even boast of our afflictions!
We know that affliction makes for endurance,
  and endurance for tested virtue, and tested virtue for hope.
And this hope will not leave us disappointed,
  because the love of God has been poured out in our hearts
  through the Holy Spirit who has been given to us.

  This is the Word of the Lord.

GOSPEL

*The cantor sings the alleluia and the people repeat it; the cantor then
sings the verse and the people repeat the alleluia. Otherwise the alleluia
may be omitted. Reference: Revelation 1, 8.*

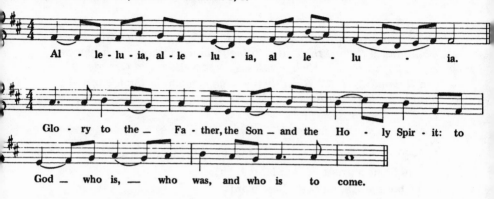

Al - le - lu - ia, al - le - lu - ia, al - le - lu - ia.

Glo - ry to the __ Fa - ther, the Son __ and the Ho - ly Spir - it: to

God __ who is, __ who was, and who is to come.

*John 16, 12-15 Whatever the Father has is mine. The Spirit will receive
what I give and tell you about it.*

*From the words of Jesus at the Last Supper. When he has left his
friends he will send them the Holy Spirit to comfort and guide them.
Read slowly and simply, with slight stress on the last sentence and
especially the last words.*

✠ A reading from the holy gospel according to John

Jesus said to his disciples:
    "I have much more to tell you,
      but you cannot bear it now.
When he comes, however,
      being the Spirit of truth
      he will guide you to all truth.
He will not speak on his own,
      but will speak only what he hears,
      and will announce to you the things to come.
In doing this he will give glory to me,
      because he will have received from me
      what he will announce to you.
All that the Father has belongs to me.
That is why I said that what he will announce to you
      he will have from me."

    This is the gospel of the Lord.

CORPUS CHRISTI

FIRST READING

Genesis 14, 18-20   Melchizedek brought bread and wine.

Melchizedec is a mysterious figure in the story of Abram (Abraham), whom the author of the Letter to the Hebrews regarded as a type or symbol of Christ our High Priest. As preparation read Genesis 14: 1-20, and Hebrews 7: 1-28. Read simply as an incident in the life of the founder of the Jewish race.

A reading from the book of Gén-e-sis

Mel-chí-ze-dek, king of Salem, brought out bread and wine,
    and being a priest of God Most High,
    he blessed Abram with these words:
"Blessed be Abram by God Most High,
    the creator of heaven and earth;
And blessed be God Most High,
    who delivered your foes into your hands."

    This is the Word of the Lord.

RESPONSORIAL PSALM

Psalm 110, 1. 2. 3. 4   After the reading the psalmist sings or says the responsorial verse and all repeat it. This response is also repeated after each verse of the psalm.

Common response:

We praise you, O Lord, for all your works are won-der-ful.

For other common responses see page 441.

Or:

℞. You are a priest for ever, in the line of Mel-chí-ze-dek.

The Lord said to my Lord: "Sit at my right hand
    till I make your enemies your footstool."   ℞.

The scepter of your power the Lord will stretch
    forth from Zí-on:
        "Rule in the midst of your enemies."   ℞.

"Yours is princely power in the day of your birth, in holy splendor;
   before the daystar, like the dew, I have begotten you." ℞.

The Lord has sworn, and he will not repent:
   "You are a priest forever, according to the order of Mel-chí-ze-dek." ℞.

SECOND READING

*1 Corinthians 11, 23-26 Every time you eat this bread and drink this
cup, you are proclaiming the death of the Lord.*

*Paul's account of the eucharist (as he had received it) occurs in a
passage where he rebukes the Corinthian converts for lack of reverence
for the sacrament. This is the earliest account known of the first
eucharist; the gospel accounts were written some years later. Read
reverently in an even tone.*

A reading from the first letter of Paul to the Cor-ín-thi-ans

I received from the Lord what I handed on to you,
   namely, that the Lord Jesus on the night in which he was betrayed
   took bread, and after he had given thanks, broke it and said,
   "This is my body, which is for you.
Do this in remembrance of me."
In the same way, after the supper, he took the cup, saying,
   "This cup is the new covenant in my blood.
Do this, whenever you drink it, in remembrance of me."
Every time, then, you eat this bread and drink this cup,
   you proclaim the death of the Lord until he comes!

   This is the Word of the Lord.

GOSPEL

*The cantor sings the alleluia and the people repeat it; the cantor then
sings the verse and the people repeat the alleluia. Otherwise the alleluia
may be omitted. Reference: John 6, 51-52.*

Al - le - lu - ia, al - le - lu - ia, al - le - lu - ia.

I am the liv-ing bread from heav-en, says the Lord; if an-y-one eats this bread he will live for-ev - er.

Luke 9, 11-17 They all ate and were filled.

Luke's record of the feeding of the five thousand is a straight account of an episode in the ministry of Jesus when he fed the hungry. Bring out the authority and power in Jesus' words and acts.

✠ A reading from the holy gospel according to Luke

Jesus spoke to the crowds of the reign of God,
    and he healed all who were in need of healing.

As sunset approached the Twelve came and said to him,
    "Dismiss the crowd so that they can go
    into the villages and farms in the neighborhood
    and find themselves lodging and food,
    for this is certainly an out-of-the-way place."
He answered them,
    "Why do you not give them something to eat yourselves?"
They replied, "We have nothing but five loaves and two fish.
Or shall we ourselves go and buy food for all these people?"
(There were about five thousand men.)
Jesus said to his disciples,
    "Have them sit down in groups of fifty or so."
They followed his instructions and got them all seated.
Then, taking the five loaves and the two fish,
    Jesus raised his eyes to heaven,
    pronounced a blessing over them, broke them,
    and gave them to his disciples for distribution to the crowd.
They all ate until they had enough.
What they had left, over and above, filled twelve baskets.

    This is the gospel of the Lord.

SACRED HEART

FIRST READING

Ezekiel 34, 11-16   I will watch over my sheep and tend them.

The passage is taken from a long chapter of denunciation of the shepherds of Israel (the rulers) who neglect their sheep (God's people).   The key word throughout is 'I' -- the Good Shepherd-- who cares for his sheep.

A reading from the book of the prophet Ezé-ki-el

Thus says the Lord God:
  I myself will look after and tend my sheep.
As a shepherd tends his flock
    when he finds himself among his scattered sheep,
    so will I tend my sheep.
I will rescue them from every place
    where they were scattered when it was cloudy and dark.
I will lead them out from among the peoples
    and gather them from the foreign lands;
    I will bring them back to their own country
    and pasture them upon the mountains of Israel
    [in the land's ravines and all its inhabited places].
In good pastures will I pasture them,
    and on the mountain heights of Israel shall be their grazing ground.
There they shall lie down on good grazing ground,
    and in rich pastures shall they be pastured
    on the mountains of Israel.
I myself will pasture my sheep;
    I myself will give them rest, says the Lord God.
The lost I will seek out, the strayed I will bring back,
    the injured I will bind up, the sick I will heal
    [but the sleek and the strong I will destroy], shepherding them rightly.

  This is the Word of the Lord.

RESPONSORIAL PSALM

Psalm 23, 1-3. 3-4. 5. 6   After the reading the psalmist sings or says the responsorial verse and all repeat it. This response is also repeated after each verse of the psalm.

Common response:

We   praise you, O Lord, for   all   your works are   won - der - ful.

For other common responses see page 441.

Or:

℟. The Lord is my shepherd; there is nothing I shall want.

The Lord is my shepherd; I shall not want.
In verdant pastures he gives me repose;
Beside restful waters he leads me;
　　he refreshes my soul.　℟.

He guides me in right paths
　　for his name's sake.
Even though I walk in the dark valley
　　I fear no evil; for you are at my side
With your rod and your staff
　　that give me courage.　℟.

You spread the table before me
　　in the sight of my foes;
You anoint my head with oil;
　　my cup overflows.　℟.

Only goodness and kindness follow me
　　all the days of my life;
And I shall dwell in the house of the Lord
　　for years to come.　℟.

SECOND READING

Romans 5, 5-11   God has entrusted his love to us.

Make clear Paul's argument that by dying for us Christ reconciled us with God.

A reading from the letter of Paul to the Romans

The love of God has been poured out in our hearts
>through the Holy Spirit who has been given to us.

At the appointed time, when we were still powerless,
>Christ died for us godless men.

It is rare that anyone should lay down his life for a just man,
>though it is barely possible that for a good man
>someone may have the courage to die.

It is precisely in this that God proves his love for us:
>that while we were still sinners, Christ died for us.

Now that we have been justified by his blood,
>it is all the more certain
>that we shall be saved by him from God's wrath.

For if, when we were God's enemies,
>we were reconciled to him by the death of his Son,
>it is all the more certain that we
>who have been reconciled will be saved by his life.

Not only that; we go so far
>as to make God our boast through our Lord Jesus Christ,
>through whom we have now received reconciliation.

>This is the Word of the Lord.

GOSPEL

The cantor sings the alleluia and the people repeat it; the cantor then
sings the verse and the people repeat the alleluia. Otherwise the alleluia
may be omitted. Reference: Matthew 11, 29.

Al - le - lu - ia, al - le - lu - ia, al - le - lu - ia.

Take my yoke up - on __ you; for I __ am gen - tle and low - ly in heart.

Luke 15, 3-7   Share my joy: I have found my lost sheep!

Emphasize that though Christ's love is for all alike yet he especially
cares for the one who at the moment most needs his help.

✠   A reading from the holy gospel according to Luke

Jesus addressed this parable to the Phár-i-sees and the scribes:
   "Who among you, if he has a hundred sheep and loses one of them,
      does not leave the ninety-nine in the wasteland
      and follow the lost one until he finds it?
And when he finds it,
      he puts it on his shoulders in jubilation.
Once arrived home, he invites friends and neighbors in
      and says to them, 'Rejoice with me
      because I have found my lost sheep.'
I tell you, there will likewise be more joy in heaven
      over one repentant sinner
      than over ninety-nine righteous people who have no need to repent."

   This is the gospel of the Lord.

CHRIST THE KING

The Christian year ends appropriately with the celebration of Christ the King. Today each reading in a very different way is a comment on that kingship.

FIRST READING

2 Samuel 5, 1-3 They anointed David king of Israel.

King Saul and Jonathan, his son, had been killed in battle by the Philistines, and the Israelites were scattered and helpless. Their elders come to David to ask him to be their king. Hereafter with David as their leader they became a great nation. But David was to be famous for another reason; the Lord promised that he would be the ancestor of the Messiah. To bring this out, stress especially the last sentence.

A reading from the second book of Sám-u-el

All the tribes of Israel came to David in Héb-ron and said:
"Here we are, your bone and your flesh.
In days past, when Saul was our king,
it was you who led the Ís-ra-el-ites out and brought them back.
And the Lord said to you,
'You shall shepherd my people Israel and shall be commander of Israel.' "
When all the elders of Israel came to David in Héb-ron,
King David made an agreement with them there
before the Lord, and they anointed him king of Israel.

This is the Word of the Lord.

RESPONSORIAL PSALM

*Psalm 122, 1-2. 3-4. 4-5   After reading the psalmist sings or says
the responsorial verse and all repeat it. This response is also repeated
after each verse of the psalm.*

Common response:

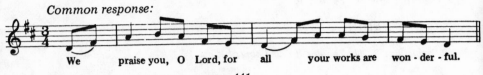

We   praise you, O Lord, for   all   your works are   won - der - ful.

For other common responses see page 441.

Or:

℟. I rejoiced when I heard them say:
    let us go the the house of the Lord.

I rejoiced because they said to me,
    "We will go up to the house of the Lord."
And now we have set foot
    within your gates, O Je-rú-sa-lem.   ℟.

Je-rú-sa-lem, built as a city
    with compact unity.
To it the tribes go up,
    the tribes of the Lord.   ℟.

According to the decree for Israel,
    to give thanks to the name of the Lord.
In it are set up judgment seats,
    seats for the house of David.   ℟.

SECOND READING

*Colossians 1, 12-20   He has taken us into the kingdom of his beloved
Son.*

*Paul reminds the Colossians that through Christ they have been
redeemed. Then, in a high strain of poetry, he breaks into a hymn
of praise of Christ, the Son of God. The language here is echoed
in the Nicene Creed. Convey the exaltation of this praise of God
the Son through whom everything on earth is created and reconciled.*

A reading from the letter of Paul to the Col-ós-si-ans

Give thanks to the Father for having made you worthy
   to share the lot of the saints in light.
He rescued us from the power of darkness
   and brought us into the kingdom of his beloved Son.
Through him we have redemption, the forgiveness of our sins.

He is the image of the invisible God,
   the first-born of all creatures.
In him everything in heaven and on earth was created,
   things visible and invisible,
     whether thrones or dominations, principalities or powers;
     all were created through him, and for him.
He is before all else that is.
In him everything continues in being.
It is he who is head of the body, the church;
   he who is the beginning, the first-born of the dead,
   so that primacy may be his in everything.
It pleased God to make absolute fullness reside in him and,
   by means of him, to reconcile everything in his person,
   everything, I say, both on earth and in the heavens,
   making peace through the blood of his cross.

This is the Word of the Lord.

GOSPEL

*The cantor sings the alleluia and the people repeat it; the cantor then
sings the verse and the people repeat the alleluia. Otherwise the alleluia
may be omitted. Reference: Mark 11, 10.*

Al - le - lu - ia, al - le - lu - ia, al - le - lu - ia.

Bless - ed   is   he   who in - her - its   the   king - dom of   Dav - id, our   fa - ther;

bless - ed   is   he   who   comes —   in   the   name   of   the   Lord.

Luke 23, 35-43   Lord, remember me when you come into your kingdom.

Jesus was first officially proclaimed King in the mocking inscription on his cross. In this bitter moment, his first act as Messiah is to welcome into his kingdom the penitent criminal who hangs beside him. Meditation and deep empathy are needed to express the irony and the triumph underlying this gospel reading.

✠   A reading from the holy gospel according to Luke

The people stood there watching,
   and the leaders kept jeering at Jesus, saying,
      "He saved others; let him save himself
      if he is the Mes-sí-ah of God, the chosen one."
The soldiers also made fun of him,
      coming forward to offer him their sour wine and saying,
      "If you are the king of the Jews, save yourself."
There was an inscription over his head:
   "THIS IS THE KING OF THE JEWS."
One of the criminals hanging in crucifixion blasphemed him,
   "Aren't you the Mes-sí-ah ?   Then save yourself and us."
But the other one rebuked him:
   "Have you no fear of God, seeing you are under the same sentence?
We deserve it, after all.
We are only paying the price for what we've done,
   but this man has done nothing wrong."
He then said, "Jesus, remember me when you enter upon your reign."
And Jesus replied, "I assure you:
   this day you will be with me in paradise."

   This is the gospel of the Lord.

PRESENTATION OF THE LORD

FIRST READING

Malachi 3, 1-4 The Lord whom you seek will come to his temple.

A prophecy of the coming of John the Baptist and of Jesus the Messiah. Proclaim as a pronouncement from God himself of his intention for his people. There is growing drama in the message. First, the messenger prepares the way, then there is the coming of the Messiah, the messenger of the New Covenant. Pause after "Lord of Hosts." The second part continues on a more intense note: when the Messiah comes, he will purge and refine his people.

A reading from the book of the prophet Mál-a-chi

The Lord God said:
Lo, I am sending my messenger
   to prepare the way before me;
And suddenly there will come to the temple
   the Lord whom you seek,
And the messenger of the covenant whom you desire.
Yes, he is coming, says the Lord of hosts.
But who will endure the day of his coming?
And who can stand when he appears?
For he is like the refiner's fire,
   or like the fuller's lye.
He will sit refining and purifying [silver],
   and he will purify the sons of Levi,
Refining them like gold or like silver
   that they may offer due sacrifice to the Lord.
Then the sacrifice of Judah and Jerusalem will please the Lord,
   as in the days of old, as in years gone by.

This is the Word of the Lord.

RESPONSORIAL PSALM

*Psalm 24, 7. 8. 9. 10 After the reading the psalmist sings or says the
responsorial verse and all repeat it. This response is also repeated after
each verse of the psalm.*

Common response:

We praise you, O Lord, for all your works are won - der - ful.

For other common responses see page 441.

Or:

℟. Who is this king of glory?   It is the Lord!

Lift up, O gates, your lintels;
    reach up, you ancient portals,
        that the king of glory may come in!   ℟.

Who is this king of glory?
The Lord, strong and mighty,
    the Lord, mighty in battle.   ℟.

Lift up, O gates, your lintels;
    reach up, you ancient portals,
        that the king of glory may come in!   ℟.

Who is this king of glory?
The Lord of hosts; he is the king of glory.   ℟.

SECOND READING

Hebrews 2, 14-18 He had to be made like his fellow men in all things.

To save mankind, the Son had first to become man and to endure human temptation and suffering. Make clear the argument: the infinite condescension of Christ, who is brother, high priest, and sacrificial offering for mankind. Be ready for the unusually long sentences.

A reading from the letter to the Hebrews

Now, since the children are men of blood and flesh,
   Jesus likewise had a full share in these,
   that by his death he might rob the devil,
   the prince of death, of his power,
   and free those who through fear of death
   had been slaves their whole life long.
Surely he did not come to help angels, but rather the children of Abraham;
   therefore he had to become like his brothers in every way,
   that he might be a merciful and faithful high priest
   before God on their behalf,
   to expiate the sins of the people.
Since he was himself tested through what he suffered,
   he is able to help those who are tempted.

This is the Word of the Lord.

GOSPEL

The cantor sings the alleluia and the people repeat it; the cantor then sings the verse and the people repeat the alleluia. Otherwise the alleluia may be omitted. Reference: Luke 2. 32.

Long Form: Luke 2, 22-40 My eyes have seen your saving power.

A straight narrative in two parts. First, the actual rite of presentation of a child, and then the recognition by two old people that this baby is indeed the long-awaited Messiah.

✠ A reading from the holy gospel according to Luke

When the day came to purify them according to the law of Moses,
    the couple brought Jesus up to Jerusalem
    so that he could be presented to the Lord,
    for it is written in the law of the Lord,
    "Every first-born male shall be consecrated to the Lord."
They came to offer in sacrifice "a pair of turtledoves or two young pigeons,"
    in accord with the dictate in the law of the Lord.

There lived in Jerusalem at the time a certain man named Sím-e-on.
He was just and pious, and awaited the consolation of Israel,
    and the Holy Spirit was upon him.
It was revealed to him by the Holy Spirit
    that he would not experience death
    until he had seen the Anointed of the Lord.
He came to the temple now, inspired by the Spirit;
    and when the parents brought in the child Jesus
    to perform for him the customary ritual of the law,
    he took him in his arms and blessed God in these words:
    "Now, Master, you can dismiss your servant in peace;
    you have fulfilled your word.
For my eyes have witnessed your saving deed
    displayed for all the peoples to see:
    A revealing light to the Gentiles,
    the glory of your people Israel."

The child's father and mother were marveling
    at what was being said about him.
Sím-e-on blessed them and said to Mary his mother:
    "This child is destined to be the downfall and the rise of many in Israel,
    a sign that will be opposed—
    and you yourself shall be pierced with a sword—
    so that the thoughts of many hearts may be laid bare."

There was also a certain prophetess, Anna by name,
   daughter of Phán-u-el of the tribe of Ásh-er.
She had seen many days,
   having lived seven years with her husband after her marriage
   and then as a widow until she was eighty-four.
She was constantly in the temple,
   worshiping day and night in fasting and prayer.
Coming on the scene at this moment,
   she gave thanks to God and talked about the child
   to all who looked forward to the deliverance of Jerusalem.

When the pair had fulfilled all the prescriptions of the law of the Lord,
   they returned to Gá-li-lee and their own town of Nazareth.
The child grew in size and strength,
   filled with wisdom, and the grace of God was upon him.

This is the gospel of the Lord.

Short Form: Luke 1, 22-32   My eyes have seen your saving power.

When the day came to purify them according to the law of Moses,
   the couple brought Jesus up to Jerusalem
   so that he could be presented to the Lord,
   for it is written in the law of the Lord,
   "Every first-born male shall be consecrated to the Lord."
They came to offer in sacrifice "a pair of turtledoves or two young pigeons,"
   in accord with the dictate in the law of the Lord.

There lived in Jerusalem at the time a certain man named Sim-e-on.
He was just and pious, and awaited the consolation of Israel,
   and the Holy Spirit was upon him.
It was revealed to him by the Holy Spirit
   that he would not experience death
   until he had seen the Anointed of the Lord.
He came to the temple now, inspired by the Spirit;
   and when the parents brought in the child Jesus
   to perform for him the customary ritual of the law,
   he took him in his arms and blessed God in these words:
   "Now, Master, you can dismiss your servant in peace;
   you have fulfilled your word.
For my eyes have witnessed your saving deed
   displayed for all the peoples to see:
   A revealing light to the Gentiles,
   the glory of your people Israel."
This is the gospel of the Lord.

ASH WEDNESDAY

FIRST READING

Joel 2, 12-18   Let your hearts be broken, and not your garments torn.

A strong call to people of all levels to repent. In this vigorous reading make the most of the short, sharp sentences, and the vivid outward signs of sorrow.

A reading from the book of the prophet Joel

Even now, says the Lord,
   return to me with your whole heart,
   with fasting, and weeping, and mourning;
Rend your hearts, not your garments,
   and return to the Lord, your God.
For gracious and merciful is he,
   slow to anger, rich in kindness,
   and relenting in punishment.
Perhaps he will again relent
   and leave behind him a blessing,
Offerings and libations
   for the Lord, your God.

Blow the trumpet in Zi-on!
   proclaim a fast,
   call an assembly;
Gather the people,
   notify the congregation;
Assemble the elders,
   gather the children
   and the infants at the breast;
Let the bridegroom quit his room,
   and the bride her chamber.
Between the porch and the altar
   let the priests, the ministers of the Lord, weep,
   And say, "Spare, O Lord, your people,
   and make not your heritage a reproach,
   with the nations ruling over them!
Why should they say among the peoples,
   'Where is their God? ' "
Then the Lord was stirred to concern for his
   land and took pity on his people.

This is the Word of the Lord.

RESPONSORIAL PSALM

*Psalm 51, 3-4. 5-6. 12-13. 14. 17   After the reading the psalmist sings or
says the responsorial verse, and all repeat it. This response is also repeated
after each verse of the psalm.*

Common response:

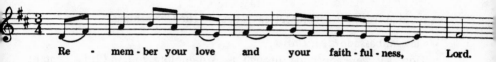

Re - mem-ber your love and your faith-ful-ness, Lord.

Or:

℟. Be merciful, O Lord, for we have sinned.

Have mercy on me, O God, in your goodness;
   in the greatness of your compassion wipe out my offense.
Thoroughly wash me from my guilt
   and of my sin cleanse me.   ℟.

For I acknowledge my offense,
   and my sin is before me always:
"Against you only have I sinned,
   and done what is evil in your sight."   ℟.

A clean heart create for me, O God,
and a steadfast spirit renew within me.
Cast me not out from your presence,
   and your holy spirit take not from me.   ℟.

Give me back the joy of your salvation,
   and a willing spirit sustain in me.
O Lord, open my lips,
   and my mouth shall proclaim your praise.   ℟.

SECOND READING

2 Corinthians 5, 20-6. 2   Be reconciled to God, now is the acceptable time.

Bring out the urgency of Paul's appeal that we must be reconciled with God. The key word is 'Now'.

A reading from the second letter of Paul to the Corinthians

We are ambassadors for Christ,
>   God as it were appealing through us. We implore you, in Christ's name:
>   be reconciled to God!

For our sakes God made him who did not know sin to be sin,
>   so that in him we might become the very holiness of God.

As your fellow workers
>   we beg you not to receive the grace of God in vain.

For he says,
>   "In an acceptable time I have heard you;
>   on a day of salvation I have helped you."

Now is the acceptable time!
Now is the day of salvation!

>   This is the Word of the Lord.

GOSPEL

The cantor sings the response and the people repeat it; the cantor then sings the verse before the gospel and the people repeat the response. Otherwise the verse befor the gospel may be omitted.
Reference: Ezekiel 18, 31

Praise   to you, Lord   Je - sus Christ,   King   of end-less   glo - ry!

For other responses to the verse see page 436.

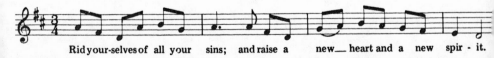

Rid your-selves of all your   sins;   and raise a   new — heart and a   new   spir - it.

Matthew 6, 1-6. 16-18   Your Father, who sees all that is done in secret, will reward you.

As often, Jesus commands us, his followers, not to parade our faith but to live it. Show the threefold commands, each introduced by

"When": let your almsgiving be anonymous, your prayer secret, and your fasting unnoticed. Pause slightly before beginning each section, and stress the key phrases -- "When you give alms. . . when you are praying. . . when you fast."

✠ A reading from the holy gospel according to Matthew

Jesus said to his disciples:

"Be on guard against performing religious acts for people to see.
Otherwise expect no recompense from your heavenly Father.
When you give alms, for example,
   do not blow a horn before you in synagogues and streets
      like hypocrites looking for applause.
You can be sure of this much,
   they are already repaid.
In giving alms
   you are not to let your left hand know what your right hand is doing.
Keep your deeds of mercy secret,
   and your Father who sees in secret will repay you.

"When you are praying,
   do not behave like the hypocrites
   who love to stand and pray in synagogues
   or on street corners in order to be noticed.
I give you my word,
   they are already repaid.
Whenever you pray, go to your room
   close your door, and pray to your Father in private.
Then your Father,
   who sees what no man sees,
   will repay you.

"When you fast,
   you are not to look glum as the hypocrites do.
They change the appearance of their faces
   so that others may see they are fasting.
I assure you,
   they are already repaid.
When you fast,
   see to it that you groom your hair and wash your face.
In that way no one can see you are fasting
   but your Father who is hidden;
   and your Father who sees what is hidden will repay you."

This is the gospel of the Lord.

JOSEPH, HUSBAND OF MARY

FIRST READING

2 Samuel 7, 4-5. 12-14. 16   The Lord will give to him the throne of his father, David.

When David had established his kingdom in Jerusalem, he wished to build a house for the Lord.   Through Nathan the prophet he was told not to build the house, but he was promised that his family would endure forever.   Straight narrative.

A reading from the second book of Samuel

The Lord spoke to Nathan and said: "Go, tell my servant David,
   'When your time comes and you rest with your ancestors,
   I will raise up your heir after you, sprung from your loins,
   and I will make his kingdom firm.
It is he who shall build a house for my name.
And I will make his royal throne firm forever.
I will be a father to him, and he shall be a son to me.
Your house and your kingdom shall endure forever before me;
   your throne shall stand firm forever.' "

   This is the Word of the Lord.

RESPONSORIAL PSALM

Psalm 89, 2-3. 4-5. 27. 29   After the reading the psalmist sings or says the responsorial verse and all repeat it.   This response is also repeated after each verse of the psalm.

Common response:

Al - le - lu - ia   al - le - lu - ia.

Or:

℟. The son of David will live for ever.

The favors of the Lord I will sing forever;
   through all generations my mouth shall proclaim your faithfulness.
For you have said, "My kindness is established forever";
   in heaven you have confirmed your faithfulness.   ℟.

"I have made a covenant with my chosen one,
    I have sworn to David my servant;
Forever will I confirm your posterity
    and establish your throne for all generations." ℟.

"He shall say of me, 'You are my father,
    my God, the Rock, my savior.'
Forever I will maintain my kindness toward him,
    and my covenant with him stands firm." ℟.

SECOND READING

Romans 4, 13. 16-18. 22   *Against all hope he believed in hope.*

In this section of the letter, Paul distinguishes between faith (believing in God's call) and justice (the right relation of man to God, brought about by faith). God promised that Abraham's descendants, the Jews, would inherit the earth, but that those who believe in Abraham's God are likewise his descendants. They inherit the promises because of their faith. To interpret the reading, careful study of the whole chapter is needed.

A reading from the letter of Paul to the Romans

Certainly the promise made to Abraham and his descendants
    that they would inherit the world did not depend on the law;
    it was made in view of the justice that comes from faith.
Hence, all depends on faith, everything is a grace.
Thus the promise holds true for all Abraham's descendants,
    not only for those who have the law but for all who have his faith.
He is father of us all, which is why Scripture says,
    "I have made you father of many nations."
Yes, he is our father in the sight of God in whom he believed,
    the God who restores the dead to life
    and calls into being those things which had not been.
Hoping against hope, Abraham believed
    and so became the father of many nations,
    just as it was once told him,
    "Numerous as this shall your descendants be."
Thus his faith was credited to him as justice.

    This is the Word of the Lord.

GOSPEL

The cantor sings the response and the people repeat it; the cantor then sings the verse before the gospel and the people repeat the response. Otherwise the verse before the gospel may be omitted. Reference: Psalm 84, 1.

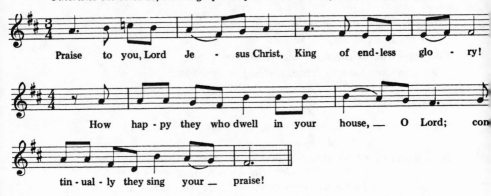

Praise to you, Lord Je - sus Christ, King of end-less glo - ry!

How hap - py they who dwell in your house, — O Lord; con-

tin - ual - ly they sing your — praise!

Matthew 1, 16. 18-21. 24   Joseph did as the angel of the Lord commanded him.

A clear account of Joseph's relationship with Mary's son.

✠ A reading from the holy gospel according to Matthew

Jacob was the father of Joseph the husband of Mary.
It was of her that Jesus who is called the Messiah was born.
Now this is how the birth of Jesus Christ came about.
When his mother Mary was engaged to Joseph,
    but before they lived together,
    she was found with child through the power of the Holy Spirit.
Joseph her husband, an upright man unwilling to expose her to the law,
    decided to divorce her quietly.
Such was his intention
    when suddenly the angel of the Lord appeared in a dream and said to him:
    "Joseph, son of David, have no fear about taking Mary as your wife.
It is by the Holy Spirit that she has conceived this child.
She is to have a son and you are to name him Jesus
    because he will save his people from their sins."
When Joseph awoke he did as the angel of the Lord had directed him.

    This is the gospel of the Lord.

OR:

Luke 2, 41-51   See how your father and I have been in sorrow seeking you.

✠ A reading from the holy gospel according to Luke

The parents of Jesus used to go every year to Jerusalem
　for the feast of the Passover,
　　and when he was twelve they went up for the celebration as was
　　　their custom.
As they were returning at the end of the feast,
　the child Jesus remained behind unknown to his parents.
Thinking he was in the party, they continued their journey for a day,
　looking for him among their relatives and acquaintances.

Not finding him, they returned to Jerusalem in search of him.
On the third day they came upon him in the temple
　sitting in the midst of the teachers,
　　listening to them and asking them questions.
All who heard him were amazed at his intelligence and his answers.

When his parents saw him they were astonished,
　and his mother said to him: "Son, why have you done this to us?
You see that your father and I have been searching for you in sorrow."
He said to them: "Why did you search for me?
Did you not know I had to be in my Father's house? "
But they did not grasp what he said to them.

He went down with them then and came to Nazareth,
　　and was obedient to them.

　　　This is the gospel of the Lord.

ANNUNCIATION

FIRST READING

Isaiah 7, 10-14   The virgin will conceive.

This prophecy of the birth of the Messiah was originally given to Ahaz, King of Judah. Two kings were advancing to attack Jerusalem; Ahaz and his people were greatly afraid. Isaiah the prophet was sent to encourage Ahaz with the message that Jerusalem would not be taken. Isaiah came again to offer the king a sign of the truth of his words. Ahaz refused thus to tempt (i.e., put to the test) the truth of the words of the Lord. Read as straight narrative.

A reading from the book of the prophet I-saí-ah

The Lord spoke to Á-haz: Ask for a sign from the Lord, your God;
   let it be deep as the nether world, or high as the sky!
But Á-haz answered, "I will not ask!
I will not tempt the Lord! "
Then he said: Listen, O house of David!
Is it not enough for you to weary men, must you also weary my God?
Therefore the Lord himself will give you this sign:
   the virgin shall be with child, and bear a son,
   and shall name him Immanuel.

   This is the Word of the Lord.

RESPONSORIAL PSALM

Psalm 40, 7-8. 8-9. 10. 11   After the reading the psalmist sings or says the responsorial verse and all repeat it. This response is also repeated after each verse of the psalm.

Common response:

Re - mem - ber your love   and   your   faith - ful - ness,   Lord.

Or:

℟. Here am I, Lord; I come to do your will.

Sacrifice or oblation you wished not,
   but ears open to obedience you gave me.

Holocausts or sin-offerings you sought not;
  then said I, "Behold I come; ℟.

In the written scroll it is prescribed for me,
  To do your will, O my God, is my delight,
  and your law is within my heart! " ℟.

I announced your justice in the vast assembly;
  I did not restrain my lips, as you, O Lord, know. ℟.

Your justice I kept not hid within my heart;
your faithfulness and your salvation I have spoken of;
I have made no secret of your kindness and your truth
in the vast assembly. ℟.

SECOND READING

*Hebrews 10, 4-10 In the scroll of the book it was written of me that
I should obey your will. O God.*

*Under the law of Moses, many bulls and goats were sacrificed as
offerings for sin. Jesus, by offering himself as the sacrifice, abo-
lished the old form of sacrifice and thereby sanctifies us. Read
distinctly and slowly to clarify this theological teaching which
may not be familiar to everyone in the congregation.*

A reading from the letter to the Hebrews

It is impossible for the blood of bulls and goats to take sins away.
Wherefore, on coming into the world, Jesus said:
"Sacrifice and offering you did not desire,
  but a body you have prepared for me;
Holocausts and sin offerings you took no delight in.
Then I said, 'As is written of me in the book,
  I have come to do your will, O God.' "
First he says,
"Sacrifices and offerings, holocausts and sin offerings
  you neither desired nor delighted in."
(These are offered according to the prescriptions of the Law.)
Then he says,
  "I have come to do your will."
In other words, he takes away the first covenant to establish the second.

By this "will," we have been sanctified
  through the offering of the body of Jesus Christ once for all.

  This is the Word of the Lord.

GOSPEL

*The cantor sings the response and the people repeat it; the cantor then
sings the verse before the gospel and the people repeat the response.
Otherwise the verse before the gospel may be omitted. Reference: John 1, 14.*

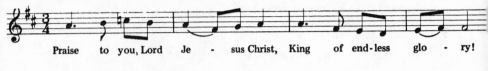

Praise to you, Lord Je - sus Christ, King of end - less glo - ry!

For other responses to the verse see page 436.

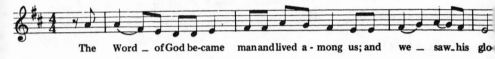

The Word _ of God be-came man and lived a - mong us; and we _ saw _ his glo

Luke 1, 26-38 You are to conceive and bear a son.

*In telling this moving story of the annunciation, bring out
especially the response and faith of Mary. At first she is
troubled by the angel's salutation. She accepts as truth the
declaration that she will be the mother of the Messiah, but
since she apparently has decided to remain a virgin, she asks
very simply: "How can this be since I do not know a man?"
The angel answers that the Holy Spirit will come upon her
and the child will be called the Son of God. Mary's reply is
complete, unquestioning acceptance of the will of God. Read
the whole passage sincerely, simply and without emotion, and
emphasize particularly Mary's final words: "I am the maidservant of the Lord. Let it be done as you say."*

✠ A reading from the holy gospel according to Luke

The angel Gá-bri-el was sent from God to a town of Gá-li-lee named Nazareth,
  to a virgin betrothed to a man named Joseph, of the house of David.
The virgin's name was Mary.
Upon arriving, the angel said to her:
  "Rejoice, O highly favored daughter!
The Lord is with you. Blessed are you among women."
She was deeply troubled by his words,
  and wondered what his greeting meant.
The angel went on to say to her: "Do not fear, Mary.
  You have found favor with God.
You shall conceive and bear a son and give him the name Jesus.
Great will be his dignity and he will be called Son of the Most High.
The Lord God will give him the throne of David his father.
He will rule over the house of Jacob forever and his reign will be
      without end."

Mary said to the angel, "How can this be since I do not know man? "
The angel answered her: "The Holy Spirit will come upon you
  and the power of the Most High will overshadow you;
  hence, the holy offspring to be born will be called Son of God.
Know tnat Elizabeth your kinswoman has conceived a son in her old age;
  she who was thought to be sterile is now in her sixth month,
  for nothing is impossible with God."

Mary said: "I am the servant of the Lord.
Let it be done to me as you say."
With that the angel left her.

  This is the gospel of the Lord.

BIRTH OF JOHN THE BAPTIST   *VIGIL MASS*

FIRST READING

Jeremiah 1, 4-10   Before I formed you in the womb, I knew you.

A stirring account of the call of a prophet. Read with zest, and pause briefly after each stanza. The key line is' "See, I place my words in your mouth. "

A reading from the book of the prophet Je-re-mí-ah

The word of the Lord came to me thus:
    Before I formed you in the womb I knew you,
    before you were born I dedicated you,
    a prophet to the nations I appointed you.
"Ah, Lord God! " I said,
    "I know not how to speak; I am too young."

But the Lord answered me,
    Say not, "I am too young."
To whomever I send you, you shall go;
    whatever I command you, you shall speak.
Have no fear before them,
    because I am with you to deliver you, says the Lord.

Then the Lord extended his hand and touched my mouth, saying,
    See, I place my words in your mouth!
This day I set you
    over nations and over kingdoms,
    To root up and to tear down,
    to destroy and to demolish,
    to build and to plant.

This is the Word of the Lord.

RESPONSORIAL PSALM

Psalm 71, 1-2. 3-4. 5-6. 15. 17 After the reading the psalmist sings or says the responsorial verse and all repeat it. This response is also repeated after each verse of the psalm.

Common response:

Hear us, O Lord, and save us.

For other common responses see page 441.

Or:

℟. Since my mother's womb, you have been my strength.

In you, O Lord, I take refuge;
let me never be put to shame.
In your justice rescue me, and deliver me;
incline your ear to me, and save me. ℟.

Be my rock of refuge,
a stronghold to give me safety,
for you are my rock and my fortress.
O my God, rescue me from the hand of the wicked. ℟.

For you are my hope, O Lord;
my trust, O God, from my youth.
On you I depend from birth;
from my mother's womb you are my strength. ℟.

My mouth shall declare your justice,
day by day your salvation.
O God, you have taught me from my youth,
and till the present I proclaim your wondrous deeds. ℟.

SECOND READING

1 Peter 1, 8-12   The prophets searched and inquired for this salvation.

*Make clear the argument of the passage: the salvation which the
Christians are now achieving through faith was predicted by the
Old Testament prophets. John the Baptist was the last in the
long line of men who prepared Israel for the coming of Christ.*

A reading from the first letter of Peter

It is true you have never seen Jesus Christ,
   but in the present age you believe in him without seeing him,
   and rejoice with inexpressible joy touched with glory
   because you are achieving faith's goal, your salvation.
This is the salvation which the prophets carefully searched out and examined.
They prophesied a divine favor that was destined to be yours.
They investigated the times and the circumstances
   which the Spirit of Christ within them was pointing to,
   for he predicted the sufferings destined for Christ and the glories
      that would follow.
They knew by revelation that they were providing,
   not for themselves but for you,
   what has now been proclaimed to you by those who preach the gospel to you
   in the power of the Holy Spirit sent from heaven.
Into these matters angels long to search.

This is the Word of the Lord.

GOSPEL

*The cantor sings the alleluia and the people repeat it; the cantor then
sings the verse and the people repeat the alleluia. Otherwise the alleluia
may be omitted. Reference John 1, 7; Luke 1, 17.*

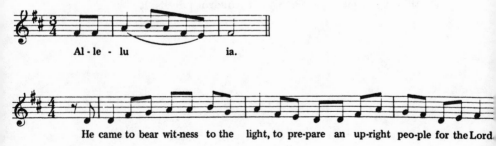

Al - le - lu   ia.

He came to bear wit-ness to the   light, to pre-pare an up-right peo-ple for the Lord

Luke 1, 5-17 A son is born to you and you will name him John.

Divide the reading into three parts. The first is explanatory intro-
duction, the second is the story of Zechariah's vision, the third,
the angel's declaration of what will happen.

✠ A reading from the holy gospel according to Luke

In the days of Herod, king of Judea,
    there was a priest named Ze-cha-rí-ah of the priestly class of A-bí-jah;
    his wife was a descendant of Aaron named Elizabeth.
Both were just in the eyes of God,
    blamelessly following all the commandments and ordinances of the Lord.
They were childless, for Elizabeth was sterile;
    moreover, both were advanced in years.

Once, when it was the turn of Ze-cha-rí-ah's class
    and he was fulfilling his functions as a priest before God,
    it fell to him by lot according to priestly usage
    to enter the sanctuary of the Lord and offer incense.
While the full assembly of people was praying outside at the incense hour,
    an angel of the Lord appeared to him,
    standing at the right of the altar of incense.
Ze-cha-rí-ah was deeply disturbed upon seeing him, and overcome by fear.

The angel said to him: "Do not be frightened, Ze-cha-rí-ah;
    your prayer has been heard.
Your wife Elizabeth shall bear a son whom you shall name John.
Joy and gladness will be yours, and many will rejoice at his birth;
    for he will be great in the eyes of the Lord.
He will never drink wine or strong drink,
    and he will be filled with Holy Spirit from his mother's womb.
Many of the sons of Israel will he bring back to the Lord their God.
God himself will go before him, in the spirit and power of E-lí-jah,
    to turn the hearts of fathers to their children
    and the rebellious to the wisdom of the just,
    and to prepare for the Lord a people well-disposed."

    This is the gospel of the Lord.

BIRTH OF JOHN THE BAPTIST *MASS DURING THE DAY*

FIRST READING

Isaiah 49, 1-6 Behold I will make you a light to the nations.

This passage is from the second of the "Servant of the Lord" songs, here applied to the mission of John the Baptist. Read as exalted, triumphant prophecy.

A reading from the book of the prophet I-saí-ah

Hear me, O coastlands,
    listen, O distant peoples.
The Lord called me from birth,
    from my mother's womb he gave me my name.
He made of me a sharp-edged sword
    and concealed me in the shadow of his arm.
He made me a polished arrow,
    in his quiver he hid me.
You are my servant, he said to me,
    Israel, through whom I show my glory.

Though I thought I had toiled in vain,
    and for nothing, uselessly, spent my strength,
    Yet my reward is with the Lord,
    my recompense is with my God.
For now the Lord has spoken
    who formed me as his servant from the womb,
    That Jacob may be brought back to him
    and Israel gathered to him;
    And I am made glorious in the sight of the Lord,
    and my God is now my strength!
It is too little, he says, for you to be my servant,
    to raise up the tribes of Jacob,
    and restore the survivors of Israel;
    I will make you a light to the nations,
    that my salvation may reach to the ends of the earth.

This is the Word of the Lord.

RESPONSORIAL PSALM

Psalm 139, 1-3. 13-14. 14-15   After the reading the psalmist sings or says the responsorial verse and all repeat it. This response is also repeated after each verse of the psalm.

Common response:

We   praise you, O Lord, for   all   your works are   won - der - ful.

For other common responses see page 441.

Or:

℟. I praise you for I am wonderfully made.

O Lord, you have probed me and you know me;
   you know when I sit and when I stand;
   you understand my thoughts from afar.
My journeys and my rest you scrutinize,
   with all my ways you are familiar.   ℟.

Truly you have formed my inmost being;
   you knit me in my mother's womb.
I give you thanks that I am fearfully, wonderfully made;
   wonderful are your works.   ℟.

My soul also you knew full well;
   nor was my frame unknown to you
When I was made in secret,
   when I was fashioned in the depths of the earth.   ℟.

SECOND READING

Acts 13, 22-26   Christ's coming was announced beforehand by the preaching of John.

On his first missionary journey, Paul preached in the Jewish synagogue in Antioch in Pisidia. He began by tracing the fulfillment
of God's promises to Abraham and to David in the person of Jesus, for whom John the Baptist had prepared the way. Show
the enthusiasm in this example of how Paul first introduced Jesus as Messiah to a Jewish audience that had not hitherto received
the good news.

A reading from the Acts of the Apostles

Paul said: "God raised up David as their king;
    on his behalf God testified, 'I have found David son of Jés-se
    to be a   man after my own heart who will fulfill my every wish.'

"According to his promise,
    God has brought forth from this man's descendants Jesus,
    a savior for Israel.
John heralded the coming of Jesus
    by proclaiming a baptism of repentance to all the people of Israel.
As John's career was coming to an end, he would say,
    'What you suppose me to be I am not.
Rather, look for the one who comes after me.
I am not worthy to unfasten the sandals on his feet.'
My brothers, children of the family of Abraham
    and you others who reverence our God,
    it was to us that this message of salvation was sent forth.'"

    This is the Word of the Lord.

GOSPEL

*The cantor sings the alleluia and the people repeat it; the cantor then
sings the verse and the people repeat the alleluia. Otherwise the alleluia
may be omitted. Reference: Luke 1, 76.*

Al - le - lu - ia.

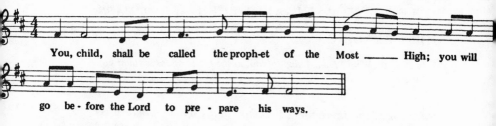

You, child, shall be called the proph-et of the Most ____ High; you will go be-fore the Lord to pre-pare his ways.

Luke 1, 57-66. 80 John is his name.

Straight account of Joseph's relationship with Mary's son.

✝ A reading from the holy gospel according to Luke

When Elizabeth's time for delivery arrived, she gave birth to a son.
Her neighbors and relatives, upon hearing that the Lord
    had extended his mercy to her,
    rejoiced with her.
When they assembled for the circumcision of the child on the eighth day,
    they intended to name him after his father Ze-cha-rí-ah.
At this his mother intervened, saying, "No, he is to be called John."

They pointed out to her, "None of your relatives has this name."
Then, using signs, they asked the father what he wished him to be called.

He signaled for a writing tablet and wrote the words, "His name is John."
This astonished them all.
At that moment his mouth was opened and his tongue loosed,
    and he began to speak in praise of God.

Fear descended on all in the neighborhood;
    throughout the hill country of Judea
    these happenings began to be recounted to the last detail.
All who heard stored these things up in their hearts, saying,
    "What will this child be? "
    and, "Was not the hand of the Lord upon him? "

The child grew up and matured in spirit.
He lived in the desert until the day when he made his public
    appearance in Israel.

    This is the gospel of the Lord.

PETER AND PAUL, APOSTLES   *VIGIL MASS*

FIRST READING

Acts 3, 1-10   What I have, I give to you; in the name of Jesus stand up and walk.

A record of the first miraculous cure made by an apostle after the descent of the Holy Spirit on the day of Pentecost. Read as a dramatic account of what happened.

A reading from the Acts of the Apostles

Once, when Peter and John were going up to the temple for prayer
   at the three o'clock hour, a man crippled from birth was being
     carried in.
They would bring him every day
   and put him at the temple gate called "The Beautiful"
   to beg from the people as they entered.
When he saw Peter and John on their way in,
   he begged them for an alms.
Peter fixed his gaze on the man; so did John.
"Look at us! " Peter said.
The cripple gave them his whole attention, hoping to get something.
Then Peter said: "I have neither silver nor gold, but what I have I give you!
In the name of Jesus Christ the Na-zo-ré-an, walk! "
Then Peter took him by the right hand and pulled him up.
Immediately the beggar's feet and ankles became strong;
   he jumped up, stood for a moment, then began to walk around.
He went into the temple with them—walking,
   jumping about, and praising God.
When the people saw him moving and giving praise to God,
   they recognized him as that beggar who used to sit at the Beautiful Gate
     of the temple.
They were struck with astonishment—
   utterly stupefied at what had happened to him.

   This is the Word of the Lord.

RESPONSORIAL PSALM

Psalm 19, 2-3. 4-5 After the reading the psalmist sings or says the responsorial verse and all repeat it. This response is also repeated after each verse of the psalm.

Common response:

We praise you, O Lord, for all your works are won - der - ful.

For other common responses see page 441.

Or:

℟. Their message goes out through all the earth.

The heavens declare the glory of God,
   and the firmament proclaims his handiwork.
Day pours out the word to day,
   and night to night imparts knowledge.   ℟.

Not a word nor a discourse
   whose voice is not heard;
Through all the earth their voice resounds,
   and to the ends of the world, their message.   ℟.

SECOND READING

Galatians 1, 11-20　God chose me while I was still in my mother's womb.

Read this passage in such a way that your hearers realize that this is Paul, giving us his own intimate account of how he was changed from a persecutor of the Church to become the apostle to the Gentiles.

A reading from the letter of Paul to the Gal-á-tians

I assure you, brothers, the gospel I proclaimed to you is no mere
    human invention.
I did not receive it from any man, nor was I schooled in it.
It came by revelation from Jesus Christ.
You have heard, I know, the story of my former way of life in Judaism.
You know that I went to extremes
    in persecuting the church of God and tried to destroy it;
    I made progress in Jewish observance far beyond most of my
        contemporaries,
    in my excess of zeal to live out all the traditions of my ancestors.

But the time came when he who had set me apart before I was born
    and called me by his favor chose to reveal his Son to me,
        that I might spread among the Gentiles the good tidings concerning him.
Immediately, without seeking human advisers
    or even going to Jerusalem to see those who were apostles before me,
    I went off to A-rá-bi-a; later I returned to Dam-ás-cus.
Three years after that I went up to Je-rú-sa-lem
    to get to know Cé-phas, with whom I stayed fifteen days.
I did not meet any other apostles except James, the brother of the Lord.
I declare before God that what I have just written is true.

This is the Word of the Lord.

GOSPEL

The cantor sings the alleluia and the people repeat it; the cantor then sings the verse and the people repeat the alleluia. Otherwise the alleluia may be omitted. Reference: John 21, 17.

Al - le - lu - ia.

Lord, you know all — things: you — know that I love ___ you.

John 21, 15-19 Feed my lambs, feed my sheep.

After his resurrection, Jesus appeared to some of his disciples while they were fishing. They breakfasted together. This gospel passage follows, one of those incidents where the meaning is conveyed subtlely and calls for a moving simplicity. It leads up to the final command: "Follow me." Peter obeyed, and thereby fulfilled the prophecy that he would die for his Master.

✠ A reading from the holy gospel according to John

When Jesus had appeared to his disciples and had eaten with them,
   he said to Simon Peter, "Simon, son of John,
    do you love me more than these? "
"Yes, Lord," Peter said, "you know that I love you."
At which Jesus said, "Feed my lambs."

A second time he put his question,
   "Simon, son of John, do you love me? "
"Yes, Lord," Peter said, "You know that I love you."
Jesus replied, "Tend my sheep."

A third time Jesus asked him, "Simon, son of John, do you love me? "
Peter was hurt because he had asked a third time, "Do you love me? "
So he said to him: "Lord, you know everything.
You know well that I love you."
Jesus told him, "Feed my sheep."
"I tell you solemnly:
   as a young man
   you fastened your belt
   and went about as you pleased;
   but when you are older
   you will stretch out your hands,
   and another will tie you fast
   and carry you off against your will."
(What he said indicated the sort of death by which Peter was to glorify
   God.)
When Jesus had finished speaking he said to him, "Follow me."

   This is the gospel of the Lord.

PETER AND PAUL, APOSTLES
MASS DURING THE DAY

FIRST READING

*Acts 12, 1-11   Now I know it is indeed true: the Lord has saved me
from the power of Herod.*

An exciting account of Peter's escape from prison.

A reading from the Acts of the Apostles

King Herod started to harass some of the members of the church.
He beheaded James the brother of John,
    and when he saw that this pleased certain of the Jews,
    he took Peter into custody too.
During the feast of Unleavened Bread he had him arrested
     and thrown into prison,
    with four squads of soldiers to guard him.
Herod intended to bring him before the people after the Passover.
Peter was thus detained in prison,
    while the church prayed fervently to God on his behalf.
During the night before Herod was to bring him to trial,
    Peter was sleeping between two soldiers,
    fastened with double chains, while guards kept watch at the door.
Suddenly an angel of the Lord stood nearby and light shone in the cell.
He tapped Peter on the side and woke him.
"Hurry, get up! " he said.
With that, the chains dropped from Peter's wrists.
The angel said, "Put on your belt and your sandals! "
This he did. Then the angel told him,
    "Now put on your cloak and follow me."

Peter followed him out,
    but with no clear realization that this was taking place through the
      angel's help.
The whole thing seemed to him a mirage.
They passed the first guard, then the second,
    and finally came to the iron gate leading out to the city,
    which opened for them of itself.
They emerged and made their way down a narrow alley,
    when suddenly the angel left him.

Peter had recovered his senses by this time, and said,
"Now I know for certain that the Lord has sent his angel
to rescue me from Herod's clutches and from all that the Jews hoped for."

This is the Word of the Lord.

RESPONSORIAL PSALM

*Psalm 34, 2-3. 4-5. 6-7. 8-9 After the reading the psalmist sings or says
the responsorial verse and all repeat it. This response is also repeated
after each verse of the psalm.*

Common response:

We   praise you, O Lord, for   all   your works are   won-- der - ful.

For other common responses see page 441.

Or:

℟. The angel of the Lord will rescue those who fear him.

I will bless the Lord at all times;
  his praise shall be ever in my mouth.
Let my soul glory in the Lord;
  the lowly will hear me and be glad.   ℟.

Glorify the Lord with me,
  let us together extol his name.
I sought the Lord, and he answered me
  and delivered me from all my fears.   ℟.

Look to him that you may be radiant with joy,
  and your faces may not blush with shame.
When the afflicted man called out, the Lord heard,
  and from all his distress he saved him.   ℟.

The angel of the Lord encamps
  around those who fear him, and delivers them.
Taste and see how good the Lord is;
  happy the man who takes refuge in him.   ℟.

SECOND READING

2 Timothy 4, 6-8. 17-18   All that remains now is the crown of righteousness.

From Paul's farewell letter, written because he knows that the day of his martyrdom is near. Bring out the pathos and the triumph, especially in the opening sentences.

A reading from the second letter of Paul to Timothy

I am already being poured out like a libation.
The time of my dissolution is near.
I have fought the good fight, I have finished the race,
    I have kept the faith.
From now on a merited crown awaits me;
    on that Day the Lord, just judge that he is, will award it to me—
    and not only to me but to all who have looked for his appearing
        with eager longing.
But the Lord stood by my side and gave me strength,
    so that through me the preaching task might be completed
    and all the nations might hear the gospel.
That is how I was saved from the lion's jaws.
The Lord will continue to rescue me from all attempts to do me harm
    and will bring me safe to his heavenly kingdom.
To him be glory forever and ever. Amen.

This is the Word of the Lord.

GOSPEL

The cantor sings the alleluia and the people repeat it; the cantor then sings the verse and the people repeat the alleluia. Otherwise the alleluia may be omitted. Reference: Matthew 16, 18.

Al - le - lu - ia.

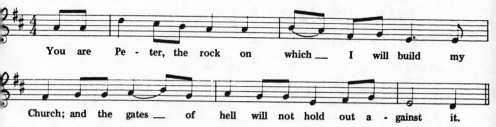

You are Pe - ter, the rock on which ___ I will build my Church; and the gates ___ of hell will not hold out a - gainst it.

Matthew 16, 13-19 You are Peter; and I will give you the keys of the Kingdom of heaven.

Peter's recognition that Jesus is indeed the Messiah is followed by the declaration that he will be the rock on which Christ's Church is to be founded. Stress especially the powers given to him. The keys are the symbol that Peter is Christ's steward on earth.

✠ A reading from the holy gospel according to Matthew

When Jesus came to the neighborhood of Cae-sa-ré-a Philippi,
    he asked his disciples this question:
    "Who do people say that the Son of Man is? "
They replied, "Some say John the Baptizer, others E-lí-jah,
      still others Jeremiah or one of the prophets."
"And you," he said to them, "who do you say that I am? "
"You are the Messiah," Simon Peter answered,
      "the Son of the living God! "
Jesus replied, "Blest are you, Simon son of John!
No mere man has revealed this to you, but my heavenly Father.
    I for my part declare to you, you are 'Rock,'
    and on this rock I will build my church,
    and the jaws of death shall not prevail against it.
I will entrust to you the keys of the kingdom of heaven.
Whatever you declare bound on earth shall be bound in heaven;
    whatever you declare loosed on earth shall be loosed in heaven."

    This is the gospel of the Lord.

TRANSFIGURATION

FIRST READING

Daniel 7, 9-10. 13-14   His raiment was as white as snow.

A vision of God (The Ancient One) on his throne in heaven, as he passes judgment on the nations of the world. The passage requires a special kind of reading—a tone of slow, solemn awe, as if the lector himself had just seen what he describes, and is still in a mood of rapture. He should bring out clearly each detail, reaching a climax on the final sentence—the kingdom of God, unlike earthly kingdoms, will last forever.

A reading from the book of the prophet Dán-i-el

As Dán-i-el watched:
Thrones were set up
    and the Ancient One took his throne.
His clothing was snow bright,
    and the hair on his head as white as wool;
    His throne was flames of fire,
    with wheels of burning fire.
A surging stream of fire
    flowed out from where he sat;
    Thousands upon thousands were ministering to him,
    and myriads upon myriads attended him.

The court was convened and the books were opened.
As the visions during the night continued, I saw
    One like a son of man coming,
    on the clouds of heaven;
When he reached the Ancient One
    and was presented before him,
    He received dominion, glory, and kingship;
    nations and peoples of every language serve him.
His dominion is an everlasting dominion
    that shall not be taken away,
    his kingship shall not be destroyed.

This is the Word of the Lord.

RESPONSORIAL PSALM

Psalm 97, 1-2. 5-6. 9 After the reading the psalmist sings or says the responsorial verse and all repeat it. This response is also repeated after each verse of the psalm.

Common response:

We praise you, O Lord, for all your works are won - der - ful.

For other common responses see page 441.

Or:

℟. The Lord is king; the most high over all the earth.

The Lord is king; let the earth rejoice;
   let the many isles be glad.
Clouds and darkness are round about him,
   justice and judgment are the foundation of his throne. ℟.

The mountains melt like wax before the Lord,
   before the Lord of all the earth.
The heavens proclaim his justice,
   and all peoples see his glory. ℟.

Because you, O Lord, are the Most High over all the earth,
   exalted far above all gods. ℟.

SECOND READING

2 Peter 1, 16-19   We heard this voice from out of heaven.

*Peter was one of the witnesses of the vision of Jesus glorified.
In this part of the letter, he reminds his hearers of the vision
and of its significance: the direct testimony of God the Father
that Jesus is his beloved Son.*

A reading from the second letter of Peter

It was not by way of cleverly concocted myths
    that we taught you about the coming in power of our Lord Jesus Christ,
    for we were eyewitnesses of his sovereign majesty.
He received glory and praise from God the Father
    when that unique declaration came to him out of the majestic splendor:
    "This is my beloved Son on whom my favor rests."
We ourselves heard this said from heaven
    while we were in his company on the holy mountain.
Besides, we possess the prophetic message
    as something altogether reliable.
Keep your attention closely fixed on it,
    as you would on a lamp shining in a dark place
    until the first streaks of dawn appear
    and the morning star rises in your hearts.

    This is the Word of the Lord.

GOSPEL

*The cantor sings the alleluia and the people repeat it; the cantor then
sings the verse and the people repeat the alleluia. Otherwise the alleluia
may be omitted. Reference:*

Al - le - lu - ia.

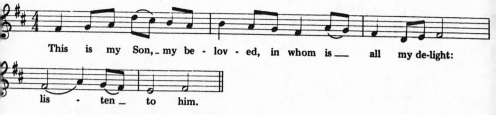

This is my Son, _ my be - lov - ed, in whom is __ all my de-light:
lis - ten _ to him.

Luke 9, 28-36 As he was praying his face was transformed.

Read this account of Jesus glorified as if you had heard it from one of the three witnesses, as the true account of an experience that is beyond analysis or explanation. Slight stress on the dazzling brightness, and the final sentence.

✠ A reading from the holy gospel according to Luke

Jesus took Peter, John and James, and went up onto a mountain
   to pray.
While he was praying, his face changed in appearance
   and his clothes became dazzlingly white.
Suddenly two men were talking with him—Moses and E-lí-jah.
They appeared in glory and spoke of his passage,
   which he was about to fulfill in Jerusalem.
Peter and those with him had fallen into a deep sleep;
   but awakening, they saw his glory
   and likewise saw the two men who were standing with him.
When these were leaving, Peter said to Jesus,
   "Master, how good it is for us to be here.
Let us set up three booths,
   one for you, one for Moses, and one for E-lí-jah."
(He did not really know what he was saying.)
While he was speaking, a cloud came and overshadowed them,
   and the disciples grew fearful as the others entered it.
Then from the cloud came a voice which said,
   "This is my Son, my Chosen One. Listen to him."
When the voice fell silent, Jesus was there alone.
The disciples kept quiet,
   telling nothing of what they had seen at that time to anyone.

   This is the gospel of the Lord.

ASSUMPTION
VIGIL MASS

FIRST READING

1 Chronicles 15, 3-4. 15. 16; 16, 1-2   They brought in the ark of God and set it inside the tent which David had pitched for it.

The ark, originally made by Moses after the giving out of the Law, was a small wooden chest, plated with gold. At either end of the cover was a gold cherub, facing inwards, with wings spread. The ark was regarded as the actual resting place of God, and was thus the most sacred of all religious symbols. When David has established the capital of his kingdom at Jerusalem, he caused the ark to be carried there. One of the titles of the Blessed Virgin Mary in her litany is "ark of the covenant."

The straight account of a stirring event.

A reading from the first book of Chronicles

David assembled all Israel in Je-rú-sa-lem
    to bring the ark of the Lord to the place which he had prepared for it.
David also called together the sons of Aaron and the Le-vites.
The Le-vites bore the ark of God on their shoulders with poles,
    as Moses had ordained according to the word of the Lord.

David commanded the chiefs of the Le-vites to appoint their brethren
        as chanters,
    to play on musical instruments, harps, lyres, and cymbals,
    to make a loud sound of rejoicing.

They brought in the ark of God
    and set it within the tent which David had pitched for it.
Then they offered up holocausts and peace offerings to God.
When David had finished offering up the holocausts and peace offerings,
    he blessed the people in the name of the Lord.

    This is the Word of the Lord.

RESPONSORIAL PSALM

Psalm 132, 6-7. 9-10. 13-14   After the reading the psalmist sings or says the responsorial verse and all repeat it. This response is also repeated after each verse of the psalm.

Common response:

We praise you, O Lord, for all your works are won - der - ful.

For other common responses see page 441.

Or:

℞. Lord, go up to the place of your rest,
    you and the ark of your holiness.

Behold, we heard of it in Éph-ra-thah;
    we found it in the fields of Já-ar.
Let us enter into his dwelling,
    let us worship at his footstool.   ℞.

May your priests be clothed with justice;
    let your faithful ones shout merrily for joy.
For the sake of David your servant,
    reject not the plea of your anointed.   ℞.

For the Lord has chosen Zion;
    he prefers her for his dwelling.
"Zion is my resting place forever;
    in her will I dwell, for I prefer her."   ℞.

SECOND READING

1 Corinthians 15, 54-57 He gives us victory through Jesus Christ.

*Through Christ Jesus, death has been overcome and our mortal
bodies take on immortality. The central idea is "Death is swallowed up in victory," and the key word is "victory," repeated
three times.*

A reading from the first letter of Paul to the Cor-ín-thi-ans

When the corruptible frame takes on incorruptibility
    and the mortal immortality,
  then will the saying of Scripture be fulfilled:
  "Death is swallowed up in victory."
"O death, where is your victory? O death, where is your sting? "
The sting of death is sin, and sin gets its power from the law.
But thanks be to God who has given us the victory through our
    Lord Jesus Christ.

    This is the Word of the Lord.

GOSPEL

The cantor sings the alleluia and the people repeat it; the cantor then sings the verse and the people repeat the alleluia. Otherwise the alleluia may be omitted. Reference: Luke 11, 28.

Al - le - lu - ia.

Bless - ed are they who hear the word of God and keep it.

Luke 11, 27-28   Blessed is the womb that bore you.

The key words are the last . . . "and keep it."

✠ A reading from the holy gospel according to Luke

While Jesus was speaking to the crowd, a woman called out,

   "Blest is the womb that bore you and the breasts that nursed you! "
"Rather," he replied, "blest are they who hear the word of God and
   keep it."

   This is the gospel of the Lord.

MASS DURING THE DAY

FIRST READING

Revelation 11, 19; 12, 1-6. 10   I saw a woman clothed with the sun and
with the moon beneath her feet.

Preparation for this reading of the woman clothed with the Sun: study
the whole chapter and meditate on its significance and depth, and how
best to convey them to the hearers. Read as if you are describing a vivid
dream as it happens. Build up the picture slowly and deliberately, phrase
by phrase, and event by event. Bring out the movement and the color, and
convey the terror and the triumph. At the same time be conscious of the
layers of meaning in the great sign. The woman personifies the peace of God in
the Old Testament and the New. The dragon is God's enemy; the serpent who
tempted Eve; the devil who tempted Christ and who is always trying to deceive
God's church. The child is the Messiah, God's son, but the child is also Jesus Christ
whose mother was Mary.

A reading from the book of Revelation

God's temple in heaven opened and in the temple could be seen the
    ark of his covenant.

A great sign appeared in the sky,
    a woman clothed with the sun, with the moon under her feet,
    and on her head a crown of twelve stars.
Because she was with child,
    she wailed aloud in pain as she labored to give birth.
Then another sign appeared in the sky:
    it was a huge dragon, flaming red, with seven heads and ten horns;
    on his head were seven diadems.
His tail swept a third of the stars from the sky
    and hurled them down to the earth.
Then the dragon stood before the woman about to give birth,
    ready to devour her child when it should be born.
She gave birth to a son—
    a boy who is destined to shepherd all the nations with an iron rod.
Her child was snatched up to God and to his throne.
The woman herself fled into the desert,
    where a special place had been prepared for her by God.

Then I heard a loud voice in heaven say:
    "Now have salvation and power come,
    the reign of our God and the authority of his Anointed One."

    This is the Word of the Lord.

RESPONSORIAL PSALM

Psalm 45, 10. 11. 12. 16   After the reading the psalmist sings or says the responsorial verse and all repeat it.   This response is also repeated after each verse of the psalm.

Common response:

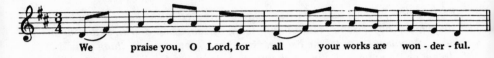

We praise you, O Lord, for all your works are won-der-ful.

For other common responses see page 441.

Or:

℟. The queen stands at your right hand, arrayed in gold.

The queen takes her place at your right hand in gold of Ó-phir.   ℟.

Hear, O daughter, and see; turn your ear,
    forget your people and your father's house.   ℟.

So shall the king desire your beauty;
    for he is your lord.   ℟.

They are borne in with gladness and joy;
    they enter the palace of the king.   ℟.

SECOND READING

1 Corinthians 15, 20-26   As members of Christ all men will be raised,
Christ first, and after him all who belong to him.

At the end of his first letter to the Corinthians Paul answers those who
deny the resurrection of Jesus, first by giving the evidence of eye
witnesses, then by showing that Christianity is meaningless if it is concerned
only with this life. Finally in this passage he shows the effect of Christ's
resurrection in God's plan. Death came into the world because of
the sin of one man, Adam; our life had to commence from the resurrection
of one man, Christ. Then Paul sees this vision of the end of all things
until death itself is destroyed and Christ triumphant hands over the
kingdom to God, his Father.

A reading from the first letter of Paul to the Cor-ín-thi-ans

Christ has been raised from the dead,
 the first fruits of those who have fallen asleep.
Death came through a man;
 hence the resurrection of the dead comes through a man also.
Just as in Adam all die, so in Christ all will come to life again,
 but each one in proper order:
 Christ the first fruits and then, at his coming,
 all those who belong to him.
After that will come the end, when,
 after having destroyed every sovereignty, authority, and power,
 he will hand over the kingdom to God the Father.
Christ must reign until God has put all enemies under his feet.

 This is the Word of the Lord.

GOSPEL

The cantor sings the alleluia and the people repeat it; the cantor then
sings the verse and the people repeat the alleluia. Otherwise the alleluia
may be omitted.

Al - le - lu - ia.

Mar - y is tak-en up to heav-en and the an - gels of God shout for joy.

Luke 1, 39-56 He who is mighty has done great things for me; he has exalted the humble.

After the great vision of the first reading, the gospel comes down to the simple story of Mary and Elizabeth; the contrast is continued in Mary's song of thanksgiving. Bring out the poetry and emphasize its theme: Mary's realization that she has been chosen to be the mother of God's Son, Jesus Christ; that God chooses the humble - not the proud and mighty to do his will; that in Christ God fulfills the promise to Abraham and his descendants.

✠   A reading from the holy gospel according to Luke

Mary set out, proceeding in haste into the hill country to a town of Jú-dah,
    where she entered Ze-cha-rí-ah's house and greeted Elizabeth.
When Elizabeth heard Mary's greeting, the baby stirred in her womb.
Elizabeth was filled with the Holy Spirit and cried out in a loud voice:
    "Blessed are you among women and blessed is the fruit of your womb.
But who am I that the mother of my Lord should come to me?
The moment your greeting sounded in my ears,
    the baby stirred in my womb for joy.
Blessed is she who trusted that the Lord's words to her would be fulfilled."

Then Mary said:
    "My being proclaims the greatness of the Lord,
    my spirit finds joy in God my savior,
For he has looked upon his servant in her lowliness;
    all ages to come shall call me blessed.
God who is mighty has done great things for me,
    holy is his name;
    His mercy is from age to age
    on those who fear him.
"He has shown might with his arm;
    he has confused the proud in their inmost thoughts.
He has deposed the mighty from their thrones
    and raised the lowly to high places.
The hungry he has given every good thing,
    while the rich he has sent empty away.
He has upheld Israel his servant,
    ever mindful of his mercy;
    Even as he promised our fathers,
    promised Abraham and his descendants forever."

Mary remained with Elizabeth about three months and then returned home.

    This is the gospel of the Lord.

TRIUMPH OF THE CROSS

FIRST READING

Numbers 21, 4-9   When those that were afflicted looked upon it, they were healed.

Treat the story as one of many told about the greatest of Jewish leaders, Moses. Remember also that in his words to Nicodemus, given in the gospel reading, Jesus took the serpent on a pole as a symbol of his own death on the cross which also will heal all who look at it. "Saraph" is often translated "fiery serpent" because its bite causes feelings of intolerable burning.

A reading from the book of Numbers

With their patience worn out by the journey,
   the people complained against God and Moses,
   "Why have you brought us up from Egypt to die in this desert,
   where there is no food or water?
We are disgusted with this wretched food! "

In punishment the Lord sent among the people saraph serpents,
   which bit the people so that many of them died.
Then the people came to Moses and said,
   "We have sinned in complaining against the Lord and you.
Pray the Lord to take the serpents from us."
So Moses prayed for the people, and the Lord said to Moses,
   "Make a saraph and mount it on a pole,
   and if anyone who has been bitten looks at it, he will recover."
Moses accordingly made a bronze serpent and mounted it on a pole,
   and whenever anyone who had been bitten by a serpent
   looked at the bronze serpent, he recovered.

This is the Word of the Lord.

RESPONSORIAL PSALM

Psalm 78, 1-2. 34-35. 36-37. 38   After the reading the psalmist sings or says the responsorial verse and all repeat it.   This response is also repeated after each verse of the psalm.

Common response:

Hear   us,   O   Lord, and   save   us.

For other common responses see page 441.

Or:

℟. Do not forget the works of the Lord!

Hearken, my people, to my teaching;
  incline your ears to the words of my mouth.
I will open my mouth in a parable,
  I will utter mysteries from of old.   ℟.

While he slew them they sought him
  and inquired after God again,
Remembering that God was their rock
  and the Most High God, their redeemer.   ℟.

But they flattered him with their mouths
  and lied to him with their tongues,
Though their hearts were not steadfast toward him,
  nor were they faithful to his covenant.   ℟.

Yet he, being merciful, forgave their sin
  and destroyed them not;
Often he turned back his anger
  and let none of his wrath be roused.   ℟.

SECOND READING

Philippians 2, 6-11   He humbled himself, therefore God has exalted him.

This reading is from a very early Christian hymn, and should be read as such. Indicate that each stanza expresses a different clause in the Nicene Creed: that Jesus is the only Son of God, he became man, he was crucified, he died and was buried, he rose again, he ascended into heaven and is seated at the right hand of the Father; all of which leads to the triumphant conclusion that we therefore worship Jesus Christ as God.

A reading from the letter of Paul to the Phil-íp-pians

Christ Jesus, though he was in the form of God,
   did not deem equality with God
   something to be grasped at.

Rather, he emptied himself
   and took the form of a slave,
   being born in the likeness of men.

He was known to be of human estate
   and it was thus that he humbled himself,
   obediently accepting even death,
   death on a cross!

Because of this,
   God highly exalted him
   and bestowed on him the name
   above every other name,
So that at Jesus' name
   every knee must bend
   in the heavens, on the earth,
   and under the earth,
   and every tongue proclaim
   to the glory of God the Father:
JESUS CHRIST IS LORD!

This is the Word of the Lord.

GOSPEL

The cantor sings the alleluia and the people repeat it; the cantor then sings the verse and the people repeat the alleluia. Otherwise the alleluia may be omitted.

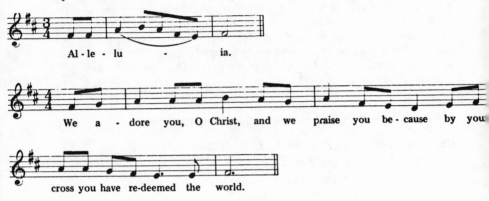

Al - le - lu - ia.

We a - dore you, O Christ, and we praise you be - cause by you cross you have re-deemed the world.

John 3, 13-17   The Son of Man must be lifted up.

Study the whole passage in John 3: 1-21 as preparation for the reading. Just as faith in the healing power of the bronze serpent saved many in the desert, so faith in the crucified Jesus will save the world. The key words of the reading are "God so loved the world."

✠ A reading from the holy gospel according to John

Jesus said to Ni-co-dé-mus:
    "No one has gone up to heaven
    except the One who came down from there—
    the Son of Man [who is in heaven].
Just as Moses lifted up the serpent in the desert,
    so must the Son of Man be lifted up,
    that all who believe
    may have eternal life in him.
Yes, God so loved the world
    that he gave his only Son,
    that whoever believes in him may not died
    but may have eternal life.
God did not send the Son into the world
    to condemn the world,
    but that the world might be saved through him."

This is the gospel of the Lord.

ALL SAINTS

FIRST READING

Revelation 7, 2-4. 9-14   I saw an immense crowd, beyond hope of counting,
of people from every nation, race, tribe and language.

The vision of the end of the world when the saints are summoned
to the presence of God from every time and place. This reading
requires great power in the lector, who should start on a note of
rapture which continues to swell until the triumphant conclusion.

The volume of sound changes to awe at, "After this . . . " and at
the end of the second paragraph, each attribute should be stressed
slowly—"praise and glory,/wisdom,/ thanksgiving and honor,/ power
and might/ to our God forever and ever."

Lower the volume at the question, and end on a note of quiet
ecstasy with "white in the blood of the lamb."

A reading from the book of Revelation

I, John, saw another angel come up from the east
   holding the seal of the living God.
He cried out at the top of his voice to the four angels
   who were given power to ravage the land and the sea,
   "Do no harm to the land or the sea or the trees
   until we imprint this seal on the foreheads of the servants of our God."
I heard the number of those who were so marked—
   one hundred and forty-four thousand from every tribe of Israel.

After this I saw before me a huge crowd
   which no one could count from every nation, race, people, and tongue.
They stood before the throne and the Lamb,
   dressed in long white robes and holding palm branches in their hands.
They cried out in a loud voice,
   "Salvation is from our God, who is seated on the throne, and from
      the Lamb! "
All the angels who were standing around the throne
   and the elders and the four living creatures
   fell down before the throne to worship God.
They said: "Amen! Praise and glory, wisdom, thanksgiving, and honor,
   power and might to our God forever and ever. Amen! "

Then one of the elders asked me,
   "Who do you think these are, all dressed in white?
And where have they come from? "
I said to him, "Sir, you should know better than I."

He then told me,
> "These are the ones who have survived the great period of trial;
> they have washed their robes and made them white in the blood
> of the lamb.

This is the Word of the Lord.

RESPONSORIAL PSALM

*Psalm 24, 1-2. 3-4. 5-6 After the reading the psalmist sings or says the
responsorial verse and all repeat it. This response is also repeated after
each verse of the psalm.*

Common response:

We praise you, O Lord, for all your works are won-der-ful.

For other common responses see page 441.

Or:

R̷. Lord, this is the people that longs to see your face.

The Lord's are the earth and its fullness;
> the world and those who dwell in it.
For he founded it upon the seas
> and established it upon the rivers.   R̷.

Who can ascend the mountain of the Lord?
> or who may stand in his holy place?
He whose hands are sinless, whose heart is clean,
> who desires not what is vain.   R̷.

He shall receive a blessing from the Lord,
> a reward from God his savior.
Such is the race that seeks for him,
> that seeks the face of the God of Jacob.   R̷.

SECOND READING

1 John 3, 1-3   We shall see God as he really is.

God our Father has called us to be his saints, which means we shall see him as he is. Read simply and clearly.

A reading from the first letter of John

See what love the Father has bestowed on us
in in letting us be called children of God!
Yet that is what we are.
The reason the world does not recognize us
   is that it never recognized the Son.
Dearly beloved,
   we are God's children now;
   what we shall later be has not yet come to light.
We know that when it comes to light
   we shall be like him,
   for we shall see him as he is.
Everyone who has this hope based on him
   keeps himself pure, as he is pure.

   This is the Word of the Lord.

GOSPEL

The cantor sings the alleluia and the people repeat it; the cantor then
sings the verse and the people repeat the alleluia. Otherwise the alleluia
may be omitted. Reference: Matthew 11, 28.

Al - le - lu - ia.

Come to me all you that la - bor and are bur - dened and

I will give you rest,_____ says the Lord.

Matthew 5, 1-12 Rejoice and be glad for your reward will be great in
heaven.

In the Sermon on the Mount, Jesus outlines the qualities of a saint.
The beatitudes should be read with a pause after each.

The key word is the repeated "blest" at the beginning of each sen-
tence, with a stronger emphasis on the last sentence of all. "Be
glad and rejoice . . . for your reward in heaven is great."

✠ A reading from the holy gospel according to Matthew

When Jesus saw the crowds he went up on the mountainside.
After he had sat down his disciples gathered around him,
     and he began to teach them:
     "How blest are the poor in spirit: the reign of God is theirs.
Blest too are the sorrowing; they shall be consoled.
[Blest are the lowly; they shall inherit the land.]
Blest are they who hunger and thirst for holiness; they shall have their fill.
Blest are they who show mercy; mercy shall be theirs.
Blest are the single-hearted, for they shall see God.
Blest too the peacemakers; they shall be called sons of God.
Blest are those persecuted for holiness' sake; the reign of God is theirs.
Blest are you when they insult you and persecute you and utter
          every kind of slander against you because of me.
Be glad and rejoice, for your reward in heaven is great."

     This is the gospel of the Lord.

THANKSGIVING DAY

FIRST READING

Deuteronomy 8, 7-18   Remember the Lord your God since it was he who gave you this strength.

Moses' solemn warning to the children of Israel as they are soon to leave the desert and the hardships of forty years.   When at last they enjoy prosperity they must remember all God has done for them, lest they grow proud and boastful.   The lector should prepare by reading the whole passage, especially verses 19-20 which follow the reading.   Be ready for two unusually long sentences and stress the message by slow and solemn proclamation.

A reading from the book of Deu-ter-ón-o-my

Moses told the people:
"The Lord, your God is bringing you into a good country,
a land with streams of water,
with springs and fountains welling up in the hills and valleys,
a land of wheat and barley,
of vines and fig trees and pomegranates,
of olive trees and of honey,
a land where you can eat bread without stint
and where you will lack nothing,
a land whose stones contain iron
and in whose hills you can mine copper.
But when you have eaten your fill,
you must bless the Lord, your God,
for the good country he has given you.
Be careful not to forget the Lord, your God,
by neglecting his commandments and decrees and statutes
which I enjoin on you today:
lest, when you have eaten your fill,
and have built fine houses and lived in them,
and have increased your herds and flocks, your silver and gold,
and all your property, you then become haughty of heart
and unmindful of the Lord, your God,
who brought you out of the land of Egypt, that place of slavery;
who guided you through the vast and terrible desert
with its saraph serpents and scorpions, its parched and waterless ground;
who brought forth water for you from the flinty rock
and fed you in the desert with manna,
a food unknown to your fathers,

that he might afflict you and test you,
but also make you prosperous in the end.
Otherwise, you might say to yourselves,
'It is my own power and the strength of my own hand
that has obtained for me this wealth.'
Remember then, it is the Lord, your God,
who gives you the power to acquire wealth,
by fulfilling, as he has now done, the covenant
which he swore to your fathers."

This is the Word of the Lord.

RESPONSORIAL PSALM

Psalm 67, 2-3. 5, 7-8 After the reading the psalmist sings or says the responsorial verse, and all repeat it. This response is also repeated after each verse of the psalm.

Common response:

We praise you, O Lord, for all your works are won - der - ful.

For other common responses see page 441.

Or:

R͗. The earth has yielded its fruits;
    God, our God, has blessed us.

May God have pity on us and bless us;
    may he let his face shine upon us.
So may your way be known upon earth;
    among all nations, your salvation.   R͗.

May the nations be glad and exult
    because you rule the peoples in equity;
    the nations on the earth you guide.   R͗.

The earth has yielded its fruits;
    God, our God, has blessed us.
May God bless us,
    and may all the ends of the earth fear him!   R͗.

SECOND READING

Colossians 3, 12-17 Giving thanks to God the Father through Christ.

Paul exhorts his hearers to remember that as chosen people they must live as Christians, full of meekness and love for each other. Read as gentle persuasion.

A reading from the letter of Paul to the Col-ós-si-ans

Because you are God's chosen ones, holy and beloved,
  clothe yourselves with heartfelt mercy,
    with kindness, humility, meekness, and patience.
Bear with one another;
  forgive whatever grievances you have against one another.
Forgive as the Lord has forgiven you.
Over all these virtues put on love,
  which binds the rest together and makes them perfect.
Christ's peace must reign in your hearts,
  since as members of the one body
  you have been called to that peace.
Dedicate yourselves to thankfulness.
Let the word of Christ, rich as it is, dwell in you.
In wisdom made perfect, instruct and admonish one another.
Sing gratefully to God from your hearts
  in psalms, hymns, and inspired songs.
Whatever you do, whether in speech or in action,
  do it in the name of the Lord Jesus.
Give thanks to God the Father through him.

  This is the Word of the Lord.

GOSPEL

*The cantor sings the alleluia and the people repeat it; the cantor then
sings the verse and the people repeat the alleluia. Otherwise the alleluia
may be omitted. Reference: Ambrosian hymn.*

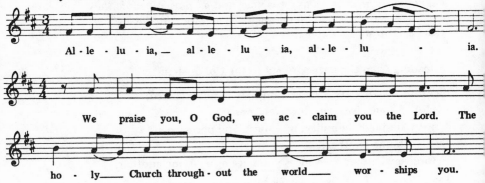

Al - le - lu - ia, — al - le - lu - ia, al - le - lu - ia.

We praise you, O God, we ac - claim you the Lord. The

ho - ly— Church through - out the world— wor - ships you.

*Luke 17, 11-19   He threw himself on his face before Jesus and thanked
him.*

*Bring out the sadness in Jesus' words that of the ten lepers healed,
only one showed any gratitude for all that he had done for them.*

✠ A reading from the holy gospel according to Luke

On his journey to Jerusalem Jesus passed along the borders of
      Sa-má-ri-a and Gál-i-lee.
As he was entering a village, ten lepers met him.
Keeping their distance, they raised their voices and said,
      "Jesus, Master, have pity on us! "
When he saw them, he responded,
      "Go and show yourselves to the priests."
On their way there they were cured.
One of them, realizing that he had been cured,
      came back praising God in a loud voice.
He threw himself on his face at the feet of Jesus and spoke his praises.
This man was a Sa-már-i-tan.

Jesus took the occasion to say,
      "Were not all ten made whole?
Where are the other nine?
Was there no one to return and give thanks to God except this foreigner"
      He said to the man, "Stand up and go your way;
      your faith has been your salvation."

      This is the gospel of the Lord.

DEDICATION OF SAINT JOHN LATERAN

FIRST READING

1 Kings 8, 22-23. 27-30   Let your eyes watch over this house.

Solomon's solemn prayer at the dedication of the great Temple at Jerusalem.   Read as an act of public worship at a supreme moment in the religious life of the people of Israel.

A reading from the first book of Kings

Solomon stood before the altar of the Lord
in the presence of the whole community of Israel,
and stretching forth his hands toward heaven, he said,
"Lord, God of Israel, there is no God like you
in heaven above or on earth below;
you keep your covenant of kindness with your servants
who are faithful to you with their whole heart.

"Can it indeed be that God dwells among men on earth?
If the heavens and the highest heavens cannot contain you,
how much less this temple which I have built!
Look kindly on the prayer and petition of your servant, O Lord, my God,
and listen to the cry of supplication
which I, your servant, utter before you this day.
May your eyes watch night and day over this temple,
the place where you have decreed you shall be honored;
may you heed the prayer which I, your servant, offer in this place.
Listen to the petitions of your servant
and of your people Israel which they offer in this place.
Listen from your heavenly dwelling and grant pardon."

This is the Word of the Lord.

RESPONSORIAL PSALM

*Psalm 84, 3. 4. 5-6. 8. 11   After the reading the psalmist sings
or says the responsorial verse, and all repeat it. This response is
also repeated after each verse of the psalm.*

Common response:

We   praise you, O Lord, for   all   your works are   won - der - ful.

For other common responses see page 441.

℟. How lovely is your dwelling-place, Lord, mighty God!

My soul yearns and pines
    for the courts of the Lord.
My heart and my flesh
    cry out for the living God.   ℟.

Even the sparrow finds a home,
    and the swallow a nest
    in which she puts her young—
Your altars, O Lord of hosts,
    my king and my God!   ℟.

Happy they who dwell in your house!
    continually they praise you.
Happy the men whose strength you are!
    They go from strength to strength.   ℟.

I had rather one day in your courts
    than a thousand elsewhere;
I had rather lie at the threshold of the house of my God
    than dwell in the tents of the wicked.   ℟.

SECOND READING

Ephesians 2, 19-22   Through the Lord, the whole building is bound together as one holy temple.

In this passage, Paul tells the pagan converts in Ephesus that through Christ Gentiles and Jews have equally become God's people; we are all parts in the structure of God's holy Temple.

A reading from the letter of Paul to the E-phé-si-ans

You are strangers and aliens no longer.
No, you are fellow citizens of the saints and members of the household
 of God.
You form a building which rises on the foundation of the apostles and
 prophets,
 with Christ Jesus himself as the capstone.
Through him the whole structure is fitted together
 and takes shape as a holy temple in the Lord;
 in him you are being built into this temple,
 to become a dwelling place for God in the Spirit.

 This is the Word of the Lord.

GOSPEL

The cantor sings the alleluia and the people repeat it; the cantor then sings the verse and the people repeat the alleluia. Otherwise the alleluia may be omitted. Reference: Ezekiel 37, 27.

Al - le - lu - ia.

My dwell - ing-place shall be with them, says the Lord, and I will be their God and they will be my peo - ple.

John 4, 19-24   True worshipers will worship the Father in spirit and in truth.

Jesus is talking to a Samaritan woman as he sits beside Jacob's well. When the woman realizes that Jesus "is a prophet," she asks him for his answer to the question much disputed between Jews and Samaritans: where ought men to worship God? Read Jesus' reply as emphatic but full of sympathy.

✝ A reading from the holy gospel according to John

The [Samaritan] woman said to Jesus:
   "Sir, I can see you are a prophet.
Our ancestors worshipped on this mountain,
   but you people claim
   that Jerusalem is the place where men ought to worship God."
Jesus told her:
   "Believe me, woman,
   an hour is coming
   when you will worship the Father
   neither on this mountain
   nor in Jerusalem.
You people worship what you do not understand,
   while we understand what we worship;
   after all, salvation is from the Jews.
Yet an hour is coming, and is already here,
   when authentic worshippers
   will worship the Father in Spirit and truth.
Indeed, it is just such worshippers
   the Father seeks.
God is Spirit,
   and those who worship him
   must worship in Spirit and truth."

   This is the gospel of the Lord.

IMMACULATE CONCEPTION

FIRST READING

*Genesis 3, 9-15. 20   I will place enmity between your seed and the seed
of the woman.*

*As used for this solemnity, the significance of the account of the
temptation of Eve lies in the prophecy: "He (that is, Eve's descendant, Christ) will strike at your head, while you (the serpent) strike
at his heel." Read as straight narrative, making a clear distinction
between each of the three persons—the Lord, Adam, and Eve. The
curse on the serpent should be especially solemn.*

A reading from the book of Gén-e-sis

After Adam had eaten of the tree
   the Lord God called to the man and asked him, "Where are you? "
He answered, "I heard you in the garden;
   but I was afraid, because I was naked, so I hid myself."
Then he asked, "Who told you that you were naked?
You have eaten, then, from the tree of which I had forbidden you to eat! "
The man replied, "The woman whom you put here with me—
   she gave me fruit from the tree, and so I ate it."
The Lord God then asked the woman,
   "Why did you do such a thing? "
The woman answered, "The serpent tricked me into it, so I ate it."

Then the Lord God said to the serpent:
   "Because you have done this, you shall be banned
   from all the animals
   and from all the wild creatures;
   On your belly shall you crawl,
   and dirt shall you eat
   all the days of your life.
I will put enmity between you and the woman,
   and between your offspring and hers;
   He will strike at your head,
   while you strike at his heel."

The man called his wife Eve, because she became the mother of all the
    living.

   This is the Word of the Lord.

RESPONSORIAL PSALM

Psalm 98, 1. 2-3. 3-4   After the reading the psalmist sings or says the responsorial verse and all repeat it. This response is also repeated after each verse of the psalm.

Common response:

Come, O   Lord,   and set   us   free.

For other common responses see page 441.

Or:

℟. Sing to the Lord a new song,
  for he has done marvelous deeds.

Sing to the Lord a new song,
  for he has done wondrous deeds;
His right hand has won victory for him,
  his holy arm.   ℟.

The Lord has made his salvation known:
  in the sight of the nations he has revealed his justice.
He has remembered his kindness and his faithfulness
  toward the house of Israel.   ℟.

All the ends of the earth have seen
  the salvation by our God.
Sing joyfully to the Lord, all you lands;
  break into song; sing praise.   ℟.

SECOND READING

*Ephesians 1, 3-6. 11-12   God chose us in Christ before the foundation
of the world.*

*Through Christ—Mary's son— we have been chosen as God's
adopted children. Straight instruction.*

A reading from the letter of Paul to the E-phé-si-ans

Praised be the God and Father of our Lord Jesus Christ,
 who has bestowed on us in Christ
 every spiritual blessing in the heavens!
God chose us in him before the world began,
 to be holy and blameless in his sight, to be full of love;
 he likewise predestined us through Christ Jesus to be his adopted sons—
 such was his will and pleasure—
 that all might praise the glorious favor he has bestowed on us
  in his beloved.

In him we were chosen; for in the decree of God,
 who administers everything according to his will and counsel,
 we were predestined to praise his glory by being the first
  to hope in Christ.

 This is the Word of the Lord.

GOSPEL

*The cantor sings the alleluia and the people repeat it; the cantor then
sings the verse and the people repeat the alleluia. Otherwise the alleluia
may be omitted. Reference: Luke 1, 28.*

Al - le - lu - ia.

Hail, Mar- y, full of grace, the Lord is with you; bless - ed are you a - mong wom-en.

Luke 1, 26-38   Rejoice, favored one, the Lord is with you.

Show that through Mary the prophecy of the First Reading is to
be fulfilled; that of all women she was chosen to bear the long-
promised Messiah, that after some natural fear and surprise,
she accepted God's will. The reading culminates in Mary's un-
questioning acquiescence: "I am the maidservant of the Lord.
Let it be done to me as you say," to be read quietly, simply
and decisively.

✤ A reading from the holy gospel according to Luke

The angel Gá-bri-el was sent from God to a town of Gá-li-lee named
        Ná-za-reth,
    to a virgin betrothed to a man named Joseph, of the house of David.
The virgin's name was Mary.
Upon arriving, the angel said to her:
    "Rejoice, O highly favored daughter! The Lord is with you.
Blessed are you among women."
She was deeply troubled by his words, and wondered what his
        greeting meant.
The angel went on to say to her: "Do not fear, Mary.
You have found favor with God.
You shall conceive and bear a son and give him the name of Jesus.
Great will be his dignity and he will be called Son of the Most High.
The Lord God will give him the throne of David his father.
He will rule over the house of Jacob forever
    and his reign will be without end."

Mary said to the angel, "How can this be since I do not know man? "
The angel answered her: "The Holy Spirit will come upon you
    and the power of the Most High will overshadow you;
    hence, the holy offspring to be born will be called Son of God.
Know that Elizabeth your kinswoman has conceived a son in her old age;
    she who was thought to be sterile is now in her sixth month,
    for nothing is impossible with God."

Mary said: "I am the servant of the Lord.
Let it be done to me as you say."
With that the angel left her.

    This is the gospel of the Lord.

THIRD SUNDAY OF LENT

FIRST READING

Exodus 17, 3-7 Give us water to drink.

A reading from the book of Éx-o-dus

In their thirst for water, the people grumbled against Moses, saying,
"Why did you ever make us leave Egypt?
Was it just to have us die here of thirst with our children and our
livestock? "
So Moses cried out to the Lord,
"What shall I do with this people?
A little more and they will stone me! "
The Lord answered Moses,
"Go over there in front of the people,
along with some of the elders of Israel,
holding in your hand, as you go,
the staff with which you struck the river.
I will be standing there in front of you on the rock in Horeb.
Strike the rock,
and the water will flow from it for the people to drink."
This Moses did, in the presence of the elders of Israel.
The place was called Más-sah and Mer-í-bah,
because the Israelites quarreled there and tested the Lord, saying,
"Is the Lord in our midst or not? "

This is the Word of the Lord.

RESPONSORIAL PSALM

*Psalm 95, 1-2. 6-7. 8-9   After the reading the psalmist sings or says
the responsorial verse, and all repeat it. This response is also repeated
after each verse of the psalm.*

Common response:

Re - mem - ber your love   and   your   faith - ful - ness,   Lord.

Or:

℟. If today you hear his voice, harden not your hearts.

Come, let us sing joyfully to the Lord;
   let us acclaim the Rock of our salvation.
Let us greet him with thanksgiving;
   let us joyfully sing psalms to him.   ℟.

Come, let us bow down in worship;
   let us kneel before the Lord who made us.
For he is our God,
   and we are the people he shepherds, the flock he guides.   ℟.

Oh, that today you would hear his voice:
   "Harden not your hearts as at Mer-i-bah,
   as in the day of Más-sah in the desert,
Where your fathers tempted me;
   they tested me though they had seen my
      works.   ℟.

SECOND READING

Romans 5, 1-2. 5-8   The love of God has been poured into our hearts
by the Holy Spirit which has been given to us.

A reading from the letter of Paul to the Romans

Now that we have been justified by faith,
  we are at peace with God through our Lord Jesus Christ.
Through him we have gained access by faith
  to the grace in which we now stand,
  and we boast of our hope for the glory of God.
And this hope will not leave us disappointed,
  because the love of God has been poured out in our hearts
  through the Holy Spirit who has been given to us.
At the appointed time, when we were still powerless,
  Christ died for us godless men.
It is rare that anyone should lay down his life for a just man,
  though it is barely possible that for a good man
  someone may have the courage to die.
It is precisely in this that God proves his love for us:
  that while we were still sinners, Christ died for us.

  This is the Word of the Lord.

GOSPEL

The cantor sings the response and the people repeat it; the cantor then
sings the verse before the gospel and the people repeat the response.
Otherwise the verse before the gospel may be omitted.

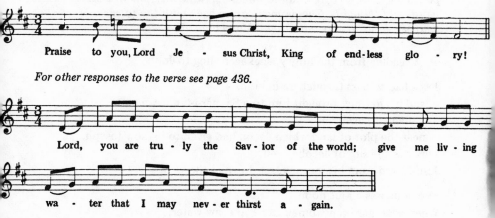

Praise to you, Lord Jesus Christ, King of endless glory!

For other responses to the verse see page 436.

Lord, you are truly the Savior of the world; give me living water that I may never thirst again.

*Long Form: John 4, 5-42   The water that I shall give will turn into a spring
of eternal life.*

*Jesus and the Samaritan woman at Jacob's Well. Tell this happy
story with zest, bringing out the vivid detail and clever character-
isation.*

*The opening lines give the scene. Jesus tired, thirsty and alone,
sits by the well. When a Samaritan woman comes to draw water,
he asks for a drink. Since there was such bitter feeling between
Samaritans and Jews, she gives him an insolent answer; but his
reply surprises her. She cannot understand his words "living water"
which she takes literally; without a bucket how does he expect
to draw "flowing water". Jesus says that anyone who drinks the
water he gives will never thirst. Her retort is mocking; if so, she
will not have to fetch any more water.*

*Jesus then tells her to call her husband, and when he shows that
he knows her private life, she reveals another side of her character.
She has no embarrassment; but she is always ready to argue about
religion, and the great quarrel between Jews and Samaritans, who
refuse to recognize Jerusalem as the Holy City.*

*He replies that a time is soon coming when true worshippers
will no longer be confined to any one place.*

*The woman is impressed, not only by what he says but by his
personality; and when he tells her that he is indeed the Messiah,
she is convinced. As the disciples come back, she leaves her
water pot and hurries back to the town to fetch the people.
The disciples, having heard nothing of the conversation, are
puzzled and as, so often, fail to understand the meaning of Jesus'
words and thoughts. The woman comes back with the townsmen
who ask Jesus to stay with them. Many are converted.*

✠ A reading from the holy gospel according to John

Jesus had to pass through Sa-má-ri-a,
    and his journey brought him to a Sa-már-i-tan town
        named Shéch-em
near the plot of land which Jacob had given to his son Joseph.
This was the site of Jacob's well.
Jesus, tired from his journey, sat down at the well.

The hour was about noon.
When a Sa-már-i-tan woman came to draw water,
    Jesus said to her, "Give me a drink."
(His disciples had gone off to the town to buy provisions.)
The Sa-már-i-tan woman said to him,
    "You are a Jew.

How can you ask me, a Sa-már-i-tan and a woman, for a drink? "
(Recall that Jews have nothing to do with Sa-már-i-tans.)
Jesus replied:
    "If only you recognized God's gift,
    and who it is that is asking you for a drink,
    you would have asked him instead,
    and he would have given you living water."
"Sir," she challenged him,
    "you don't have a bucket and this well is deep.
Where do you expect to get this flowing water?
Surely you don't pretend to be greater than our ancestor Jacob,
    who gave us this well and drank from it
    with his sons and his flocks? " Jesus replied:
    "Everyone who drinks this water
    will be thirsty again.
    But whoever drinks the water I give him
    will never be thirsty;
    no, the water I give
    shall become a fountain within him,
    leaping up to provide eternal life."
The woman said to him, "Give me this water, sir,
    so that I won't grow thirsty
    and have to keep coming here to draw water."

He told her,
    "Go, call your husband, and then come back here."
"I have no husband," replied the woman.
"You are right in saying you have no husband! " Jesus exclaimed.
"The fact is, you have had five,
    and the man you are living with now is not your husband.
What you said is true enough."

"Sir," answered the woman, "I can see you are a prophet.
Our ancestors worshiped on this mountain,
    but you people claim that Jerusalem is the place
    where men ought to worship God."
Jesus told her:
    "Believe me, woman,
    an hour is coming
    when you will worship the Father
    neither on this mountain
    nor in Jerusalem.
You people worship what you do not understand,
    while we understand what we worship;
    after all, salvation is from the Jews.

Yet an hour is coming, and is already here,
  when authentic worshipers
  will worship the Father in Spirit and truth.
Indeed, it is just such worshipers
  the Father seeks.
God is Spirit,
  and those who worship him
  must worship in Spirit and truth."

The woman said to him: "I know there is a Mes-sí-ah coming.
(This term means Anointed.)
When he comes, he will tell us everything."
Jesus replied, "I who speak to you am he."

His disciples, returning at this point,
  were surprised that Jesus was speaking with a woman.

No one put a question, however, such as "What do you want of him? "
    or "Why are you talking with her? "
The woman then left her water jar and went off into the town.
She said to the people:
  "Come and see someone who told me everything I ever did!
Could this not be the Més-si-ah? "
With that they set out from the town to meet him.

Meanwhile the disciples were urging him,
  "Rabbi, eat something."
But he told them:
  "I have food to eat
  of which you do not know."
At this the disciples said to one another,
  "You do not suppose anyone has brought him something to eat
Jesus explained to them:
  "Doing the will of him who sent me
  and bringing his work to completion
  is my food.
Do you not have a saying:
  'Four months more
  and it will be harvest! '?
Listen to what I say:
  Open your eyes and see!
The fields are shining for harvest!
The reaper already collects his wages
  and gathers a yield for eternal life,
  that sower and reaper may rejoice together.
Here we have the saying verified:

'One man sows; another reaps.'
I sent you to reap
  what you had not worked for.
Others have done the labor,
  and you have come into their gain."

Many Sa-már-i-tans from that town believed in him
  on the strength of the woman's word of testimony:
  "He told me everything I ever did."
The result was that, when these Samaritans came to him,
  they begged him to stay with them awhile.
So he stayed there two days,
  and through his own spoken word many more came to faith.
As they told the woman:
  "No longer does our faith depend on your story.
We have heard for ourselves,
  and we know that this really is the Savior of the world."

  This is the gospel of the Lord.

*Short Form: John 4, 5-15. 19-26. 39. 40-42   The water that I shall give will
turn into a spring of eternal life.*

✠   A reading from the holy gospel according to John

Jesus had to pass through Sa-má-ri-a,
  and his journey brought him to a Sa-már-i-tan town named Shéch-em
  near the plot of land which Jacob had given to his son Joseph.
This was the site of Jacob's well.
Jesus, tired from his journey, sat down at the well.

The hour was about noon.
When a Sa-már-i-tan woman came to draw water,
  Jesus said to her, "Give me a drink."
(His disciples had gone off to the town to buy provisions.)
The Sa-már-i-tan woman said to him,
  "You are a Jew.
How can you ask me, a Sa-már-i-tan and a woman, for a drink? "
(Recall that Jews have nothing to do with Sa-már-i-tans.)
Jesus replied:
  "If only you recognized God's gift,
  and who it is that is asking you for a drink,
  you would have asked him instead,
  and he would have given you living water."
"Sir," she challenged him,
  "you don't have a bucket and this well is deep.

Where do you expect to get this flowing water?
Surely you don't pretend to be greater that our ancestor Jacob,
    who gave us this well and drank from it with his sons and his flocks? "

Jesus replied:
    "Everyone who drinks this water
    will be thirsty again.
But whoever drinks the water I give him
    will never be thirsty;
    no, the water I give
    shall become a fountain within him,
    leaping up to provide eternal life."
The woman said to him, "Give me this water, sir,
    so that I won't grow thirsty
    and have to keep coming here to draw water.
I can see you are a prophet.
Our ancestors worshiped on this mountain,
    but you people claim that Jerusalem is the place
    where men ought to worship God."
Jesus told her:
    "Believe me, woman,
    an hour is coming
    when you will worship the Father
    neither on this mountain
    nor in Jerusalem.
You people worship what you do not understand,
    while we understand what we worship;
    after all, salvation is from the Jews.
Yet an hour is coming, and is already here,
    when authentic worshipers
    will worship the Father in Spirit and truth.
Indeed, it is just such worshipers
    the Father seeks.
God is Spirit,
    and those who worship him
    must worship in spirit and truth."
The woman said to him: "I know there is a Mes-sí-ah coming.
(This term means Anointed.)
When he comes, he will tell us everything."
Jesus replied, "I who speak to you am he."

Many Sa-már-i-tans from that town believed in him
    on the strength of the woman's word of testimony.

The result was that, when these Sa-már-i-tans came to him,
    they begged him to stay with them awhile.
So he stayed there two days,
    and through his own spoken word many more came to faith.
As they told the woman: "No longer does our faith depend on
        your story.
We have heard for ourselves,
    and we know that this really is the Savior of the world."

This is the gospel of the Lord.

FOURTH SUNDAY OF LENT

FIRST READING

1 Samuel 16, 1. 6-7. 10-13 In the presence of the Lord God, they anointed David king of Israel.

A reading from the first book of Samuel

The Lord said to Samuel:
    "I am sending you to Jés-se of Béth-le-hem,
    for I have chosen my king from among his sons.

As Jés-se and his sons came to the sacrifice,
    Sám-u-el looked at E-lí-ab and thought,
    "Surely the Lord's anointed is here before him."
But the Lord said to Sám-u-el:
    "Do not judge from his appearance or from his lofty stature,
    because I have rejected him.
Not as man sees does God see, because man sees the appearance
    but the Lord looks into the heart."
In the same way Jés-se presented seven sons before Sám-u-el,
    but Sám-u-el said to Jés-se,
"The Lord has not chosen any one of these."
Then Sám-u-el asked Jés-se,
    "Are these all the sons you have? "
Jés-se replied,
    "There is still the youngest, who is tending the sheep."
Sám-u-el said to Jés-se, "Send for him;
    we will not begin the sacrificial banquet until he arrives here."
Jés-se sent and had the young man brought to them.
He was ruddy,
    a youth handsome to behold and making a splendid appearance.
The Lord said,
    "There—anoint him, for this is he! "
Then Sám-u-el, with the horn of oil in hand,
    anointed him in the midst of his brothers;
    and from that day on, the spirit of the Lord rushed upon David.

    This is the Word of the Lord.

RESPONSORIAL PSALM

*Psalm 23, 1-3. 3-4. 5. 6 After the reading the psalmists sings or says
the responsorial verse, and all repeat it. This response is also repeated
after each verse of the psalm.*

Common response:

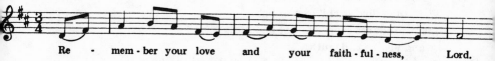

Re - mem - ber your love   and   your   faith - ful - ness,   Lord.

Or:

℟. The Lord is my shepherd, there is nothing I shall want.

The Lord is my shepherd; I shall not want.
In verdant pastures he gives me repose;
Beside restful waters he leads me;
   he refreshes my soul.   ℟.

He guides me in right paths
   for his name's sake.
Even though I walk in the dark valley
   I fear no evil; for you are at my side
With your rod and your staff
   that give me courage.   ℟.

You spread the table before me
   in the sight of my foes;
You anoint my head with oil;
   my cup overflows.   ℟.

Only goodness and kindness follow me
   all the days of my life;
And I shall dwell in the house of the Lord for years to come.   ℟.

SECOND READING

Ephesians 5, 8-14   Rise from the dead and Christ will shine on you.

A reading from the letter of Paul to the E-phés-ians

There was a time when you were darkness,
  but now you are light in the Lord.
Well, then, live as children of light.
Light produces every kind of goodness
  and justice and truth.
Be correct in your judgment of what pleases the Lord.
Take no part in vain deeds done in darkness;
  rather, condemn them.
It is shameful even to mention the things
    these people do in secret;
  but when such deeds are condemned,
    they are seen in the light of day,
    and all that then appears is light.
That is why we read:
  "Awake, O sleeper,
  arise from the dead,
  and Christ will give you light."

This is the Word of the Lord.

GOSPEL

*The cantor sings the response and the people repeat it; the cantor then
sings the verse before the gospel and the people repeat the response.
Otherwise the verse before the gospel may be omitted.*

Praise to you, Lord Jesus Christ, King of end-less glo-ry!

For other responses to the verse see page 436.

I am the light of the world, says the Lord: the
man who fol-lows me will have the light of life.

*Long Form: John 9, 1-41   The blind man went off and washed himself
and came away with his sight restored.*

*As in other stories told by John in his gospel, there is an acute
feeling for event and character, especially in the once blind
man who holds his own, even against the experts.*

*The question asked by the disciples is natural because there
was a general belief that prosperity or adversity revealed God's
approval or disapproval of a man's deeds - a belief which Jesus
denied several times.*

*Read the story with zest, with each incident properly emphasised
. . . the anointing with mud of the man's eyes. The man washes
and is able to see. The surprise of the neighbors. The man's
excited account of what Jesus did to him.*

*Then his first appearance before the Pharisees who make him
tell again what had happened. Their disapproval that a deed
of healing should be done on the Sabbath; their disagreement
with each other. Their question to the man - "what do you
have to say about him? " and the decisive reply "He is a
prophet."*

*The disbelief of the Jews. They send for the parents who try
to avoid becoming involved. The man's second appearance
before the Pharisees and the argument that follows in which
the man once blind, irritated by their attitude and disbelief,
jeers at them: "Do not tell me you want to become his
disciple too! " The argument gets hotter until the Pharisees
are reduced to mere abuse.*

*Stress the conclusion - that this story is an illustration of the
truth that Jesus came to make the blind see.*

✠ A reading from the holy gospel according to John

As Jesus walked along,
   he saw a man who had been blind from birth.
His disciples asked him,
   "Ráb-bi, was it his sin or his parents'
   that caused him to be born blind? "
"Neither," answered Jesus:
   "It was no sin, either of this man or of his parents.
Rather, it was to let God's works show forth in him.
We must do the deeds of him who sent me while it is day.
The night comes on
   when no one can work.
While I am in the world
   I am the light of the world."

With that Jesus spat on the ground,
    made mud with his saliva,
    and smeared the man's eyes with the mud.
Then he told him, "Go, wash in the pool of Sil-o-am "
(This name means "One who has been sent.")
So the man went off and washed,
    and came back able to see.

His neighbors and the people
    who had been accustomed to see him begging began to ask,
    "Isn't this the fellow who used to sit and beg? "
Some were claiming it was he;
    others maintained it was not
    but someone who looked like him.
The man himself said,
    "I'm the one."
They said to him then,
    "How were your eyes opened? "
He answered: "That man they call Jesus made mud and smeared it
      on my eyes,
    telling me to go to Sil-o-am and wash.
When I did go and wash, I was able to see."
"Where is he? " they asked.
He replied, "I have no idea."

Next, they took the man who had been born blind, to the Pharisees.
(Note that it was on a sabbath
    that Jesus had made the mud paste and opened his eyes.)
The Pharisees, in turn, began to inquire
    how he had recovered his sight.
He told them, "He put mud on my eyes.
I washed it off, and now I can see."
This prompted some of the Pharisees to assert,
    "This man cannot be from God because he does not keep the sabbath."
Others objected, "If a man is a sinner,
    how can he perform signs like these?"
They were sharply divided over him.
Then they addressed the blind man again:
    "Since it was your eyes he opened,
    what do you have to say about him? "
"He is a prophet," he replied.

The Jews refused to believe
    that he had really been born blind and had begun to see,
    until they summoned the parents of this man who now could see.

"Is this your son? " they asked,

"and if so, do you attest that he was blind at birth?
How do you account for the fact that he now can see? "
His parents answered, "We know this is our son,
and we know he was blind at birth.
But how he can see now,
or who opened his eyes, we have no idea.
Ask him. He is old enough to speak for himself."
(His parents answered in this fashion
because they were afraid of the Jews,
who had already agreed among themselves
that anyone who acknowledged Jesus as the Mes-sí-ah
would be put out of the synagogue.
That was why his parents said, "He is of age—ask him.")

A second time they summoned the man who had been born blind
and said to him, "Give glory to God!
First of all, we know this man is a sinner."
"I would not know whether he is a sinner or not," he answered.
"I know this much: I was blind before; now I can see."
They persisted: "Just what did he do to you?
How did he open your eyes:"
"I have told you once,
but you would not listen to me," he answered them.
"Why do you want to hear it all over again?
Do not tell me you want to become his disciples too? "
They retorted scornfully,
"You are the one who is that man's disciple.
We are disciples of Moses.
We know that God spoke to Moses,
but we have no idea where this man comes from."
He came back at them:
"Well, this is news!
You do not know where he comes from,
yet he opened my eyes.
We know that God does not hear sinners,
but that if someone is devout and obeys his will he listens to him.
It is unheard of that anyone ever gave sight
to a person blind from birth.
If this man were not from God,
he could never have done such a thing."
"What! " they exclaimed,
"You are steeped in sin from your birth,

and you are giving us lectures? "
With that they threw him out bodily.

When Jesus heard of his expulsion,
   he sought him out and asked him,
     "Do you believe in the Son of Man? "
He answered, "Who is he, sir, that I may believe in him? "
"You have seen him," Jesus replied.
"He is speaking to you now."
["I do believe, Lord," he said, and bowed down to worship him.

Then Jesus said:]
   "I came into this world to divide it,
   to make the sightless see
   and the seeing blind."
Some of the Pharisees around him picked this up, saying,
   "You are not counting us in with the blind, are you? "
To which Jesus replied:
   "If you were blind
   there would be no sin in that.
'But we see,' you say,
   and your sins remains.

This is the gospel of the Lord.

*Short Form: John 9, 1. 6-9. 13-17. 34-38   The blind man went off and
washed himself and came away with his sight restored.*

✠   A reading from the holy gospel according to John

As Jesus walked along,
   he saw a man who had been blind from birth.
Jesus spat on the ground, made mud with his saliva,
   and smeared the man's eyes with the mud.
Then he told him, "Go, wash in the pool of Sil-o-am. "
(This name means "One who has been sent.")
So the man went off and washed,
   and came back able to see.

His neighbors and the people
   who had been accustomed to see him begging began to ask,
   "Isn't this the fellow who used to sit and beg? "
Some were claiming it was he;
   others maintained it was not
   but someone who looked like him.
The man himself said, "I'm the one."

Next, they took the man who had been born blind, to the Pharisees.
(Note that it was on a sabbath
   that Jesus had made the mud paste and opened his eyes.)
The Pharisees, in turn, began to inquire
   how he had recovered his sight.

He told them, "He put mud on my eyes.
I washed it off, and now I can see."
This prompted some of the Pharisees to assert,
   "This man cannot be from God because he does not keep the sabbath."
Others objected, "If a man is a sinner,
   how can he perform signs like these? "
They were sharply divided over him.
Then they addressed the blind man again:
   "Since it was your eyes he opened,
   what do you have to say about him? "
"He is a prophet," he replied.

"What! " they exclaimed,
   "You are steeped in sin from your birth,
   and you are giving us lectures? "
With that they threw him out bodily.

When Jesus heard of his expulsion,
   he sought him out and asked him,
   "Do you believe in the Son of Man? "
He answered, "Who is he, sir, that I may believe in him? "
"You have seen him," Jesus replied.
"He is speaking to you now."
["I do believe, Lord," he said,
   and bowed down to worship him.]

   This is the gospel of the Lord.

FIFTH SUNDAY OF LENT

FIRST READING

Ezekiel 37, 12-14   I shall put my spirit in you, and you will live.

A reading from the book of the prophet E-zé-ki-el

Thus says the Lord God:
    O my people, I will open your graves
    and have you rise from them,
    and bring you back to the land of Israel.
Then you shall know that I am the Lord,
    when I open your graves
    and have you rise from them,
O my people!
I will put my spirit in you that you may live,
    and I will settle you upon your land;
    thus you shall know that I am the Lord.
I have promised, and I will do it, says the Lord.

    This is the Word of the Lord.

RESPONSORIAL PSALM

*Psalm 130, 1-2. 3-4. 5-6. 7-8   After the reading the psalmist sings or says
the responsorial verse, and all repeat it. This response is also repeated after
each verse of the psalm.*

Common response:

Re - mem - ber your love   and   your   faith - ful - ness,   Lord.

Or:

℟. With the Lord there is mercy, and fullness of redemption.

Out of the depths I cry to you, O Lord;
    Lord, hear my voice!

Let your ears be attentive
   to my voice in supplication. ℟.

If you, O Lord, mark iniquities,
   Lord, who can stand?
But with you is forgiveness,
   that you may be revered. ℟.

I trust in the Lord;
   my soul trusts in his word.
More than sentinels wait for the dawn,
   let Israel wait for the Lord. ℟.

For with the Lord is kindness
   and with him is plenteous redemption;
And he will redeem Israel
   from all their iniquities. ℟.

SECOND READING

Romans 8, 8-11   *If the Spirit of him who raised Jesus from the dead is living in you then he will give life to your own mortal bodies.*

A reading from the letter of Paul to the Romans

Those who are in the flesh cannot please God.
But you are not in the flesh;
   you are in the spirit,
   since the Spirit of God dwells in you.
If anyone does not have the Spirit of Christ,
   he does not belong to Christ.
If Christ is in you,
   the body is indeed dead because of sin,
   while the spirit lives because of justice.
If the Spirit of him who raised Jesus from the dead dwells in you,
   then he who raised Christ from the dead
   will bring your mortal bodies to life also
   through his Spirit dwelling in you.

   This is the Word of the Lord.

For the Gospel please turn to page 442.

ALLELUIA MELODIES

These five "Alleluia" melodies which precede and close the sung Verses before the Gospel will be found in three keys — D, Bb and Eb. These keys will also be found in the Verses.

None of these keys is arbitrary. Through transposition they will adapt to any Verse in any situation or occasion at the discretion of the Cantor or Choirmaster.

The structure of the "Alleluias" is twofold: the first is a single Alleluia; the second, a multiple or threefold Alleluia. Either may be used at the will of those who plan the Liturgy.

ALLELUIA I

LLELUIA IV

Single

Al - le - lu - ia.

Multiple

Al - le - lu - ia, al - le - lu - ia, al - le - lu - ia.

LLELUIA V

Single

Al - le - lu - ia.

Multiple

Al - le - lu - ia, al - le - lu - ia, al - le - lu - ia.

r communities when a greater variety of settings is practical the
owing are included:

LELUIA FOR CHRISTMAS

Single

Al - le - lu - ia.

Multiple

Al - le - lu - ia, al - le lu - ia, al - le - lu - ia.

ALLELUIA FOR EASTER

Single

Al - le - lu - ia.____

Multiple

Al - le-lu - ia, al - le - lu ia, al - le - lu - ia.____

ALLELUIA FOR PENTECOST

Single

Al - le - lu - ia.

Multiple

Al - le - lu - ia, al - le - lu - ia, al - le - lu - ia

RESPONSES FOR VERSES BEFORE THE GOSPEL

Praise to you, Lord Je - sus Christ, King of end - less glo - ry!

Praise and hon - or to you, Lord____ Je - sus Christ.

Glo - ry and praise to you, Lord Je - sus Christ.

Glo - ry to you,____ Word of God, Lord ___ Je - sus Christ.

ALLELUIA VERSES FOR SUNDAYS OF THE YEAR

1. *I Samuel 3, 9; John 6, 69*

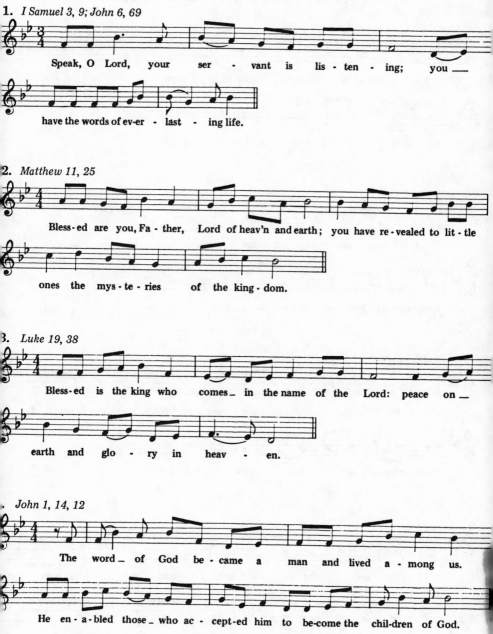

Speak, O Lord, your ser - vant is lis - ten - ing; you __ have the words of ev-er - last - ing life.

2. *Matthew 11, 25*

Bless - ed are you, Fa - ther, Lord of heav'n and earth; you have re - vealed to lit - tle ones the mys - te - ries of the king - dom.

3. *Luke 19, 38*

Bless - ed is the king who comes __ in the name of the Lord: peace on __ earth and glo - ry in heav - en.

John 1, 14, 12

The word __ of God be - came a man and lived a - mong us. He en - a - bled those __ who ac - cept - ed him to be - come the chil - dren of God.

ALLELUIA VERSES FOR SUNDAYS OF THE YEAR *(Continued)*

5. *John 6, 64, 69*

Your words, O Lord, __ are __ spir - it and life, __

you have the words of ev - er - last - ing life.

6. *John 8, 12*

I am the light of the world, __ says the Lord; the

man who fol-lows me will have the light __ of life.

7. *John 10, 27*

My sheep _____ lis - ten to my voice, says the Lord; I

know them __ and __ they __ fol - low me.

8. *John 14, 5*

I am __ the way, the truth __ and the __ life, says the

Lord; no one comes __ to the Fa - ther, ex - cept __ through me.

ALLELUIA VERSES FOR SUNDAYS OF THE YEAR *(Continued)*

John 14, 23

If an-y-one loves me, he will hold to my words, and my

Fa-ther will love him and — we — will come — to him.

John 15, 5

I call you my friends, — says the Lord, for I have made known to

you all that the Fa-ther has told _____ me.

John 17, 7

Your word, — O Lord, — is — truth; make us ho-ly in — the truth.

See Acts 16, 14

O-pen our hearts, — O — Lord, — to lis-ten to the words of your Son.

See Ephesians 1, 17-18

May the Fa-ther of our Lord, — Je-sus Christ, — en-light-en the

eyes of our hearts that we might see how great — is the hope to which we are called.

ALLELUIA VERSES FOR THE LAST SUNDAYS

14. *Matthew 24, 42, 44*

Be watch - ful and read - y: you know not when the Son of Man is com - ing.

15. *Luke 21, 36*

Be watch-ful, pray _ con-stant - ly that you _ may be wor - thy to stand be - fore the Son _ of Man. _

16. *Revelation 2, 10*

Be faith-ful un - til death, says the Lord, and _ I _ will _ give _ you the crown _ of life. _

SEASON OF THE YEAR *a.) for use with a psalm of praise:*

Praise the Lord for he is good.

We praise you, O Lord, for all your works are won - der - ful.

Sing to the Lord a new song.

) with a psalm of petition:

The Lord is near to all who call on him.

Hear us, O Lord, and save us.

The Lord is kind and mer - ci - ful.

GOSPEL

*The cantor sings the response and the people repeat it; the cantor then
sings the verse before the gospel and the people repeat the response.
Otherwise the verse before the gospel may be omitted.*

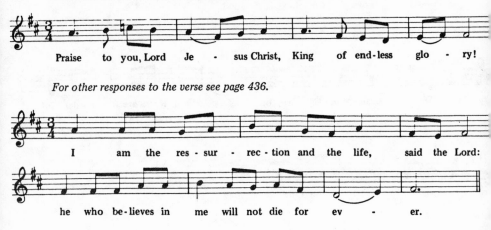

Praise to you, Lord Je - sus Christ, King of end-less glo - ry!

For other responses to the verse see page 436.

I am the res - sur - rec - tion and the life, said the Lord:

he who be - lieves in me will not die for ev - er.

Long Form: John 11, 1-45 I am the resurrection and the life.

*The raising of Lazarus is told by John with great feeling
and vivid detail. Read the story as if it was being told by
one of the disciples who relates it stage by stage as he saw
it happen.*

*The first lines give the setting. Lazarus with Martha and
Mary, his sisters, live together at Bethany; Jesus loves them;
he is told that Lazarus is very ill. Nevertheless at first he
does not go to them. At last he says he will go. The disciples
are troubled, for Bethany is near Jerusalem, and Jesus'
enemies in Jerusalem are planning to kill him. Jesus tells
them that Lazarus is dead.*

*Martha goes back to the house to fetch Mary. Jesus is greatly
moved by her faith, and all go towards the tomb.*

*At this point bring out Jesus' two natures. As a man he is
overcome by natural sorrow at the death of a friend; and
he weeps. As God he commands even death: "Take away the
stone". . ."Lazarus, come out." "Untie him, and let him go."*

*Emphasise especially the words of Jesus: "This sickness. .
glorified" "Are there not twelve hours. . .no light in him"
"I am the resurrection and the life. . .Father, I thank you. .
sent me."*

✠ A reading from the holy gospel according to John

There was a certain man named Láz-a-rus who was sick.
He was from Béth-a-ny, the village of Mary and her sister Martha.
(This Mary whose brother Láz-a-rus was sick
    was the one who anointed the Lord with perfume and dried his
       feet with her hair.)
The sisters sent word to Jesus to inform him,
    "Lord, the one you love is sick."
Upon hearing this, Jesus said:
    "This sickness is not to end in death;
    rather it is for God's glory,
    that through it the Son of God may be glorified."

Jesus loved Martha and her sister and Láz-a-rus very much.
Yet, after hearing that Láz-a-rus was sick,
    he stayed on where he was for two days more.
Finally he said to his disciples,
    "Let us go back to Judea."
"Rabbi," protested the disciples,
    "with the Jews only recently trying to stone you,
    you are going back up there again? "

Jesus answered:
    "Are there not twelve hours of daylight:
If a man goes walking by day he does not stumble,
    because he sees the world bathed in light.
But if he goes walking at night he will stumble,
    since there is no light in him."
After uttering these words, he added,
    "Our beloved Láz-a-rus has fallen asleep,
    but I am going there to wake him."
At this the disciples objected,
    "Lord, if he is asleep his life will be saved."
Jesus had been speaking about his death,
    but they thought he meant sleep in the sense of slumber.
Finally Jesus said plainly,
    "Láz-a-rus is dead.
For your sakes I am glad I was not there,
    that you may come to believe.
In any event, let us go to him."
Then Thomas (the name means "Twin") said to his fellow disciples,
"Let us go along, to die with him."

When Jesus arrived at Béth-a-ny,
  he found that Láz-a-rus had already been in the tomb four days.
The village was not far from Jerusalem—
  just under two miles—
  and many Jewish people had come out
  to console Martha and Mary over their brother.
When Martha heard that Jesus was coming she went to meet him,
  while Mary sat at home.
Martha said to Jesus,
  "Lord, if you had been here, my brother would never have died.
Even now, I am sure
  that God will give you whatever you ask of him."
"Your brother will rise again," Jesus assured her.
"I know he will rise again," Martha replied,
  "in the resurrection on the last day."
Jesus told her:
"I am the resurrection and the life:
whoever believes in me,
though he should die, will come to life;
and whoever is alive and believes in me will never die.
Do you believe this? "
"Yes, Lord," she replied.
"I have come to believe that you are the Mes-sí-ah, the Son of God:
  he who is to come into the world."

When she had said this
  she went back and called her sister Mary.
"The Teacher is here, asking for you," she whispered.
As soon as Mary heard this,
  she got up and started out in his direction.
(Actually Jesus had not yet come into the village
  but was still at the spot where Martha had met him.)
The Jews who were in the house with Mary consoling her
  saw her get up quickly and go out,
    so they followed her, thinking she was going to the tomb to
      weep there.
When Mary came to the place where Jesus was,
  seeing him, she fell at his feet and said to him,
    "Lord, if you had been here my brother would never have died."
When Jesus saw her weeping,
  and the Jewish folk who had accompanied her also weeping,
  he was troubled in spirit,
    moved by the deepest emotions

"Where have you laid him? " he asked.

"Lord, come and see," they said.

Jesus began to weep, which caused the Jews to remark,

"See how much he loved him! "

But some said, "He opened the eyes of that blind man.

Why could he not have done something to stop this man from dying? "

Once again troubled in spirit, Jesus approached the tomb.

It was a cave with a stone laid across it.

"Take away the stone," Jesus directed.

Martha, the dead man's sister, said to him,

"Lord, it has been four days now;
surely there will be a stench! "

Jesus replied, "Did I not assure you
that if you believed you would see the glory of God displayed? "

They then took away the stone
and Jesus looked upward and said:
"Father, I thank you for having heard me.

I know that you always hear me
but I have said this for the sake of the crowd,
that they may believe that you sent me."

Having said this, he called loudly, "Láz-a-rus, come out! "

The dead man came out,
bound hand and foot with linen strips,
his face wrapped in a cloth.

"Untie him." Jesus told them, "and let him go free."

This caused many of the Jews who had come to visit Mary,
and had seen what Jesus did,
to put their faith in him.

This is the gospel of the Lord.

*Short Form: John 11, 3-7. 17. 20-27. 33-45 I am the resurrection and
the life.*

✠ A reading from the holy gospel according to John

The sisters of Láz-a-rus sent word to Jesus to inform him,
"Lord, the one you love is sick."
Upon hearing this, Jesus said:
"This sickness is not to end in death;
rather it is for God's glory,
that through it the Son of God may be glorified."

Jesus loved Martha and her sister and Láz-a-rus very much.
Yet, after hearing that Láz-a-rus was sick,
he stayed on where he was for two days more.
Finally he said to his disciples,
"Let us go back to Judea."
When Jesus arrived at Béth-a-ny,
he found that Láz-a-rus had already been in the tomb four days.
When Martha heard that Jesus was coming she went to meet him,
while Mary sat at home.
Martha said to Jesus, "Lord, if you had been here,
my brother would never have died.
Even now, I am sure that God will give you whatever you ask of him."
"Your brother will rise again," Jesus assured her.
"I know he will rise again," Martha replied,
"in the resurrection on the last day."

Jesus told her:
"I am the resurrection and the life:
whoever believes in me,
though he should die, will come to life;
and whoever is alive and believes in me will never die.
Do you believe this? "
"Yes, Lord," she replied.
"I have come to believe that you are the Messiah, the Son of God
he who is to come into the world."
Jesus was troubled in spirit, moved by the deepest emotions
'Where have you laid him? " he asked.

"Lord, come and see," they said.
Jesus began to weep, which caused the Jews to remark,
 "See how much he loved him! "
But some said, "He opened the eyes of that blind man.
Why could he not have done something to stop this man from dying? "
Once again troubled in spirit, Jesus approached the tomb.

It was a cave with a stone laid across it.
"Take away the stone," Jesus directed.
Martha, the dead man's sister, said to him,
 "Lord, it has been four days now;
 surely there will be a stench! "
Jesus replied, "Did I not assure you that if you believed
 you would see the glory of God displayed? "
They then took away the stone and Jesus looked upward and said:
 "Father, I thank you for having heard me.
I know that you always hear me
 but I have said this for the sake of the crowd,
 that they may believe that you sent me."
Having said this, he called loudly, "Láz-a-rus come out! "
The dead man came out,
 bound hand and foot with linen strips,
 his face wrapped in a cloth.
"Untie him," Jesus told them, "and let him go free."

This caused many of the Jews who had come to visit Mary,
 and had seen what Jesus did,
 to put their faith in him.

 This is the gospel of the Lord.

PRONUNCIATION GUIDE

Pronunciation follows the guide of Webster's International Dictionary of the English language. Hebrew and Greek names are followed by their phonetic rendering in parentheses.

Hebrew and Greek names are followed by their English Pronunciations in Parentheses.

Pronunciation

Phonetic spelling was used. The vowel system was as follows:

ā as in dāte
ă as in ăsk
à as in àrm
â as in râve
ē as in Eden
ĕ as in ĕnd
êr as in fathêr
ī as in mīle
ĭ as in hĭm
î as in mîrth
ō as in gō
ŏ as in tŏp
ô as in hôrn
ōō as in trōōp
ŏŏ as in fŏŏt
ū as in tūne
ŭ as in bŭt
û as in fûr

Aaron (âr'ŭn)
Abel-meholah (ā'bĕl-mē-hō'là)
Abijah (àbī'jà)
Abilene (ăb'-ĭ-lēn)
Abishai (à-bĭsh'ā-i)
Abiud (à-bī'ûd)
Abner (ăb'nêr)
Achim (ă'kĭm)
Ahaz (ă'hăz)
Amminadab (ă-mĭn'-à-dăb)
Amalek (ăm'à-lĕk)
Ammonite (ăm'ŏn-īt)
Amos (ā'mŏs)
Annas (ăn'năs)
Antioch (ăn'tĭ-ŏk)
Arabia (à-rā'bĭ-à)
Arimathea (â'rĭ-mà-thē'à)
Asa (ā'sà)
Asher (ăsh'êr)
Attalia (ăt'tà-lī'à)
Azor (ā'zôr)

Barabbas (bà-răb'ăs)
Barnabas (bàr'nà-băs)
Baruch (bâr'ŭk)
Bethany (bĕth'à-nē)
Bethlehem (bĕth'lĕ-hĕm)
Bethphage (bĕth'fà-jā)
Boaz (bō'ăz)

Caesar Augustus (sē'zêr ô-gŭs'tŭs)
Caesarea Philippi (sĕs'à-rē'à fĭ-lĕp'ī)
Caiaphas (kā'yà-fàs)
Capernaum (kà-pûr'nā-ŭm)
Cappadocia (kăp'à-dō'shĭ-à)
Cephas (sĕ'fàs)
Chaldeans (kăl-dē'ăns)
Chuza (kū'zà)
Cilicia (sĭ-lĭsh'ĭ-à
Clopas (klō'pàs)
Colossians (kŏ-lŏsh'ănz)
Corinthians (kô-rĭn'thĭ-ănz)
Cushite (kūsh'īt)
Cyrenean (sī-rē'nĭ-ăn)

Damascus (dȧ-măs′kŭs)
Derbe (dûr′bē)
Deuteronomy (dū-têr-ŏn′ō-mē)
dromedaries (drŏm-ĕ-dā′rēs)

Ebed-melech (ĕ′bĕd-mĕ-lĕk)
Ecclesiastes (ĕ-klē-zĭ-ăs′tēz)
Egyptians (ē-gip′shăns)
Elamites (ē′lăm-īts)
Eleazar (ĕ-lē′ȧ-zár)
Eliab (ĕ-lī′ăb)
Eliakim (ĕ-lī′ȧ-kĭm)
Elijah (ē-lī′jȧ)
Elisha (ĕ-lī′shȧ)
Eliud (ĕ-lī′ŭd)
Emmanuel (ē-măn′ū-ĕl)
ephah (ĕ′fȧ)
Ephesians (ĕ-fē′shŭnz)
Ephrathah (ĕf′rȧ-thȧ)
Euphrates (ū-frā-tēz)
Exodus (ĕgs′ō-dŭs)
Ezechiel (ē-zĕk′yĕl)

Gabbatha (găb′ȧ-thȧ)
Gabriel (gā′brĭ-ĕl)
Galatia (gȧ-lā′shĭ-ȧ)
Galatians (gȧ-lā′shĭ-ȧns)
Galileans (găl-ĭ-lē′ăns)
Galilee (găl′ĭ-lē)
Genesis (jĕn′ĕ-sĭs)
Gilgal (gĭl′găl)
Golgotha (gŏl′gō-thȧ)
Gomorrah (gō-mŏr′ȧ)

Habakkuk (hȧ-băk′ŭk)
Hadad-rim-mon (hă′dăd-rĭm′ŏn)
Hebron (hĕ′brŏn)
Herod Tet-rarch (hĕr′ŭd tĕt-rárch)
Hezekiah (hĕz′ē-kī′ȧ)
Hezron (hĕz′rŏn)
Hittite (hĭt′īt)
Hur (hûr)

Isaac (ī′zȧk)
Isaiah (ī-sā′ȧ)
Israelites (ĭz′rȧ-ĕl-īts)
Itaraea (it-ū-rē′a)

Jaar (jā′ar)
Javon (jă′văn)
Jechoniah (jĕk-ō-nī′ȧ)
Jehoshaphat (je-ho′shȧ-făt)
Jeremiah (jĕr-e-mī′ȧ)

Jericho (jĕr-ĭ-ko′)
Jesse (jĕs′sē)
Jethro (jĕth′rō)
Joanna (jō′ăn-nȧ)
Joram (jo′ram)
Joshua (josh′ū-ȧ)
Josiah (jō-sī′ȧ)
Jotham (jō′thăm)
Judea (jū-dē′ȧ)
Judah (jū′dȧ)

Kidron (kĭd′rŏn)

Lazarus (lăz′ȧ-rŭs)
Levites (lē′vĭts)
Lysanias (lĭ-săn-ĭ-as)
Lystra (lĭs′trȧ)

Maccabees (măk′ȧ-bēs)
Magdalene (măg′dȧ-lēn)
Malachi (măl′ȧ-chī)
Malchiah (măl-kī′ȧ)
Malchus (măl′kŭs)
Mamre (măm′rē)
Manasseh (mȧ-năs′sĕ)
Massah (măs′ȧ)
Mathan (mă′thăn)
Megiddo (mĕ-gĭd′ō)
Melchizedek (mĕl-kĭz′ĕ-dĕk)
Meribah (mĕr-ĭ′bȧ)
Mesopotamia (mĕs-ō-pō-tā′mĭ-ȧ)
Messiah (mĕ-sī′ȧ)
Midian (mĭd′ĭ-ăn)
Moriah (mō-ri′ȧ)
Mosoch (mŏs′ōk)

Naaman (nā′ăm-ȧn)
Nahshon (nă′shōn)
Naim (nā′ĭm)
Nathan (nā′thăn)
Nathanael (nȧ-thăn′ā-ĕl)
Nazareth (năz′ȧ-rĕth)
Nazorean (năz-ō-rē′ăn)
Ner (nûr)
Nicodemus (nĭk-ō-dē′mŭs)

Obed (ō′bĕd)
Olivet (ŏl′ĭ-vĕt)
Ophir (ō′fêr)

Pamphylia (păm-fĭl′ĭ-ȧ)
Parthians (par′thĭ-ănz)
Patmos (păt′mŏs)

Perez (pĕr-ez)
Perga (pûr'gȧ)
Phanuel (fȧ-nū'ĕl)
Pharaoh (fār'ō)
Philemon (fĭl-ā'mŏn)
Philippians (fĭl-ĭp'pĭ-ȧnz)
Phrygia (frĭj'ĭ-ȧ)
Pisidia (pĭ-sĭd'ĭ-ȧ)
Pontus (pŏn'tŭs)
Presbyters (prĕz'bĭ-têrs)

Qoheleth (kō-hā'lĕth)
Quirinius (kwi-rē'nĭ-ŭs)

Rabbi (răb'bī)
Rahab (rā'hăb)
Ram (răm)
Rehoboam (rē'hō'bō-ăm)

Sadducees (săd'yū-sēz)
Salmon (săl'mŏn)
Samaria (sȧ-măr'ĭ-ȧ)
Samaritan (sȧ-măr'ĭ-tăn)
Samuel (săm'ŭ-ĕl)
Sanhedrin (săn'hĕ-drĭn)
Scythian (sĭth'ĭ-ăn)
Shaphat (shă'făt)
Shealtiel (shē-ăl'tĭ-ĕl)
Sidon (sī'dŏn)
Silas (sī'lȧs)
Siloam (sĭl'ō-ăm)
Simeon (sĭm'ē-ŭn)
Simon (sī'mŭn)
Simon Iscariot (sī-mŭn ĭs-căr'ĭ-ŏt)
Sinai (sī'nī)
Sirach (sī'răk)
Sodom (sŏd'ŭm)
Solomon (sŏl'ō-mŭn)
Susanna (sū-zăn'ȧ)

Tamar (tȧ'mȧr)
Tarshish (tȧr'shĭsh)
Theophilus (thē-ŏf'ĭ-lŭs)
Thessalonians (thĕs-sȧ-lō'nĭ-ănz)
Tiberias (tĭ-bēr'ĭ-ăs)
Tiberius (tĭ-bēr'ĭ-ŭs)
Tibetius (tĭ-bē'shŭs)
Titus (tī'tŭs)
Trachonitis (trăk-ō-nī'tĭs)
Tubal (tū'bȧl)
Tyre (tĭr)

Uriah (ū-rī'ȧ)
Uzziah (ū-zī'ȧ)

Yah-weh-yi-reh (yȧ'wā-yĭr'ā)

Zachaeus (ză-kē'ŭs)
Zadok (ză'dŏk)
Zareph (zăr'ĕf)
Zarephtah (ză'rĕf-tȧh)